Birds of Gloucestershire

Above Young Heron. Birds of this species may be found in the Wye Valley, along the Severn Vale, at cotswold streams and in the Water Park.

Left Great Crested Grebe: a species which has increased greatly in Gloucestershire during the present century.

Below The Moorhen is a common breeding bird in the county. Many early nests are built in very conspicuous situations.

Birds of Gloucestershire

Christopher M. Swaine

Formerly Head of Science Department,
Rendcomb College

ALAN SUTTON
1982

Alan Sutton Publishing Limited
17a Brunswick Road
Gloucester

First published 1982

Copyright © 1982 Christopher M. Swaine

All rights reserved. No part of this publication may be reproduced, stored in a retrieval system, or transmitted, in any form or by any means, electronic, mechanical photocopying, recording or otherwise, without the prior permission of the publishers and copyright holder.

British Library Cataloguing in Publication Data
Swaine, Christopher M.
   Birds of Gloucestershire.
   1. Birds—Gloucestershire
   I. Title
   598.29424'1   QL690.G7

ISBN 0-86299-012-2

Typesetting and origination by
Alan Sutton Publishing Limited.
Photoset Imprint 10/11
Printed in Great Britain
by Page Bros (Norwich) Limited.

Contents

Author's Preface and Acknowledgements		3
List of Illustrations		5
Introduction		7
Chapter One:	The Wye Valley and the Forest of Dean	13
Chapter Two:	The Severn Vale	22
Chapter Three:	The Cotswolds	33
Chapter Four:	The Thames Area	43
Chapter Five:	Migratory and other movements in relation to Gloucestershire	52
Chapter Six:	Ornithology in Gloucestershire: A Brief History	65
Chapter Seven:	The Work of some Organisations based in Gloucestershire	75
Chapter Eight:	Changes in the Status of Birds in Gloucestershire	84
Chapter Nine:	*The Atlas of Breeding Birds in Britain and Ireland*	95
Systematic Section:		
Introductory Notes		99
Annotated List of Species		104
Appendices:		
List of birds reputed to have occurred in Gloucestershire but not accepted for present purposes		213
Scientific names of plants mentioned in the text		215
Bibliography		217
Gazetteer: place-names		223
Index		230

To the memory of
Guy L. Charteris and Howard H. Davis

Author's Preface and Acknowledgements

During the 1950s Guy L. Charteris, Howard H. Davis and I started work on a book to be entitled *The Birds of Gloucestershire*. A basic draft of the introductory chapters describing the county was prepared and an annotated list of species was completed up to the end of 1958. In the 1950s, however, we had far less knowledge of the county's birds at our disposal than is now the case, and for this reason and others the project was discontinued before completion. In retrospect this was perhaps a good decision, for a great mass of new data has accumulated in the intervening years, now enabling a much more detailed and thorough account to be written.

To the sorrow of many Guy Charteris died in September 1967 and Howard Davis early in 1974, and it is with regret that I have had to prepare this book without the current help and guidance of these two fine naturalists and good friends. Their efforts, however, have not been wasted, for although this book has been entirely reconstructed, it incorporates much of the material and many of the ideas which we discussed in the 1950s.

During the past two years I have received help from many people on many topics concerning Gloucestershire and its ornithology. A glance at the *Gloucestershire Bird Report* over the years, and at the *Journal* of the Gloucestershire Naturalists' Society,[31] will give some idea of the large number of observers who have contributed records from within the county. These records, together with contributions from the Bristol Naturalists' Society, the Wildfowl Trust and other sources, constitute the main body of data since about 1950, upon which the Systematic Section of this book has been built. A Table setting out the main annual lists and *Reports* concerning Gloucestershire birds since 1948, together with their editors, is given in Chapter Six, page 72, while the editors of the *Journal* of the Gloucestershire Naturalists Society are listed in the Bibliography (and see *Journal*, June-July 1978)[31].

I wish particularly to thank Malcolm Ogilvie of the Wildfowl Trust for his unstinting encouragement and advice throughout the whole period of writing this book. In addition he read all the introductory chapters, supplying comments and constructive criticism. I am especially grateful also to John Sanders, my successor since March 1979 as Ornithological Secretary of the Gloucestershire Naturalists' Society. He dealt promptly with the many and varied questions which I sent to him: nothing, it seems, was too much trouble for his careful attention, and this was especially manifest in his examination of the Systematic Section in typescript.

Dr. Bruce Campbell made helpful comments on Chapters Six and Eight; Mrs. S.C. Holland on Chapter Four, part of Chapter Six and on various other matters, and J.D. Sanders on Chapters Two and Five. R.K. Bircher and J.D. Sanders furnished data on bird ringing and supplied a draft on the work of the Severn Vale Ringing Group, while the accounts of the activities of other organisations were prepared or checked by Mrs. S.C. Holland (Gloucestershire Naturalists' Society), M.J. Penistan (Gloucestershire Trust for Nature Conservation), P.G. Hadley (Dursley Birdwatching and Preservation Society) and M.A. Ogilvie (Wildfowl Trust). See Chapter Seven.

Other information on a variety of topics came from the following: B. Campbell on Pied Flycatchers; P.H. Dymott on the B.T.O. *Atlas* project; J.W. Hale on Nightingale and other species; Mrs. S.C. Holland, D.V. Mardle and G.L. Webber on the Cotswold Water Park; M.A. Ogilvie on the Anatidae; L.C. Pierce on Rooks; D.S.J. Price on the history of agriculture in Gloucestershire; G.M. Shearman and Miss C.E. Williams on references from the library of the Gloucestershire Naturalists' Society. Thanks are due also to Staff members of the public libraries and museums of Cheltenham and Gloucester for assistance rendered.

A special note of appreciation must go to Mrs. Carol Ogilvie for providing the many drawings which liven the text. She generously offered to do these without any request from me; she also prepared finished copies of the various maps.

I am grateful to Philippa Scott for permission to use the photograph on page 82 of waterfowl on "Swan Lake", Slimbridge, and to the Wildfowl Trust for that of White-fronted Geese on page 59. All other photographs were taken by the author, who wishes to thank Jonathan Leach of the Wildfowl Trust for preparing enlargements.

In all a great deal of information and general help has been supplied by many people, too numerous for all to be named. Omissions in this field are due to lack of space, not of gratitude. The ways in which data and ideas have been used in this book are, of course, the final responsibility of the author.

C.M. Swaine.

List of Illustrations

Photographs

Heron; Great Crested Grebe; Moorhen .... Frontispiece
River Wye in Devonian sandstone country 14
River Wye and limestone cliffs, Woodcroft 14
The Forest of Dean near Staunton 18
The Forest of Dean: Cannop Ponds 20
Frampton Pools 25
Coombe Canal area in summer 27
Combe Canal area during winter floods 27
The Severn estuary near Slimbridge 29
The Severn Vale from Coaley Peak 32
Pope's Wood, Cranham 35
Leckhampton Hill, Cheltenham 36
Cleeve Hill 37
Dipslope scenery near Farmington 37
Lower Slaughter 39
River Churn at Rendcomb 41
Rendcomb Lake in summer 41
Gravel extraction: the drag-line 45
A South Cerney gravel-pit in winter 45
A long-established deep water gravel-pit 49
White-fronted Geese on the New Grounds 59
Ringing Pied Flycatchers in the Dean 70

The Wildfowl Trust: "Swan Lake" 82
Marsh Warbler 86
Little Ringed Plover 93
Barn Owl 98
Nightjar in the Forest of Dean 169
Swift on a Cotswold Tower 170
Woodlark 175
Grasshopper Warbler 188
Spotted Flycatcher 194

Maps, etc

Gloucestershire: topography 8
Gloucestershire: geology 9
Table of Geological Periods 12
Section through a Water Park gravel-pit 46
Spring migration 54
Autumn migration 58
Gloucestershire: ornithological regions 100

Introduction

The year 1902 saw the publication of *A Treatise on The Birds of Gloucestershire*[41] by W.L. Mellersh, until now the only book devoted solely to the avifauna of this county. There has been a remarkable growth of interest in birds during the past 35 or 40 years, and the same period has witnessed a continued increased in the pressures which are imposed upon birds and other forms of wild life by man's technological advance.

This, therefore, seems a good time for a new statement on Gloucestershire's bird life. Far more is now known in this field than even 30 years ago, and it is hoped that the present work may provide a much-needed baseline against which future changes in the bird populations of the county may be judged. It may also serve as an historical record to assist in some way those planning for future conservation and protective measures. For this reason, as well as for general interest, chapters are included on the history of ornithology and on changes in the status of birds in the county.

Underlying all such studies of wild life is the need for adequate understanding of habitats and the general geographical background of the region. The first part of this book is therefore concerned with these aspects of Gloucestershire, seen with an ornithological eye.

Formerly Gloucestershire included land on the left bank of the Severn estuary, and in the southern Cotswolds, as far south as the City of Bristol and the Bristol Avon. Under the Local Government Act of 1972, however, a large area of south Gloucestershire became transferred to the new county of Avon when the Act came into effect on 1 April 1974 (see map, page 8).

The present work is therefore an account of the birds of "new" Gloucestershire. All records from that part of the former county which is now in Avon have been omitted, no matter when they were made, and they are now retained by the Bristol Naturalists' Society for future use.

In this context it is important to realise that all numbers of the *Gloucestershire Bird Report* from 1963 to 1973 inclusive were compiled from data collected in all parts of the "old" county, and consequently contain many records which were used also by the Bristol Naturalists' Society in compiling the annual *Britsol Bird Report*. From 1 January 1974 onwards, the *Gloucestershire Bird Report* refers only to the county within its new

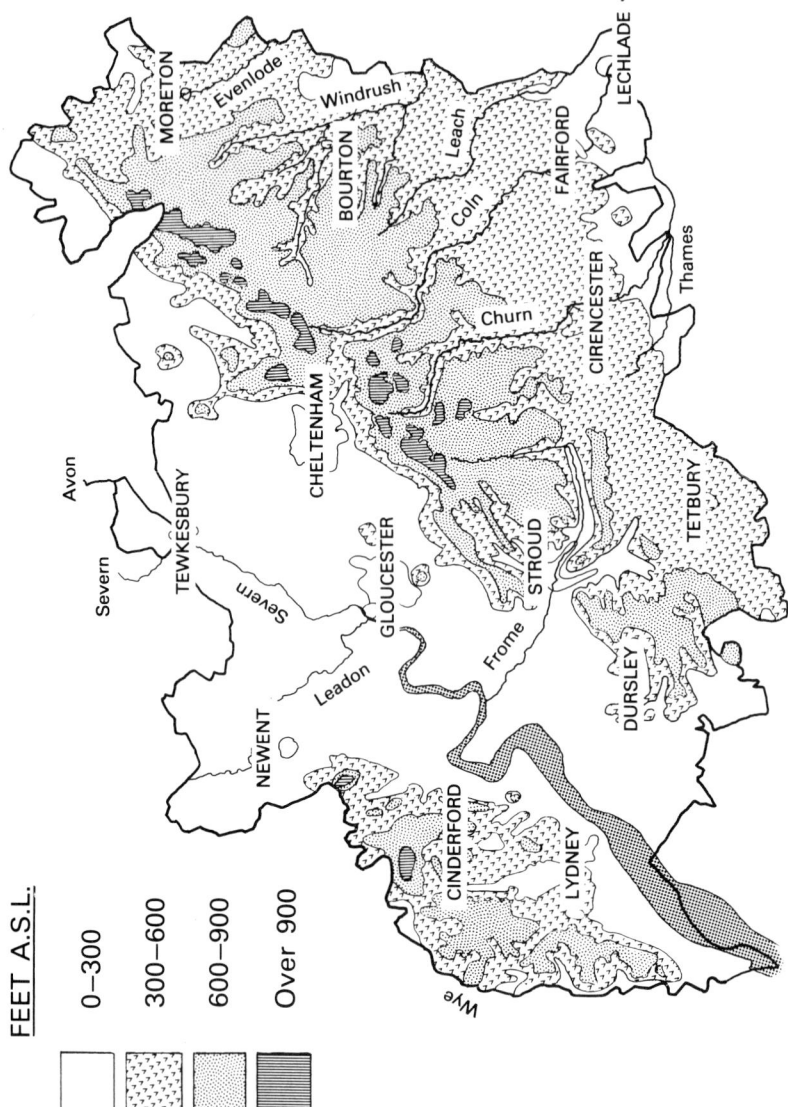

Gloucestershire: topography

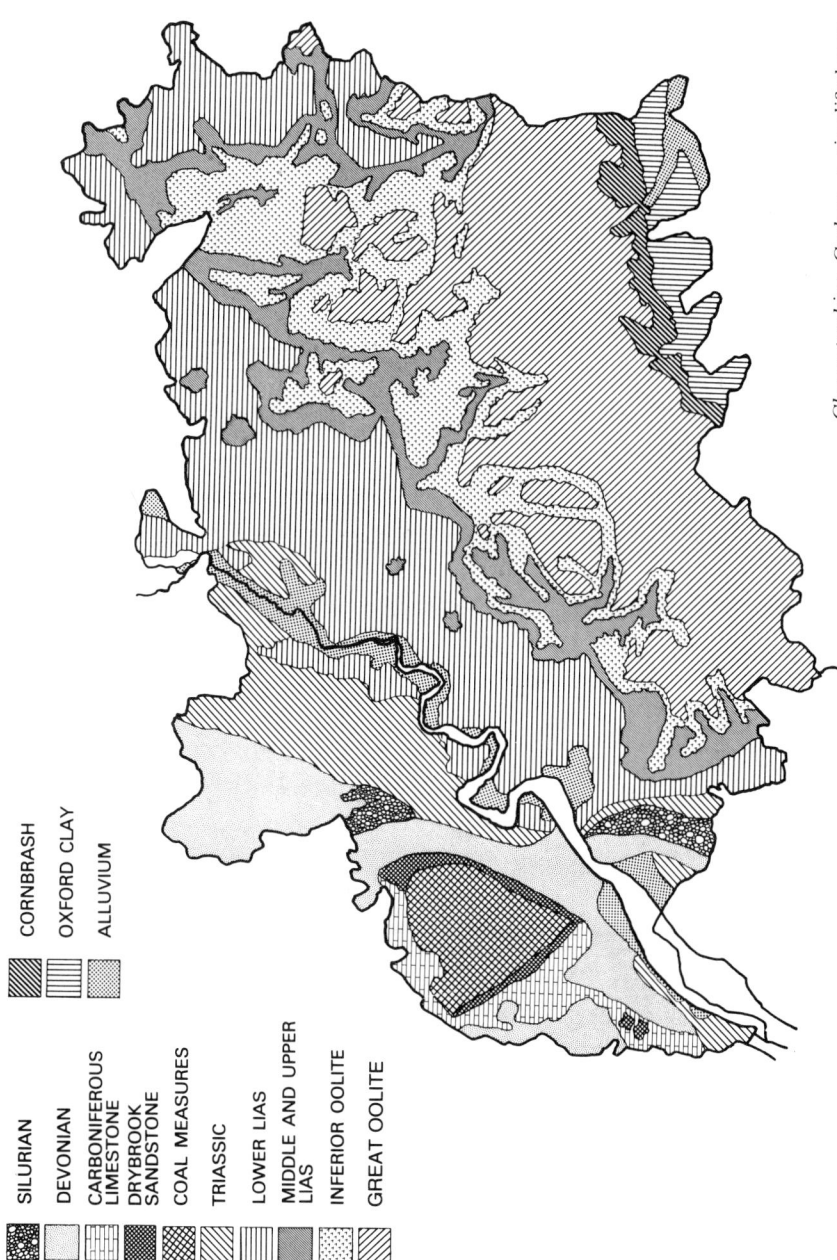

Gloucestershire: Geology, a simplified map

boundaries, thus ending the former overlap (see page 72). Since each Bird Report covers one complete year, it was considered advisable to effect this change in the pattern of ornithological recording on 1 January 1974, rather than the 1st April.

Gloucestershire is often referred to as a West Midland county. In fact the City of Gloucester is almost equidistant from St. Davids, Caernarfon, King's Lynn, Southend and Brighton, each at a distance of about 125 miles. The county is of a somewhat irregular outline (see map, page 8), and about 40 miles across, whether measured from north-east to south-west or along the diagonal at right angles.

Few counties of comparable size show greater diversity of scenery and wild life habitats. The lower Wye Valley, forming the western limit of the county, is famous for its limestone cliff scenery, and the adjacent Forest of Dean is an outstanding area of semi-natural woodland; the Severn is Britain's longest river and its estuary one of the largest; the Cotswolds provide superb views from vantage points along the escarpment edge, while the gentle streams of the dipslope seem to typify the best of rural England. The gravel-pits in the east of the county constitute a remarkable series of recently opened artificial lakes.

Gloucestershire is deeply penetrated in the south-west by the upper part of the Severn estuary which, with its wide flood-plain, forms a kind of ecological barrier between the Forest of Dean on ancient Palaeozoic rocks to the west, and the Jurassic limestone country of the Cotswolds on the east side of the river. The habitats of western Gloucestershire show some affinity with parts of south-east Wales; those of the Cotswolds are more closely allied to areas of central and southern England, while between the two the Severn Vale comes under estuarine influences and those of the prevailing winds which blow unhindered up the estuary.

Climatic conditions vary to some extent throughout the county.[53] The heaviest rainfall, over 40 inches a year, falls on the high ground to the west of the Forest of Dean; the lowest is in the upper part of the Severn Vale, where less than 25 inches may be recorded. The higher Cotswolds receive about 34 inches, declining eastwards towards Lechlade, where annual precipitation is, on average, less than 30 inches.

Gloucestershire is one of the warmer counties of England, with average mean temperatures of about 40°F (4.4°C) and 62°F (16.7°C) in January and July respectively. Summer maxima in excess of 90°F (32.2°C) are exceptional, and in very severe winter weather, as in the early months of 1940 and 1963, temperatures may fall to near zero Fahrenheit (−17.8°C) with serious consequences for several species of birds. The average mean daily sunshine is a little over four hours at both Cirencester and Cheltenham, and somewhat lower in the Forest of Dean.

The main geological and topographical features of the county run from north-east to south-west. In consequence its boundaries enclose large areas of three distinctive types of countryside and a smaller part of a fourth. Each has a well-defined flora and fauna, even the bird life showing clear regional variation in spite of the great potential for dispersal which flight bestows on birds. (See maps, pages 8–9).

For ornithological purposes Gloucestershire may therefore be divided into the following regions (see map, page 100):

The Wye Valley and Forest of Dean: This district includes about 25 miles of the terminal part of the river Wye, together with the hilly country, much of it heavily wooded, which lies between the Wye and the Severn estuary. It forms the most westerly of the four regions. The sandstone country to the north-east of the Forest is also considered here.

The Severn Vale: A wide belt of low-lying country flanking the river on both sides from Tewkesbury in the north to the southern county boundary with Avon. It includes the upper part of the Severn estuary, and separates the hills of the Forest of Dean in the north-west from the Cotswold escarpment to the south-east.

The Cotswolds: These form a long, high limestone escarpment whose steep western *scarp-face* lies parallel to the river Severn. The gentle *dipslope* falls gradually eastwards towards the borders of Wiltshire and Oxfordshire.

The Thames Area: A small region in the extreme eastern corner of the county, lying south of a line from Poole Keynes to near Lechlade. This has no sharp demarkation from the Cotswolds to which, however, it is less related geologically and ecologically than to the Thames Basin. It includes the recently designated Cotswold Water Park.

Each of these regions contains geographical features which are of special interest for local ornithology, and brief explanations of these help in understanding the distribution within the county of many bird species. In the following account of each of the four Ornithological Regions, a short statement of the relevant geological history is therefore included as background to the description of the county and its birds. The Table of Geological Periods on page 12 is included for reference; also a simplified geological map on page 9, and readers are invited to consult these in connection with each of the next four chapters.[22][23][69][79]

TABLE OF GEOLOGICAL PERIODS

ERA	PERIOD	START OF PERIOD (MILLIONS OF YEARS)	MAIN FEATURES
CENOZOIC	QUATERNARY	2	Pleistocene ice-ages. Modern mammals. Dominance of man. Decline of forests.
CENOZOIC	TERTIARY	65	Rise of birds and gradual dominance of mammals and insects. Forests and grasslands
MESOZOIC	CRETACEOUS	135	Extinction of many reptiles. Early mammals Flowering Plants become dominant.
MESOZOIC	JURASSIC	195	First birds; also primitive mammal-like reptiles. Climax to Age of Reptiles.
MESOZOIC	TRIASSIC	225	Progressive dominance of reptiles and, among plants, of cycads and conifers.
PALAEOZOIC	PERMIAN	280	Diversification of reptiles. Development of coniferous forests.
PALAEOZOIC	CARBONIFEROUS	345	Ferns and other Pteridophyta. Early insects and reptiles. Coal swamps.
PALAEOZOIC	DEVONIAN	395	Primitive land-plants reached tree-size. Age of fishes. Primitive amphibia.
PALAEOZOIC	SILURIAN	440	Invasion of land by primitive plants and some invertebrate animals.
PALAEOZOIC	ORDOVICIAN	500	Primitive jawless fishes. Algae.
PROTEROZOIC	CAMBRIAN	570	Establishment of all phyla of invertebrate animals. Great variety of Algae.
PROTEROZOIC	PRE-CAMBRIAN		First living organisms appeared more than 3.5 thousand million years ago.

ORIGIN OF EARTH : ABOUT 4.6 THOUSAND MILLION YEARS AGO

Time-scale based on that in *Scientific American,* Vol. 239, No. 3, pp. 46–47.

CHAPTER ONE
The Wye Valley and The Forest of Dean

Peregrine

Geological history of the lower Wye

The lower Wye valley forms the western boundary of Gloucestershire and provides some strikingly beautiful scenery. The river is unusual in having cut right across the rock strata of various ages, and now flows in steep-sided valleys flanked by "old red sandstone" of Devonian age and impressive cliffs of Carboniferous limestone. The explanation of this anomalous course is that the Wye is a *rejuvenated river,* having cut deeply into underlying strata during the past million years or so as a result of falling sea-level. Conversion of water to ice in polar regions at the approach of the Pleistocene ice-ages initiated this change in ocean level, and the remains of the pre-ice-age plain over which the ancestral Wye used to meander can still be traced in and around the Forest area at an altitude of about 600 feet above present sea-level.

The river Wye in Devonian sandstone country. Dense deciduous woodland clothes the steep slopes in many places.

The river Wye near Woodcroft. Ravens and a few pairs of Herring Gulls nest here, and Peregrines used to do so. The steep tidal mud attracts few birds.

The influence of this rejuvenation process upon a landscape depends, among other factors, upon the hardness and chemical nature of the affected strata. Along the lower Wye the important beds are Devonian sandstones and Carboniferous limestones. Where the river flows through the former the result tends to be a somewhat V-shaped valley with sides inclined at steep angles. More spectacular effects are to be seen where the flow of water has produced incised meanders with high vertical cliffs of limestone. Such features provide natural habitats which would not otherwise be represented in the county.[22] [69]

The first cliffs to be encountered upstream from the mouth of the Wye are on both sides of the river near Chepstow, and here there is a long-standing colony of Herring Gulls. Most pairs nest on the Gloucestershire side of the river, using ledges on the limestone. A further two miles upstream limestone cliffs are again found in the vicinity of Lancaut, those at Wintour's Leap reaching 300 feet in height. Herring Gulls may be found breeding here also in some years, while Ravens regularly nest on the Wye rocks, including those still further up-river at Symond's Yat to the north-east of Monmouth. Ravens also occupy tree-sites in west Gloucestershire, but the former presence of breeding Peregrines in the county is directly attributable to the presence of these high precipitous cliffs, where eyries were located on numerous occasions in the past.

The Wye, like the Severn, is extremely tidal, high water sometimes having an effect twelve miles up-stream at Redbrook. Mud banks are exposed at low water in the terminal reaches of the river, but these are dwarfed by the vast expanses of sand and mud of the nearby Severn. The river Wye, by comparison, attracts very few estuarine birds. Shelduck regularly visit the lower reaches and no doubt breed there annually. Cormorant, Heron, Kingfisher, Dipper and Grey Wagtail are often noted along the river, while Common Sandpipers are regular on migration.

For much of its course in Gloucestershire the Wye runs through Devonian sandstones which have not given rise to cliffs, although the slopes are often steep and therefore uncultivated. Clothed chiefly in semi-natural woodland, they are well-managed for forestry purposes in some parts, but elsewhere remain more or less untouched. These woods may be so dense that few birds find them suitable, but in other places, as near Symond's Yat, sylviculture has produced mature forest conditions where woodland species thrive. Buzzard, Redstart, Wood Warbler and Hawfinch are among the birds which may be found, while the Nightingale used to breed until fairly recently near Tidenham and along the lower parts of the Wye.

Geological history of the Forest area

The Forest of Dean with its outlying woods and heathland, lies to the east of the lower Wye valley. Much of this region is characterised by steep-sided ridges and vales, heavily forested. The basic reason for this is to be sought as far back as the Pre-Cambrian era, more than 600 million years ago, when a mountain chain was elevated in this region, part of it being represented today by the Malverns and May Hill. These hard and unyielding rocks presented a resistance to subsequent earth-movements, notably the Hercynian interude of mountain building at the close of the Carboniferous Period. The result was the formation of wave-like folds, with a north-south trend, in what is now the Forest of Dean and lower Wye area. In consequence the strata still tend to be sharply tilted. Following these events there has been much erosion and filling-in of hollows, but the general result is the steeply uneven ground of the present-day Forest, unsuited to agricultural but favourable to the development of woodland habitats. Most of the modern Forest lies in a shallow depression on the Coal Measures, surrounded by a narrow zone of sandstones with limestone becoming prominent between the Forest and the Wye (see map, page 9).

Little is known of the ice-age vegetation in this part of England which lay close to the southern fringe of the Pleistocene ice-sheet. When the prevailing tundra conditions receded northwards, however, woodland slowly extended over much of the country. Pollen analysis from local deposits indicates that oak was already the dominant tree in the Dean some 4,000 years ago.

Human activity in this region developed slowly, but by Roman times this deciduous forest already held many human settlements, and modification of the natural woodland was in progress. Since then the region has had a chequered history, with extensive exploitation in the production of charcoal for iron-smelting and the provision of timber for the English Navy. Almost all large oaks had been felled by 1667 when, after a period of private ownership, the Crown again acquired the Forest.

Oak and beech were planted about that time, but progress was slow and irregular until early in the nineteenth century, when several other tree species were introduced, including some conifers. From the ornithologist's point of view it is fortunate that a plan produced in 1916 to convert three-quarters of the Forest to conifers was not fully implemented. The area still contains much broad-leaved woodland including some fine oak-woods, although by the 1950s the proportion of conifers in the whole area had risen to about 50%.[25] [49]

The modern Dean woodlands

It is clear that the Forest of Dean cannot be regarded as natural woodland. Perhaps the primitive condition was that of a "sessile" oakwood, with *Quercus petraea* the dominant tree, but both the common species of oak (*Q.petraea* and *Q.robur*) are now plentiful, together with several other tree species brought in and managed by man: beech, ash, sweet chestnut, larch, Norway spruce and smaller numbers of other kinds are widely grown.

The management of the Dean woodlands was taken over by the Forestry Commission in 1924, and in 1938 a large area was declared the first National Forest Park. The Commission's aim of maintaining productivity while having due regard to public amenity and scenic value has been ably maintained up to the present, but there is a continuing risk that broadleaved woodland may decline still further in proportion to conifers.

Modern forestry ensures that every stage of development from newly cleared ground to mature woodland is always represented. These, together with ancient common-lands, spoil-heaps from old mines, disused quarries, streams and artificial pools, provide a wealth of avian habitats.

All the bird species which in Britain are specifically associated with the deciduous forest community are to be found in the Dean woodlands. Most are common and widespread, but a few call for special mention. The Buzzard is scarce but nests annually in the Forest, while the elusive Hawfinch is probably more numerous here than elsewhere in the county. The erection of nest-boxes in various woods, notably near Parkend, led to the extraordinary build-up of a large population of Pied Flycatchers, a species previously regarded as quite uncommon in the Forest.[13] Sylvicultural practice in the Dean eliminates most old and dying trees so that natural nesting sites for woodpeckers, tits, Redstarts and other hole-nesting birds are much reduced. This goes far to explain the success of nest-box schemes in the Forest.

The Woodcock is a fairly common breeding species in these woods, while the Wood Warbler is numerous but distinctly local in distribution. This

Pied Flycatcher

18   BIRDS OF GLOUCESTERSHIRE

The Forest of Dean near Staunton in spring. The bird community is that typical of deciduous woodland in Britain generally.

warbler is greatly influenced by the nature of the ground-cover beneath the trees which, in turn, is determined by the amount of light reaching the ground and also by grazing activities of sheep, rabbits and deer. There is still a considerable area of free grazing for sheep in the Forest, but deer were virtually exterminated in the Forest proper by about 1855.[25][39][47] In former years their part in checking regeneration of forest growth must have had a considerable indirect influence on the distribution of birds such as the Wood Warbler and Tree Pipit.

In some summers these deciduous woodlands may be severely defoliated by the larvae of certain Lepidoptera and at these times huge numbers of Rooks, Jackdaws and Starlings arrive from elsewhere to feed upon the caterpillars. In autumn and winter the usual feeding flocks of tits, Treecreepers and Nuthatches are widespread, and parties of Siskins may often be seen in alders or among birch and larch trees. A few Siskins stay on into April and breeding has been reported recently.

Coniferous plantations are now extensive in the Forest. The species of spruce and fir all cast deep shade so that their ground vegetation tends to be very sparse, while pines and the deciduous larches provide a more open canopy, with greater variety of plants on the woodland floor. Birds characteristic of these coniferous woods include Coal Tit and Goldcrest, while Crossbills are now reported almost annually and sometimes breed. Sparrowhawks may be found throughout the Forest area but prefer conifers for nesting, and Woodcock breed in the more open parts of these plantations.

Marginal ground and heathland

Clearance of woodland is followed by a process of *plant succession* in which a series of communities of increasing complexity eventually leads back to natural forest, provided that the area is left to itself. In practice, however, felled woodland in the Dean is enclosed against sheep and then replanted with small trees a foot or so in height. Eventually it returns to one or other of the managed woodand types already mentioned.

At an early stage in the process the habitat becomes temporarily suitable for Tree Pipit and Whinchat, while Nightjars will breed provided some relatively bare patches of ground are available. Isolated trees and bushes provide perches and song-posts for these birds. With the development of more shrubby conditions Willow Warbler, Whitethroat and Grasshopper Warbler join the community, followed later by Lesser Whitethroat, Garden Warbler, Turtle Dove and other species. Until fairly recently Red-backed Shrikes were also to be found in this habitat. As scrub progresses towards woodland, the earlier bird colonisers drop out, the habitat no longer being suitable.

Spoil heaps, thrown out from old mines and quarry workings, were slow to develop a covering of vegetation, although some have now been planted with pine and larch. In former years these huge mounds provided breeding sites for a few pairs of Wheatear and Woodlark. The former also used old stone walls in the region,[47] and a few pairs of the latter bred in very young plantations until the 1960s (see page 86).

True heathland in and around the Forest is not extensive, much of it now having been planted with trees. The best known heath is on Tidenham Chase, part of which is a nature reserve managed by the Gloucestershire Trust for Nature Conservation (page 79). Heathland vegetation includes areas of grassland, gorse, bracken and heather, usually with scattered trees and bushes. The typical birds are Willow Warbler, Tree Pipit, Whinchat and Nightjar, while a variable number of Stonechats may also be found.

There are many old quarries in the Forest region, inhabited chiefly by Jackdaws but also used as breeding places by small numbers of Stock Doves, Kestrels and, occasionally, Ravens. Barn Owls have been suspected of nesting in at least one quarry, but this is an uncommon bird and more likely to be encountered around the perimeter of the Forest. The Tawny Owl is the only member of this group of predators which occurs in any numbers in the Dean woodlands.

Streams and pools

Few aquatic habitats in this region are notable for their bird-life. The main Forest streams drain south-eastwards to the Severn and are inhabited by small numbers of Dipper and Grey Wagtail. These birds also breed at or near some of the pools within the district. The most important Forest lakes are Cannop Ponds in the centre of the Forest, Soudley Ponds, south of Cinderford, and Noxon Pond near Bream. Apart from the Mallard, few

The Forest of Dean: Cannop Ponds. Only small numbers of water birds are attracted to the tree-ringed Forest pools.

duck visit these waters. Coot, Moorhen and Little Grebe breed there, but not in large numbers; Reed Warblers are seldom noted and even Sedge Warblers are uncommon. The pool at Noxon Park is notable as a regular winter resort of Whooper Swans.

The Newent-Redmarley area

To the north-east of the Forest of Dean and its outlying woodlands is a large area of sandstone country, much of it Triassic "new red sandstone", which forms an undulating countryside now used largely for pasture with some orchards, for woodlands are no longer extensive here. The main stream is the slow-flowing river Leadon which, like the Forest streams, runs in a south-easterly direction to the Severn (see pages 22–23).

The bird life is much as would be expected in this type of lowland English countryside, although most of the district appears not to have been studied in detail. A small population of Woodlarks used to breed in the general area of Redmarley, and the woods near Highnam were the subject of prolonged investigations by Price.[56]

This district merges gradually with the lower, more level ground of the Severn Vale.

CHAPTER TWO
The Severn Vale

White-fronted Geese

Geological history

During the period following the Triassic, the whole of this part of Britain was inundated by the great Jurassic Sea in which were laid down not only the Lias clays now so characteristic of the Severn Vale but also the oolitic limestones of the Cotswolds.

At this time the Severn estuary as we know it did not exist and the Jurassic deposits must have extended right across the region which is now Gloucestershire, and possibly even beyond the borders of Wales. Following emergence of the land, the present-day river systems of the district had their origins upon a surface gently sloping to the south-east. As a result of this dip in the rock strata, the rivers formed part of the Thames drainage system which then occupied a much greater area of southern Britain than now. This south-easterly flow of local rivers is still a feature of the Wye, the Forest of Dean streams and the river Leadon, even though these waters now form part of the Britsol Channel drainage. On the far side of the Severn, the rivers of the Cotswold dipslope also demonstrate the southerly or south-easterly trend of the older system.

It is evident that the great Severn estuary of today has cut across and interrupted the former drainage pattern. Local streams, flowing south-westwards towards the Irish Sea, must have cut back into the land and captured the head-waters of the Thames system, deflecting them one by one to the Bristol Channel and, at the same time, starting to form the steep face of the Cotswold escarpment. The Warwickshire Avon and other waters of the lower Severn area eventually became involved in the same process.

Still later, during the ice-ages, the whole of the upper Severn drainage from central Wales, which previously flowed towards the Cheshire Plain, or possibly into the Trent catchment, became deflected southwards from a glacier-lake near the site of Shrewsbury, cutting the gorge at Iron Bridge and converting the Severn into Britain's longest river.

During and after the Pleistocene glaciation, the movement of ice and melt-water from this huge area of Wales and central England deepened and widened the Severn estuary, emphasising the scarp-face of the Cotswolds and cutting it back towards its present position. These events prepared the way for the development of the wide variety of habitats which are now so important for birds in the Severn Vale.[23,69,79]

Non-riverine habitats

The Vale may be defined as the low-lying ground, little of it exceeding 150 feet above sea-level and much considerably lower, extending from the edge of the Forest of Dean hills to the foot of the Cotswolds. This gently undulating plain is about sixteen miles wide at Cheltenham, narrowing to six near Sharpness where hard Silurian and Devonian rocks restricted the erosive force of the river.

Much of the Vale is floored by Lias clay with some Triassic sandstone, chiefly west of the river. Until the early middle-ages the resulting poorly-drained soils were clad in continuous forest, but this had in large measure been cleared by the early fourteenth century, to be replaced by permanent pasture. When viewed today from the edge of the Cotswold escarpment, the many old cider orchards and hedgerow trees create the illusion of a well wooded country, an impression now much reduced by the almost total destruction of elms by fungus attack in the 1970s, the so-called Dutch elm disease. The most noticeable effect of this loss of hedgerow-trees on the bird-life is a marked reduction and redistribution of the Rook population. The Vale in fact now carries few woods of any size, the largest being Michael Wood close to the southern county boundary, and now cut in half by the busy M5 motorway. Michael Wood is the largest remnant of the ancient forest cover of the Vale. Although it is much modified, woodland birds are still well represented, and Nightjars have bred there in the recent past.

Nightingales nest in scattered sites along the Severn Vale, and the Hobby breeds sparingly and irregularly, probably on both sides of the river. In former years Cirl Buntings were to be found in a number of localities, but there are no recent records. The Corn Bunting, on the other hand, shows signs of spreading southwards in the Vale, although nowhere so common as on parts of the Cotswolds.

Hobby

The chief urban areas of the region are Cheltenham, Gloucester and Stroud, where well-timbered parks and gardens attract many birds. Large urban Pied Wagtail roosts (page 62) may be observed here, while most reports of Black Redstarts and of wintering Blackcaps come from these and other towns. Lesser Black-backed Gulls began to nest on roofs in the city of Gloucester in 1967, joined by Herring Gulls four years later, and numbers of both species are now large. Urban refuse-tips are important sources of food, especially in winter, for these and other birds.

Aquatic habitats close to the river

Gloucestershire has no large reservoirs to supply town water requirements, but the small reservoirs at Dowdeswell and Hewletts near Cheltenham, and at Witcombe, attract some aquatic birds, including occasional rarities, but these waters are of no great importance to birds, attracting species mainly on account of their proximity to the river Severn.

Other man-made habitats of aquatic type are found on the low-lying flood-plain of the river. These include a variety of ponds, slow-flowing waterways and osier beds. Excavations for Lias clay formed the pools at Walham and Sandhurst, while extraction of gravel near Frampton-on-Severn has produced the large lakes now known as Frampton Pools. This gravel deposit consists of oolitic limestone detritus brought down off the Cotswolds by the river Frome during and immediately following the ice-ages of the Pleistocene period. The underlying clay ensures that the excavations remain water-filled even in dry seasons. (*cf*: Thames Area, pages 43–44).

Pools, drainage ditches, the terminal parts of the old Thames-Severn Canal and Coombe Canal, and disused osier-beds provide habitats attractive to Sedge, Reed and Marsh Warblers. The best reed-beds in the Vale are in the region of Frampton-on-Severn, but Reed Warblers are by no means restricted to reeds and may be found nesting in mixed marsh vegetation, including old osier beds, at various sites close to the river. When Marsh

Frampton Pools, close to the estuary, are old gravel-pits and attract a great variety of birds throughout the year.

Warblers were not uncommon from Frampton-on-Severn northwards, the two species could often be heard singing in the same habitat, but the Marsh Warbler is now a very scarce bird in Gloucestershire (see page 85).

Frampton Pools lie quite close to the Severn and this, together with their large areas of open water and marsh vegetation, makes them one of the most important sites of ornithological interest in the county. The breeding-bird population includes Great Crested Grebe, Little Grebe, Tufted Duck, Gadwall and Reed Warbler, while Water Rail may nest more frequently than records suggest. The main attraction of these waters, however, lies in the great variety of non-breeding birds to be seen during spring and autumn migration and in winter.

Passage migrants, moving along the nearby Severn, frequently stop at Frampton Pools, and these birds include some waders and passerine species whenever the water level is sufficiently low. Black Terns are regular in spring and autumn, sometimes in considerable numbers (page 56), while other species of tern and the Little Gull are now frequently reported.

A large autumn and winter population of Coot and the commoner species of ducks often includes a few Goldeneye and Goosander, occasional Scaup, Long-tailed Duck and Red-breasted Merganser, while Smew may also appear at the Pools in severe weather. Divers and grebes of several species are irregular in their visits and other infrequent arrivals include the Bittern, Marsh Harrier, Osprey, Temminck's Stint and Bearded Tit. From time to time much rarer species have been noted at Frampton Pools, and these are included in the list on page 30.

The Severn pastures and Hams

The river Severn, close to its junction with the Wye, has the second greatest tidal range in the world, but upstream from Gloucester the effects of this are controlled to some extent by a lock system. The famous Severn Bore,[23] which develops with tides in excess of 26 feet, seems to cause only temporary disturbance to birds on the river, which either ride out the rough water, or move to the banks and adjacent fields. A good view of the Bore may be had from near Stonebench.

The combination of great tidal range and large fluctuations in the volume of water coming down the Severn makes flooding a common phenomenon along the estuary and the lower reaches of the river. Parts of the alluvial flood-plain have been protected for many years by sea-wall embankments from all but occasional inundation, and such areas now constitute the fertile Severn pastures, nowhere better seen than at the New Grounds, Slimbridge. Several other low-lying districts, where flooding is still usual in autumn and winter, are known as "hams" and these may lie under water for considerable periods. Thus they may serve as breeding grounds for Lapwing, Redshank, Curlew, Yellow Wagtail and Meadow Pipit in summer, while attracting various kinds of ducks, Bewick's Swans, wild geese and other aquatic species during the winter. Important localities of

The Severn Vale

The flood-plain of the Severn near Coombe Canal in summer. Such places attract Redshank, Curlew, Yellow Wagtail and other breeding birds.

The Coombe Canal area flooded in winter. Ducks, geese and swans may appear in large numbers on these temporary waters.

this type are the Severn Ham at Tewkesbury, a former breeding ground for Corncrake and Marsh Warbler; Hasfield Ham, part of which is now the Ashleworth Ham Nature Reserve; the Coombe Canal marshes; the hams at Maisemore, Minsterworth and Elmore and Walmore Common to the north-east of Westbury-on-Severn.

Most of these low-lying areas are threatened by drainage schemes, as at Ashleworth a few years ago, when the nature reserve was saved only after much effort, including a Public Enquiry. Plans have been published for the prevention of flooding at Coombe Canal, and Walmore Common has been threatened with drainage on a number of occasions during the past thirty years.

The protected "New Grounds" near Slimbridge are now famous as one of Britain's leading wildfowl resorts and as the home of the Wildfowl Trust. For centuries wild geese have visited this area in autumn and winter. The dominant species is the White-fronted Goose, and numbers in excess of 7,000 birds have been recorded in a single season. Their favoured feeding grounds are the flood-plain pastures between the Severn and the Wildfowl Trust's enclosures, and fields closer to the Gloucester-Berkeley canal. Many geese may also be observed at rest on the exposed mud-banks of the river and, especially when disturbed at the Slimbridge area, considerable flocks may appear at Walmore Common, Coombe Canal and elsewhere in the Vale.

Pink-footed Geese used to occur in some numbers, but few are now reported (see page 60). All other British species of wild geese occur from time to time, including the rare Red-breasted and Snow Geese, while the Lesser White-front, doubtless overlooked in earlier years, is now known to occur almost every year in very small numbers. (See also Chapter Five.)

Drainage ditches and small flooded depressions in the riverside pastures attact a variety of ducks, including a few Garganey on passage, while many hundreds or thousands of Wigeon feed in the grassland during autumn and winter. Large winter populations of Curlew and Golden Plover are also present at the New Grounds and, in smaller numbers, on the opposite side of the river, while Whimbrel pass in spring and autumn. The sea-wall embankments and rough ground immediately above high-tide level attract visits from Rock Pipits and migrating Wheaters, while Snow Buntings and Short-eared Owls are less regular in occurrence. Peregrine and Merlin are autumn and winter predators of this district, and harriers are occasionally noted.

An interesting habitat known as Frampton Marsh lies at the northern end of the New Grounds and attracts many birds. It includes a fair-sized reed bed and some rough ground which tends to remain wet even when most of the region has little standing water. On a winter's day in 1967 the Frampton Hundred Acre field, adjacent to the marsh, held nearly 7,000 birds of at least seventeen species — ducks, geese, swans, waders and Starlings — on and around its flood-waters, clearly demonstrating the importance of such conditions for birds.[73]

The river Severn

Many of the species found on the riverside pastures and hams also visit the Severn itself, while other birds are more restricted to the river and its immediate margins. The Severn broadens suddenly at the southern end of the great horse-shoe bend at Arlingham, reaching a mile and a half in width off the New Grounds. After narrowing again at Sharpness it widens once more towards the southern county boundary. In these broad reaches great quantities of mud and sand have been deposited and now form exposed flats at low tide.

These are winter feeding grounds for many Shelduck, some of which remain to breed along the river margins before departing overland on their moult-migration (page 56). The exposed stretches of riverine deposits are also frequented by many waders and gulls. The former include small numbers of Oystercatcher, Grey Plover, Knot, Little Stint, Curlew

The Severn estuary near Slimbridge. Birds of many species are attracted at all levels of the tide. The hills of the Forest of Dean are seen across the river.

Sandpiper and Spotted Redshank, while both kinds of godwit are sometimes numerous. Scarcer species such as the Kentish Plover and Avocet are occasionally recorded. Rocky areas along the river are few, but Turnstones are not uncommon and the Purple Sandpiper has been seen at Guscar Rocks on the west bank.

Although the commoner waders such as the Dunlin and Ringed Plover may occur in considerable numbers at times, the total wader population of the estuary is less than might be expected from so large an area. The explanation lies in the great tidal range and the powerful currents of the Severn, which tend to keep the supply of food organisms in the surface mud at a relatively low level.

An enormous autumn and winter gull-roost is present every year off the New Grounds. The number of Common Gulls varies much, sometimes reaching 30,000, while estimates in excess of 50,000 have been made. Several hundred Black-headed Gulls and rather greater totals of Herring Gulls and Lesser Black-backs are also present at times. By day these birds spread far and wide, chiefly along the Vale and over the Cotswolds, to feed in fields, at refuse tips and along the river margins.

Common, Arctic, Sandwich and Little Terns may be seen over the river in spring and autumn, and all four British species of skua have been noted, although only the Arctic Skua is at all regular. Rough weather frequently brings maritime species up the estuary, notably the Gannet, Shag, petrels, Manx Shearwater and auks. Many no doubt find their way back to the sea, but other may be blown inland. The Kittiwake, however, which sometimes occurs over the Severn in large flocks, is seldom found exhausted or dead and it is possible that some at least are involved in an overland migration (see page 56).

Thus the whole of this estuary, together with its flood-plain and minor habitats on both sides of the river, supports a large and varied bird population which undergoes considerable seasonal changes. It is not surprising, therefore, that scarce and rare visitors are frequently noted. The following is a list of such species which currently come under the notice of the *British Birds* Rarities Committee (*Brit. Birds:* 67, p. 347), and which have been observed from time to time in various flood-plain and river localities. The majority of these records are from the New Grounds, Frampton Pools and the Wildfowl Trust enclosures, and all are detailed in the Systematic Section:

Little Bittern	White-rumped Sandpiper
Night Heron	Baird's Sandpiper
Squacco Heron	Broad-billed Sandpiper
Cattle Egret	Buff-breasted Sandpiper
Little Egret	Great Snipe
Purple Heron	Lesser Yellowlegs
Lesser White-fronted Goose	Wilson's Phalarope
Red-breasted Goose	Long-tailed Skua
American Wigeon	Ivory Gull
Blue-winged Teal	Gull-billed Tern
Ring-necked Duck	Caspian Tern
Red-footed Falcon	White-winged Black Tern
Gyrfalcon	Pallas's Sandgrouse
Little Crake	Red-throated Pipit
Baillon's Crake	Aquatic Warbler
Crane	Serin
Lesser Golden Plover	

The Wildfowl Trust enclosures

The formation of the Severn Wildfowl Trust (now the Wildfowl Trust) at Slimbridge in November 1946, and its subsequent development, was an event of great importance in the history of ornithology, and an account of the Trust's work is given on page 80. The buildings and enclosures on the New Grounds overlook the feeding areas of the wild geese, and are the headquarters of the world's largest and most comprehensive collection of living water-fowl. This began with a mere fifty birds in 1946, but by 1963 it held some 2,500 birds of 126 species. Most of the birds are pinioned to prevent escape, but some are free-flying and a few species appear to be in process of establishing feral breeding populations in Gloucestershire. This is true of the Gadwall, Red-crested Pochard, Ruddy Duck and Mandarin.

This open-air collection of birds kept in a series of constructed ponds under semi-natural conditions and close to the estuary, is a constant attraction to wild birds which frequently alight and remain in the enclosures for considerable periods. While it is the presence of tame birds which attracts the wild ones initially, it is the ample food supply, provided for the collection, which tempts them to stay.

The most conspicuous of these visitors are without doubt the many Bewick's Swans which now spend every winter in the Rushy Pen, commuting between this haven and feeding grounds along the river, and returning year after year with their families. Many of the commoner ducks standing within a few feet of human visitors are also free although no longer so wild as they were, having lost much of their fear of man. The same may be said of the numerous Greenfinches, Chaffinches, Collared Doves and Moorhens which thrive on the food and safety which the system proffers. A sense of security is perhaps as important to birds as it is to humans.

There are also records from the enclosures of exceptional visitors such as the Little Egret, Night Heron, Blue-winged Teal and Little Crake (see page 30). The first Ring-necked Duck ever to be accepted as a wild visitor to Europe alighted in March 1955 on the waters of the Rushy Pen, and was present during the two days following.

If one looks eastwards from one of the observation towers at the Wildfowl Trust, or indeed from any minor eminence in the Severn Vale, the skyline is seen to be formed at no great distance by a long line of level hills clad in a patchwork of downland and woodland. This is the steep north-westward facing *scarp-slope* of the Cotswolds which form the subject of the next Chapter. This high ground marks the eastern edge of the Severn Vale just as the Forest of Dean hills indicate its western limits.

The view back from the Cotswold escarpment edge towards the west and north-west gives a very good impression of the character of the Severn Vale outlined in this chapter, and an observer can readily appreciate the sudden alteration in the countryside as one moves from the Vale either westwards to the Forest or eastwards on to the Cotswold Hills. The marked change in patterns of habitat between these three regions readily accounts for the notable differences in their bird populations.

The Severn Vale from Coaley Peak on the Cotswold edge. The limestone downland drops sharply to the clay and sandstone of the Vale. The river and the Dean hills are seen in the distance.

CHAPTER THREE
The Cotswolds

Wheatear

Geological history

The Cotswolds furnish a good example of an escarpment composed of oolitic limestone, a rock much softer than the older Carboniferous limestone of the Wye valley, and one which has been freely eroded to give the steep slopes and low cliffs of the scarp-face, overlooking the Severn Vale.

The highest point of the Cotswolds is at 1083 feet above sea-level on Cleeve Common, near Cheltenham, and close to the scarp-face where the ground rises more than 700 feet over a distance of one mile. Several other areas near the edge of the escarpment between Stroud and Chipping Campden exceed 900 feet, but at the lower edge of the Cotswolds in the Thames area, at a distance of some twelve to twenty miles down the dipslope, most of the ground lies below the 300 foot contour.

Reference has already been made to the geological history of this region (pp. 22–23). The Pleistocene ice-sheet in the Severn Vale scarcely topped the Cotswold escarpment, although a small incursion of ice reached the Moreton-in-Marsh district from the north. The Cotswolds, however, must have experienced severe tundra conditions and, as the climate ameliorated some 10,000 years ago and forest conditions slowly spread throughout southern England, these limestone hills eventually become clad in some sort of open deciduous woodland, probably with beech and ash as the most important trees. About 5,000 years ago, in the Neolithic period, forest clearance in relation to primitive agriculture gradually developed, and by Bronze Age times, 3,500 years ago, much of this local Cotswold woodland had probably been removed.

From then onwards emphasis at different times has been on sheep-rearing or on arable farming. One consequence of the westward spread of the English in the sixth and seventh centuries A.D. was a shift from pasturage to arable, and the maximum area under plough was reached in the thirteenth century. There followed a swing back to sheep-farming, with a marked acceleration resulting from the great outbreaks of plague in the fourteenth century, which reduced the labour force by more than half.[53] (D.S.J. Price[1]).

Throughout the whole of this long period the really important ecological change was the continued loss of woodland, and considerable areas of the present-day Cotswolds still have the appearance of open and relatively treeless country. The lower lying regions, however, and particularly the river valleys, now carry an abundance of trees, while the indented edge of the escarpment, facing the Severn Vale, supports some of the finest seminatural "beech-hangers" in the country, on slopes too steep to be readily cultivated.

The scarp-face

These beautiful beechwoods are seen at their best on the steep, well-drained slopes near Cranham, Sheepscombe and Dursley. The deep shade under beeches limits the development of ground flora and, in these conditions, Wood Warblers breed in scattered localities along the scarp-slope, but the woodland avifauna in general is much less rich than that of the more varied woods in the dipslope valleys or in the Forest of Dean.

Popes Wood, Cranham: a typical scarp-edge beechwood. Birds tend to be less plentiful than in the Forest of Dean woodlands.

Some Cotswold edge woodland has been cleared and replanted. In such places a *plant succession* occurs, comparable with that seen under similar circumstances in the Forest of Dean (page 19), leading to scrub conditions and so, in time, back to woodland. As in the Dean, Tree Pipits, Grasshopper Warblers and (now very rarely) Nightjars are early arrivals, while Woodlarks adopted this habitat up to the early 1960s, but have not been reported since then.

The Woodlark used to nest also in very sparse vegetation on the downland slopes on or near the scarp-face, and in a few places further down the dislope. In fact these steep limestone banks, if not given over to woodland, were maintained as dry downland by the grazing of sheep and rabbits. Nowadays, however, rough grassy and bush vegetation tends to develop, especially since the great reduction in the rabbit population following the 1954 outbreaks of myxomatosis. This change in the vegetation may have hastened the disappearance of the Woodlark (see page 86), but has aided colonisation by Willow Warbler, Grasshopper Warbler, Whitethroat, Garden Warbler and other scrub-land birds. Another "lost" species is the Red-backed Shrike, which formerly nested in some numbers, especially where hawthorn was an important component of the vegetation.

The escarpment cliffs of oolitic limestone which overlook parts of the Severn Vale are of no great height. Those of Cleeve Hill, Leckhampton Hill and Crickley Hill provide nesting sites for many Jackdaws, but Ravens, although sometimes seen, have not resumed regular nesting on the

Leckhampton Hill, Cheltenham. In a few places the Cotswold edge has been eroded to form low cliffs, but these are too small to attract such birds as the Raven and Buzzard.

Cotswolds, either in cliffs or trees. Buzzards also are few and those which do breed select tree-sites along the scarp-face or at some distance down the dislope.

The open Cotswolds

The plateau-like summit of Cleeve Hill near the scarp-edge is a bleak expanse of short, dry vegetation which includes some heather and gorse on sandy deposits near the summit. Meadow Pipits breed here in greater numbers than elsewhere in the county, while a few pairs of Wheatear nest in most years in old walls and in the screes of the Postlip Valley. Ring Ouzels are probably regular on migration and, while old reports of nesting are open to doubt, it is here if anywhere that a pair might remain to breed. Stonechats nest irregularly in gorse-clad areas here and elsewhere on the wolds, but this bird is more sensitive than most to severe winters and may be absent for periods of many years.

The high, open nature of Cleeve Hill gives it an almost moorland appearance, and attracts occasional unusual visitors such as the Dotterel and Short-eared Owl, but the lack of extensive peat and the rapid drainage through the limestone are perhaps sufficient to explain the general paucity of bird-life here, as in other similar high ground.

Much of the elevated land between the main river valleys of the Cotswold

Cleeve Hill provides the nearest approach to high moorland scenery to be found in Gloucestershire, but its bird-life is sparse.

Dipslope scenery near Farmington. Land between the Cotswold rivers is dissected by small dry "bottoms". The bird-life of the whole area is that of agricultural land.

dipslope appears flat or gently undulating, and the general south-eastward dip of this country is not obvious. There are, in fact, many small dry valleys or "bottoms", whose sides are usually too steep for cultivation, and which dissect the plateau-like land between the rivers. Their steep sides are grazed by sheep, cattle and rabbits, producing downland vegetation, rich in limestone flora but rather poor in birds. Scrub, however, has developed on some of these slopes, and it was in one such place that a winter roost of Long-eared Owls was recently discovered, following a long period in which this species was unrecorded in Gloucestershire.

The country between the river systems is largely agricultural. It is divided into fields, often large and bounded either by stone walls or hedgerows. Small woods and plantations are present in sufficient numbers to make a long uninterrupted skyline unusual, but still sparse enough to give the impression of an open landscape.

Characteristic birds of the farmlands are the Skylark, Yellowhammer, Lapwing, Partridge and Red-legged Partridge, all widely distributed throughout the region, and the Corn Bunting which is not uncommon but of more local occurrence. Quail are often reported from the agricultural land, but are numerous only in some years, while both the Corncrake and the Stone-curlew are vanished Cotswold birds.

Common and Black-headed Gulls visit the upland fields from August to March in great numbers. The constant stream of small parties heading away from the Severn in the early mornings and returning to roost in the late afternoons is a familiar sight over the hills. Of recent years this pattern has been complicated by the development of another large roost in the Thames

Gulls and the plough

Area (page 50). Golden Plovers also visit certain restricted localities on spring and autumn passage, while winter feeding flocks of finches and other birds are common and widespread.

Storm-driven sea-birds and waders are not infrequently found on the Cotswolds. Severe gales in September 1974, for example, produced reports of a Puffin at Guiting Power, a Manx Shearwater at Barrington Park and, surprisingly, twelve Ringed Plovers and six Sanderlings apparently attempting to feed on the wet tarmac of Little Rissington airfield, 700 feet above sea-level (see also page 62).

Kestrel, Little Owl and Barn Owl are the best known birds of prey on the open wolds, but for breeding purposes they show a distinct preference for territories along the sides of the main river valleys and their subsidiary streams, where old trees provide nesting holes. The Hobby may also be found in such localities, a few pairs nesting in small woods and isolated clumps of trees, using old nests of Carrion Crow, Rook or Magpie.

The Cotswold river valleys

Of the principal dipslope streams, the Frome runs south from its source near Brimpsfield and then turns westwards through the Stroud valley to the Severn. The other rivers also rise on high ground near to the scarp-face, but flow south or south-eastwards, eventually joining the upper Thames (pages

Lower Slaughter: a characteristic Cotswold scene. Swifts still nest under loose stone roof-tiles in some villages, and the faster streams are the home of Dipper and Grey Wagtail.

22–23). From south to north, these rivers are the Churn, Coln, Leach, Windrush and the upper streams of the Evenlode. Their valleys are among the most attractive anywhere in Britain and provide a wide variety of bird habitats including, in addition to the streams themselves, artificial pools, mixed woodland, parkland, downland slopes and the old houses and gardens so characteristic of Cotswold villages and small towns.

Most of the birds usually associated with human dwellings are found here, including a declining number of Swifts, some of which still nest under loose-fitting stone tiles on cottage roofs. These colonies disappear when manufactured tiles are fitted to replace the old hand-cut stones. Swallows breed throughout the district; House Martins more locally, while Spotted Flycatchers are typical village birds. Lesser Spotted Woodpeckers are thinly distributed in the district and the Great Spotted is a frequent visitor to bird-tables, where Nuthatches are also regular in gardens with big trees in the vicinity.

Although examples of beechwood are to be found in and near these valleys, most woodland is now composed of a variety of tree species, frequently including some conifers. More light reaches the ground here than under pure stands of either beech or conifers, and the ground flora is dense and varied. Wood Warblers, preferring thinner plant cover, are therefore uncommon on the Cotswold dipslope, whereas most birds of the broad-leaved forest community are present in large numbers. Tawny Owl and Sparrowhawk are relatively numerous predators, while Garden Warbler, Blackcap, Chiffchaff, Treecreeper and various species of tits are common. The Willow Tit, however, although widespread is not numerous. Redstarts are perhaps more frequent in parkland habitats than in dense woodland; Nightingales are very local and increasingly scarce on the dipslope, and the evasive Hawfinch is now seldom reported. Woodcock breed in scattered woodland localities over a considerale area of the Cotswolds, and are even more widespread during autumn and winter, when Siskins and small numbers of Redpolls may also be found in woods and along the streams.

In a few places, woodlands are maintained on a much larger scale, although nowhere so extensively as in the Forest of Dean. The principal areas are Withington and Chedworth Woods, and those to the west of Cirencester Park. Honey Buzzard and Goshawk have been noted in these woods in the past and might colonise them if given the chance, but even the "common" Buzzard is not readily tolerated in a part of the country where game-rearing is still practised.

The rivers themselves are typically slow-flowing, alder-fringed streams, with deep trout-pools and occasional weirs and sluices, usually associated with old corn mills. Moorhen and Mallard are the common riverside birds, while the Heron is quite numerous, usually nesting singly or in very small groups in neighbouring woodland. Except, perhaps, in the Windrush valley, there is little sign of migratory movements by waterside birds through these valleys and even Sedge Warblers seldom if ever nest here (see page 53).

The Cotswolds 41

The river Churn at Rendcomb. Slow-flowing reaches of the dipslope streams attract Moorhen, Mallard and perhaps Coot and Little Grebe for breeding.

Rendcomb Lake in summer. The bird-life of artificial pools on the Cotswolds depends greatly upon the degree of colonisation by marsh vegetation.

Dipper and Grey Wagtail are attracted to rapid broken water, and both species nest, sometimes close together, beside mill-races and the outlets from artificial lakes. The Dipper is close to the eastern fringe of its British distribution here, and probably owes its existence on the Cotswolds to the presence of man-made structures along the streams. In some years from five to seven pairs of Dippers can be found along the first twelve miles of the river Churn, more than on the whole 27 miles of the Coln which, being longer, is also a slower river.

There are no large natural lakes on the limestone dipslope of the Cotswolds, but artificial pools have been established in various places, chiefly on private estates. Those in Woodchester and Cirencester Parks are breeding localities for Great Crested Grebes, while Little Grebes are found on a number of waters, including some broader reaches of the rivers. Other pools are partly silted up or even completely overgrown with marsh vegetation but, where open water still exists, Coot breed and a few of the commoner duck species, in addition to Mallard, may be found as passing visitors. Kingfishers are noted quite frequently at pools and along the rivers, but few nest here, owing to a lack of suitable banks.

A small gravel-pit system has been opened up at Bourton-on-the-Water, where oolitic limestone gravel deposits have accumulated near the confluence of the Windrush with its tributary, the Dikler. These waters attract a number of bird species which, however, are more numerous in the very extensive gravel-pits of the Cotswold Water Park in the Thames Area of the county, now to be described.

Dipper

CHAPTER FOUR
The Thames Area

Slavovian Grebe — Black necked Grebe

Geological history

The uppermost deposit laid down in the Jurassic Sea some 140 million years ago is known as Oxford clay. It is found extensively in the Thames Basin and its western fringe reaches the lower Cotswold dipslope in Gloucestershire. Here it forms a narrow belt to the south of a line passing close to Poole Keynes, South Cerney, Fairford and on to the county boundary a mile or so north of Lechlade. This is the region described here as the Thames Area, and is nowhere more than about three miles in width from north to south.

Much of the Oxford clay in Gloucestershire, however, which one might expect to find close to the surface of the ground, is now covered by extensive gravel beds. This gravel is composed of disintegrated oolitic limestone, eroded from the Cotswold plateau during glacial and post-glacial times, and washed down the main river valleys to be deposited over the much younger Oxford clay. This erosion was responsible also for the innumerable dry valleys of the dipslope, referred to on page 38.

The ground in the Thames Area is flat or gently undulating; the water-table is often only a foot or two beneath the surface, and the soil water is alkaline in reaction. The land is divided by hedgerows into numerous small fields and traversed in some districts by water-filled ditches. In contrast to the Cotswolds, woods are few and small, and the common tree along the streams and drainage dykes is the crack willow rather than the alder. Close to the Thames and the terminal reaches of its main tributaries, fields are larger and subject to the periods of flooding characteristic of so-called water meadows.

Many of the willows and other trees are pollarded and ancient, providing nesting sites for such birds as the Tree Sparrow, Redstart, Little Owl and Green Woodpecker. Close to the larger streams, the vegetation on the damp ground may be very dense, here and there attracting Nightingales to moist copses and withy-beds, while Sedge Warblers are plentiful and small colonies of Reed Warblers may be found.

Gravel pits: the Cotswold Water Park

The real ornithological interest of this small region, however, centres upon the extensive system of large gravel pits which has been developed since the 1920s. The industry grew slowly until about 1950, but since then more and more excavations have been made in two main areas, one between Poole Keynes and Cerney Wick in the west, the other in the Fairford-Lechlade region to the east. The underlying Oxford clay impedes drainage of water from the district, and this explains why permanent lakes are formed wherever gravel is removed (see diagram, page 46; and *cf.* Frampton Pools, page 25).

In the late 1960s the concept of a "Cotswold Water Park" became firmly established, and the Park now encompasses both sets of pits, sometimes referred to as "CWP West" and "CWP East". The intervening ground, however, carries unworked gravel beds and these may yet be opened up. In any event, the two series of waters form a single ecological unit and are treated as such for present purposes.[35]

By 1980 the number of gravel pits potentially available for birds and other forms of wild life, not to mention human recreation, exceeded 90, three-quarters of them in the western section. The total area of these waters is not far short of 1,500 acres (some 600 hectares), the Water Park itself occupying more than 14,000 acres (about 5,700 hectares).[35] Prior to gravel extraction the Thames Area was totally lacking in large sheets of standing water, so that a whole range of new habitats has been created in this corner of the county as a result of human activity.

The depth of the gravel beds seldom exceeds twenty feet and most of the pits are therefore from ten to twenty feet deep. In the early days, bulldozers and mechanical shovels were the principal means of excavation, while pumping was employed to keep down the water-level, thus producing shallow pits with uneven floors. By 1960, however, the dragline or "wet-dig" method was in use, crane-grabs being employed to deepen superficial excavations by scraping gravel from under the water. In these circumstances pumping becomes unnecessary and pits with vertical sides are the result. These differences in technique have important effects upon the consequent habitats and their bird-population.

The Thames Area 45

The drag-line method of gravel extraction produces steep marginal banks. Pumping may maintain relatively dry conditions, but if discontinued the pit soon fills with water.

South Cerney: a pit such as this usually attracts many kinds of birds throughout the year, but snow and ice may cause complete desertion.

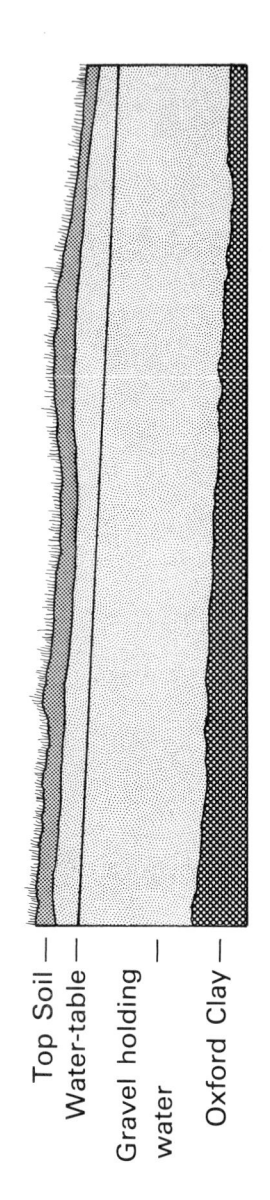

BEFORE EXTRACTION

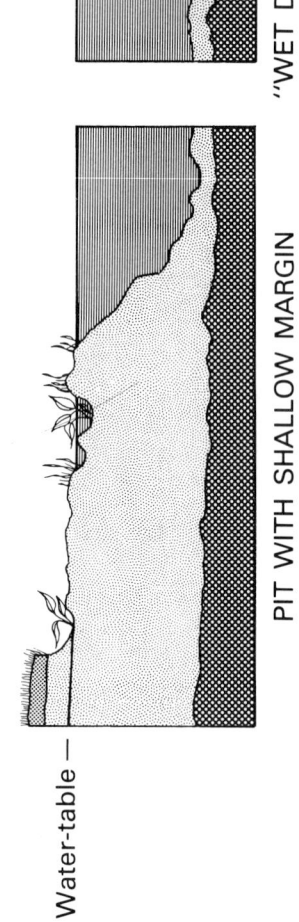

Top Soil —
Water-table —
Gravel holding water —
Oxford Clay —

PIT WITH SHALLOW MARGIN

"WET DIG" METHOD

AFTER EXTRACTION

Water-table —

Vertical section through a Water Park gravel-pit (see text)

Shallow, drained pits

Pits opened up by shallow digging methods and those kept relatively dry by pumping have large areas of exposed gravel interspersed with pools and shallow channels. Algae, notably species of *Chara,* and various forms of invertebrate animal life soon appear in the water, while invasion by Flowering Plant colonisers, both on gravel and in the water, soon follows. In these early stages, the pits attract a variety of waders, especially during overland spring and autumn passage. In all, some 30 kinds have been reported in the gravel pit area since 1952, including uncommon species such as Kentish Plover, Temminck's Stint, Pectoral Sandpiper and Wood Sandpiper. During a ten-day period in May 1975, seventeen species of wader were encountered, three at that time new to the Water Park list of birds, and most being seen at one pit which happened to be in a suitable condition (Glos. Nat. Soc. *Journal,* June 1975). This draws attention to the fact that gravel-pit habitats tend to alter rather rapidly, especially during the earlier stages.

Breeding birds of the open gravel are very few. The Lapwing may be found nesting, but more characteristic is the Little Ringed Plover, first reported here in 1953 and now occurring in some numbers. This bird is very intolerant of vegetation on its nesting ground, so that breeding pairs decrease in number as the plant-cover increases. The continued presence of Little Ringed Plovers in the area will depend upon provision of extensive stretches of fresh gravel, either by the opening of new pits or by maintenance techniques under nature reserve conditions.

The plant species which colonise these partially flooded pits are numerous. Wind-borne seeds introduce sow-thistles, coltsfoot and various willow-herbs, while grasses and weeds of agricultural land encroach from surrounding fields. The shallow pools gradually develop a varied marsh flora which may include species of rush and sedge, reedmace, bulrush and reed, while water-milfoil and various kinds of water-crowfoot and pondweed grow more or less submerged. Amphibious bistort may form dense mat-like growths in some places.*

During this process of *plant succession* visits by most of the wading birds decline in frequency, although Snipe and Jack Snipe show an increase, while Green and Wood Sandpipers, Greenshank and Redshank may continue to visit for some years, Redshanks remaining in spring to breed in some localities in and around the pits.

At this stage, provided there is a large enough area of open water, Moorhen, Coot and Little Grebe may be found nesting, and in recent years a large breeding population of Tufted Duck has developed, the birds nesting in rough vegetation around the pits or on islands, and usually quite close to the water. Other breeding birds, whose numbers increase under

---

*For scientific names of plant species see Appendix Two.

Tufted Duck

these conditions, include Reed Bunting and Sedge Warbler, both of which are common; the Yellow Wagtail which nests in variable numbers, and the Reed Warbler, of which there are several small colonies. As in the Severn Vale, Reed Warblers are not restricted to reed-beds but also inhabit marsh vegetation beneath osiers and other willow species, often with reeds nearby. There are also a few records of Marsh Warblers nesting in such places in the Water Park, and Nightingales are now increasingly frequent at gravel-pit sites.

The arrival of willow seedlings in the plant succession may have far-reaching consequences because, if left undisturbed, the habitat then develops into a dense willow-thicket or "carr", which may eventually extend into quite deep water, producing conditions unsuitable for most species of marsh and water birds.

The sequence of events outlined above was studied in some detail at South Cerney between 1952 and 1967, and also at gravel pits near Lechlade which became the Edward Richardson Nature Reserve (B. Campbell and C.M. Swaine).[1]

Deep-water pits

The willow-carr stage seldom develops over extensive areas, for the great majority of gravel pits are now deepened by the drag-line method (page 44) and so, after a variable period of time, the worked-out pits become permanently and deeply flooded when pumping is discontinued.

Flooded pits eventually develop marginal vegetation, and the presence of islands helps to attract Great Crested Grebe, Tufted Duck and Kingfisher to breed, while the Hobby may come in search of hirundines and large insects.

Many deep pits nevertheless retain some shallow marginal areas with emergent growth of reeds, reedmace and bulrushes, and these are the breeding grounds of Moorhen, Coot, Little Grebe and Great Crested Grebe. The latter prefers the larger waters and has increased steadily in this part of Gloucestershire, so that it is now a characteristic bird at all seasons.

Shallow-water vegetation is also the favoured foraging habitat of the surface-feeding ducks. The Mallard is the only regular breeding members of this group, but Wigeon and Teal are plentiful in winter, while Shoveler, Pintail and Gadwall, which were formerly very uncommon, show recent signs of increase. Garganey occur in small numbers on passage.

All these gravel pits are "marl lakes", resulting from the extraction of limestone gravel. The consequent high lime content of the water results in a deposit of marl on the bottom, a process which involves removal of most of the available phosphate from the water. Submerged plants, rooted in the marl, have access to this phosphate, but the general deficiency in the lake-water inhibits rapid development of small suspended and floating algae (phytoplankton). The lake-water is therefore clear and the rooted plants do well under these well-lit conditions. Further development of the vegetation, however, and of the animal life associated with it, is slow, depending upon depth of water and the gradual build-up of a humus cover to the marl. This rather complex sequence of events probably explains why populations of birds such as Coot and Pochard, which benefit from the rich underwater plant-life, develop earlier than those of animal feeders such as the Great Crested Grebe.

Extensive open waters of this type, devoid of emergent vegetation, are now the autumn and winter haunts of a big population of diving ducks, together with small numbers of other species which require deep water in which to feed. Large gatherings of Pochard and Tufted Duck are often present, and these may be joined by considerable flocks of Wigeon, Mallard and other surface-feeding ducks, which frequently rest on open water when not in search of food. Goldeneye and Goosander are now regular winter visitors in small numbers, with several other diving ducks occurring more rarely. Holland and Mardle,[35] in 1977, published a list of Wildfowl Counts and Peak Figures in the Water Park for the years 1973–77, and other data appear in the *Gloucestershire Bird Reports*.[31] All wildfowl counts in Gloucestershire made under the National Wildfowl Count Scheme are deposited at the Wildfowl Trust, Slimbridge.

Open-water visitors outside the breeding season also include various species of grebe and diver, the Cormorant and an occasional Osprey, while in recent years a large gull-roost has developed on the big pit near South Cerney. Many thousands of gulls now gather there on autumn and winter evenings. Most are Black-headed Gulls, but hundreds of Lesser Black-backs and Common Gulls may be present, with small numbers of Herring Gulls. Some of these birds evidently move on over the Cotswolds before dusk to the huge roost on the river Severn (page 30).

Spring and autumn passage may bring flocks of Black Tern to these waters, with smaller numbers of other tern species. The recent nesting of Black-headed Gull and Ringed Plover in this region, and of Common Tern just beyond the county boundary, encourages the hope that these and perhaps other species may one day establish breeding grounds in the Water Park gravel-pits of Gloucestershire. Two breeding species, already familiar in the area, owe their presence to the drag-line method of gravel-winning, for this tends to produce more or less vertical banks or small cliffs round the margins of the pits. The Kingfisher breeds in greater concentration here than elsewhere in the county while Sand Martins are common colonial nesters. The large numbers of these and other hirundines, which hawk for insects over and around the lakes, attract that high-speed falcon the Hobby which is now often seen in the district in summer, feeding on small birds and large insects.

The South Cerney sewage-farm, close to the northern edge of the Water Park and just outside the gravel-pit region, includes a number of damp fields, sometimes more or less flooded. This extensive area has for long attracted marsh-loving birds in greater numbers than in equivalent areas elsewhere in the region. These include Teal, Wigeon, Shoveler, a variety of waders, a few Garganey, wild geese and swans, and occasional rarities of various kinds. The Thames Water Authority has recently constructed a modern plant at the site, but so far this has not reduced its value for ornithologists.

The Cotswold Water Park, and the Thames Area as a whole, have produced records of a number of scarce and rare species which have not so far been mentioned. These include the following which appear on the current list drawn up by the *British Birds* Rarities Committee (*Brit. Birds*, 67, p. 347): White Stork, Ring-necked Duck, Red-footed Falcon, Collared Pratincole, Buff-breasted Sandpiper, White-winged Black Tern, Alpine Swift, Bee-eater, White's Thrush, and Great Reed Warbler. This is a short list compared with that for the Severn estuary (page 30), but the Thames Area gravel pits constitute a relatively new and expanding series of wetland habitats, and one of great potential.

Kingfisher

CHAPTER FIVE
Migration and Other Movements in Relation to Gloucestershire

(For references see the end of this chapter, and consult also the Systematic Section).

Swallows

It may be said at the outset that this account must contain a considerable element of speculation, especially where migration routes are discussed. Evidence in this field has to be sought outside as well as from within the county, and the list of references given at the end of the chapter therefore contains a number of publications, mostly in *British Birds,* reporting observations from other counties which have a bearing on this subject.

Sources of information within Gloucestershire include the Severn Vale Ringing Group,[61] whose work covers a wide variety of species; the Wildfowl Trust,[78] mainly concerned with the Anatidae; and a number of individuals who have made observations at scattered places, especially in recent years in the Severn Vale and the Cotswold Water Park.[35]

Recoveries of ringed wildfowl at the Wildfowl Trust, Slimbridge, must now exceed 4,000 in number, with up to 25% recovery rate for some species. The Severn Vale Ringing Group, however, concentrating mainly on passerines and waders, must be content with a much lower percentage of returns, and the construction of a comprehensive migration picture for these birds is of necessity much slower than for ducks, geese and swans. Where ringing data warrant it, comments on individual species have been included in the Systematic Section (page 104), but details of single recoveries have usually been omitted. (See maps on pages 54, 58).

Spring migration

The main spring arrivals in Gloucestershire are those on a broad front from directions between south-east and south-south-west, and those on a much narrower pathway from the south-west along the Severn estuary and its margins.

Small night-flying migrants may cover more than 300 miles in a single spring night, and they are therefore quite capable of travelling overnight from France or, under ideal conditions, from Spain or Italy to any part of Gloucestershire. It is significant in this context that early individuals of such birds as Chiffchaff, Willow Warbler, Blackcap, Nightingale and Redstart are reported more or less simultaneously in the Cotswold Water Park and in the Severn Vale on opposite sides of the Cotswolds, and in each case several days before members of the same species appear on the Cotswold dipslope. Movement of these passerines on to the dipslope tends to be slow, probably because of the exposed nature of the hills. Even the sheltered north-south river valleys of the dipslope transmit only small or moderate numbers of birds from the Thames Area and these are probably heading for local breeding grounds.

Many small birds bound for Wales and the north-west must pass over Gloucestershire by night and undetected, but it seems reasonable to suppose that a proportion, which varies with the weather conditions, break their journey for a few hours of feeding before continuing northwards. Some of the Water Park birds may fall into this category. This appears to be the case with Wheatear and Whinchat and may be so for other species, such as Yellow Wagtail and Turtle Dove, which sometimes appear temporarily in numbers which seem too large to be accounted for by potential local breeders. On the north-west side of the Cotswolds, the Severn Vale Ringing Group has established peak passage times for a number of passerine species, chiefly warblers (Table, below). Some of these are doubtless local birds; others may have farther to go.

Peak passage times of warblers in the Severn Vale area of Gloucestershire

	Spring	Autumn
Sedge Warbler	Early May	Mid-August
Reed Warbler	Early May	Late August
Lesser Whitethroat	Early May	Late August to early September
Whitethroat	Early May	Early August
Garden Warbler	–	Late August to early September
Blackcap	Mid-April	Late August to early September
Chiffchaff	Early to mid-April	Early to mid-September
Willow Warbler	Mid- to late April	Mid- to late August

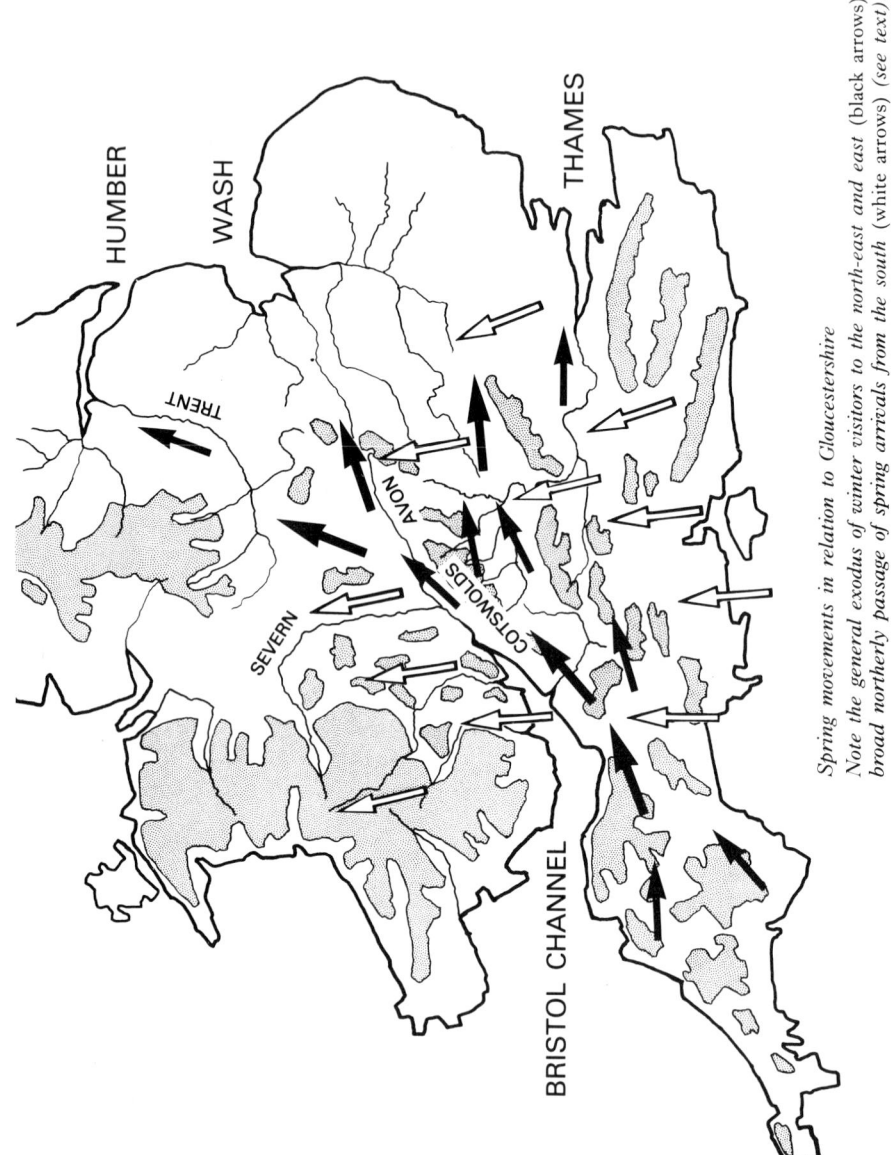

Spring movements in relation to Gloucestershire
Note the general exodus of winter visitors to the north-east and east (black arrows) and the broad northerly passage of spring arrivals from the south (white arrows) (see text).

A case of particular local interest is that of the Pied Flycatcher. The autumn migration of this species takes the birds down the western margin of Europe, but there is some evidence to support a more easterly return route in spring. Few Pied Flycatchers are recorded at south coast observatories, and passing birds on the Cotswolds or in the Severn Vale are seldom seen, so it seems probable that the Forest of Dean and Welsh breeding populations arrive by non-stop overnight flights from the south-east.

Swifts and hirundines present a somewhat different situation. The major spring movement of these birds into Gloucestershire is up the Severn estuary where huge numbers are sometimes seen (Moyser, G. and Sellers, R.M.: *Journal,* Glos. Nat. Soc., Aug. 1980). How far to the south-west and north-east this narrow flyway extends is at present under investigation. Birds of these species also arrive in the Thames Area of the county as part of a broad-front movement from the south. Swallows and Swifts may be seen to move on up the Cotswold dipslope, but House Martins tend to appear suddenly and rather late on the hills, while very few Sand Martins are reported passing over the Cotswolds or, except for the Windrush, along their river valleys.

The considerable variety of waders noted in small numbers on passage through the Water Park has already been mentioned (page 47). Some of these birds do cross the Cotswolds, for a few Common and Green Sandpipers are noted passing up the dipslope valleys in spring, and there is a thin movement of Curlew and Whimbrel over the high ground. It is probable also that spring and autumn records of Dunlin and Ringed Plover at these gravel pits refer to birds moving up or down the west side of Britain (but see pages 143, 147). Ringing returns show that some members of both species pass northwards along the middle Severn valley. Waders, however, often migrate at considerable heights above the ground and frequently by night, so that passage to the north-west and north across Gloucestershire may be heavier than appears to be the case, many of the birds not alighting even along the Severn estuary.

Spring migration on a narrow pathway up the estuary is much more obvious and therefore better known than some of the broad front movement just discussed. The existence of a flyway between the Severn estuary and the east coast between the Humber and the Wash was recognised many years ago. The birds using this route are chiefly those which breed in northern and eastern Europe and north Russia, and which have wintered in Gloucestershire and the south-west of Britain. Black-headed, Common and Lesser Black-backed Gulls are involved, and perhaps also small numbers of Common and Arctic Terns and Arctic Skuas. The route is probably followed also by waders of several species, notably those wintering in the south-west, such as the godwits, Green Sandpiper, Spotted Redshank, Greenshank and Little Stint; and less consistently by the Wood Sandpiper, Curlew Sandpiper and other birds which may have drifted farther to the west than the majority of their species.

An interesting case is that of the Black Tern. In some years these birds reach western Britain in greater numbers than normal and then apparently move eastwards towards the Thames estuary and the Wash, thus enabling a short sea-crossing to the Continent (Dickens, *Brit. Birds,* XLVIII, pp. 148–169). This would explain the passage of Black Terns both up the Severn estuary and through the Cotswold Water Park on the opposite side of the hills. Indeed it seems plausible to suppose that wader movement through the Water Park is also, in part, a southern component of the larger north-east passage up the Severn estuary to the east coast via the Warwickshire Avon and across the Cotswolds.

There seems to be little if any indication that warblers and other small visitors make this journey from Severn to Wash and Humber, and any which might occasionally do so are likely to be re-orientated birds which had drifted too far to the west. There is, however, some ringing evidence involving Willow Warbler and Blackcap in a northward movement up the Middle Severn towards the Cheshire Plain.

Early spring arrival in Gloucestershire may coinide with, or even precede the departure of birds which have wintered in the county. Fieldfares, Redwings, Bramblings and other species which are winter visitors to this part of Britain now move away to the east and north-east. The exodus includes individuals of some species which also breed in Gloucestershire, such as the Curlew, Skylark, Meadow Pipit and Reed Bunting, thus complicating the picture.

Many of the duck which have wintered in the Severn and the Water Park also leave in the same general direction, while the Vale sees the departure of the many White-fronted Geese and Bewick's Swans which have spent the cold months on the estuary. The geese and swans leave along a rather narrow belt over the northern Cotswolds, heading first for the Netherlands and West Germany before moving on to western Russia and finally to their tundra breeding grounds. They desert the Severn in February or March, the actual departures (and arrivals in autumn) being much influenced by weather conditions, notably wind-direction: Bewick's Swans, and probably White-fronts and other large birds, show a marked preference for tail-winds.[27]

Two other rather peculiar migratory movements are worthy of mention. The first concerns Kittiwakes which, between March and May, sometimes appear in large flocks in the Severn estuary, and which may form part of the overland migration of birds to the east coast. There is little evidence of a return movement in autumn (Hume, *Brit. Birds,* 69, pp. 62–63).

The second case is that of the moult-migration of Shelduck. During early July great numbers of Shelduck, presumably from the coasts of Wales and south-west England, gather in Bridgwater Bay. This, however, is chiefly a "staging-post" for although many remain to moult there the majority move up the Severn, perhaps joined as they go by the Gloucestershire birds, and so pass north-eastwards to the Wash or, following a more easterly course, cross the north Cotswolds to the Thames estuary. Their flight then continues to the main moulting grounds on the Knechtsand in the south-eastern corner of the North Sea. This is a specialised mid-summer migration, unrelated to spring movements although following one of the spring passage routes. As a post-breeding migration it seems more akin to autumn passage in spite of its anomalous direction and early date. A clearly defined return route from September onwards has not been identified.

Autumn migration

Autumn passage between the east coast and the Severn is more obvious, or at least better documented (pp. 63–64) than are spring movements and it is clear that ducks, waders, gulls, terns and certain passerine species all pass through the English midlands in considerable numbers in autumn.

The normal autumn migration of small summer visitors from Scandinavia and northern Europe in general is in directions between south-west and south-east towards Africa and Arabia, and under ordinary circumstances few would cross the North Sea to Britain. Under certain weather conditions, however, large numbers may be deflected westwards and reach our eastern coasts. On arrival these birds quickly redirect their flight to the south, and few continue inland for any great distance. Raines (see page 63), however, noted many migrant species, including warblers, Whinchats, hirundines and Swifts, in the Trent valley heading south-west, but it cannot be assumed that these were necessarily of continental origin. Simms' autumn observations[63][64] at the northern end of the Cotswolds (i.e. still further to the south-west), indicate some movement towards the Severn estuary by Swifts, hirundines and Yellow Wagtails, but are chiefly concerned with gulls, Skylarks, Meadow Pipits and finches which are potential winter visitors to Gloucestershire and beyond.

Thus passerine summer visitors seen in Gloucestershire in autumn are most likely to be of British stock moving south or south-east towards France (see Table, page 53), and few of continental origin are likely to drift as far to the south-west as this county. This conclusion is supported by the absence of ringing data to the contrary, and by the extreme scarcity of Gloucestershire records for east-coast drift-migrants such as the Bluethroat, Barred Warbler, Yellow-browed Warbler and Red-breasted Flycatcher.

Those passerines which do travel from the east coast to Gloucestershire are mainly winter visitors to this county and to the south-west of Britain generally. They include Redwing, Fieldfare, Skylark, Meadow Pipit, Yellowhammer and Chaffinch. These birds often travel on a broad front and in flocks. Non-passerines which may follow narrower flyways to the Severn estuary and the Cotswold Water Park include Curlew, Whimbrel, several small and medium-sized wader species, Common, Arctic and perhaps Sandwich Terns, and various kinds of gulls.

Birds following this route from the Humber tend to pass up the valley of the Trent and either cross to the middle Severn or into the Avon catchment area, both these movements leading to the Severn estuary in Gloucestershire. Birds flying south-west from the Wash may pass down either side of

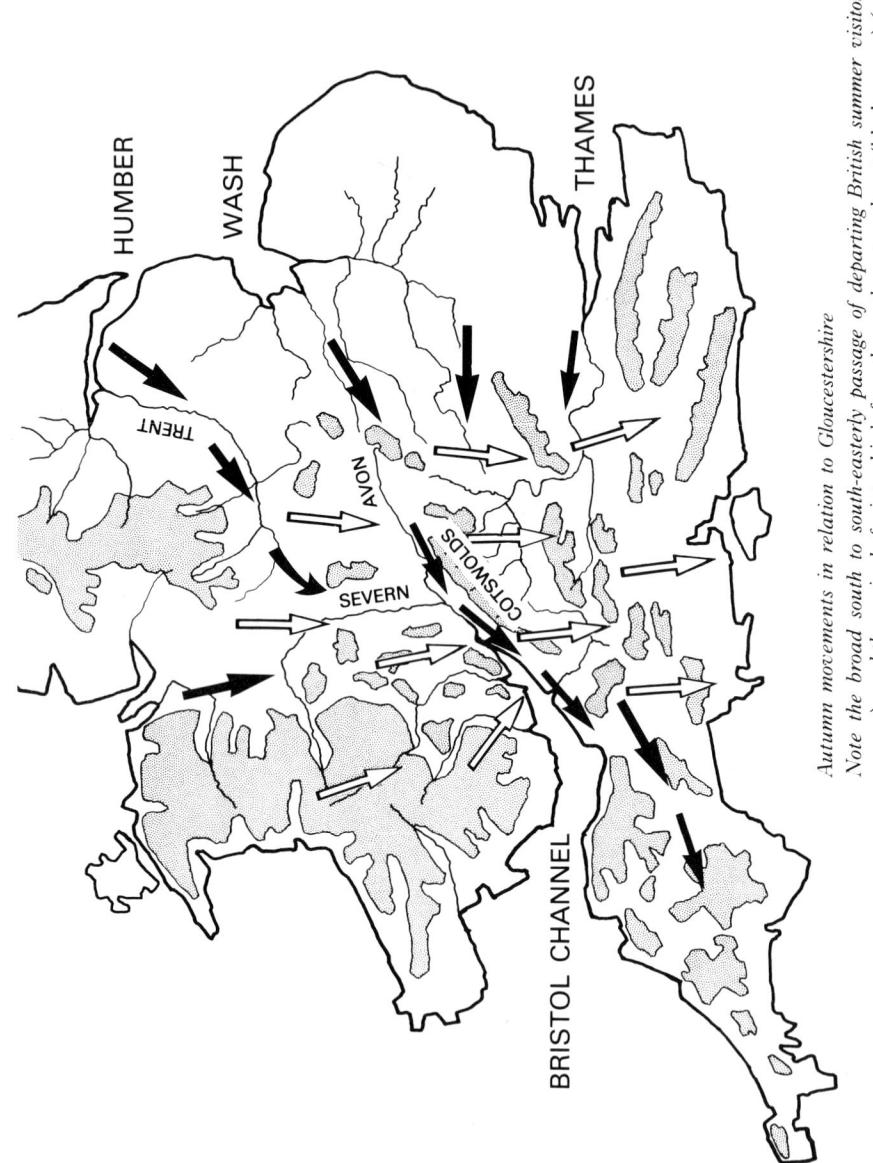

Autumn movements in relation to Gloucestershire
Note the broad south to south-easterly passage of departing British summer visitors (white arrows), and the arrival of winter birds from the north-east and east (black arrows) (see text).

the Cotswolds. Those to the north side also reach the lower Severn via the Warwickshire Avon, while some birds passing south of the hills may arrive at the gravel pits of the Cotswold Water Park in the Thames Area of Gloucestershire. Birds of either group may then continue to the south-west. On the other hand many may pass above the hills which form no great obstacle to migration.

Indeed the suggestion that birds migrate along set pathways must not be applied too widely. Many do not follow "leading lines" or other clearly defined routes, either because they are "broad-front" migrants or because they travel high enough to be independent of topographical features when crossing lowland Britain. Good examples of the latter group are the geese, swans and ducks. Thanks largely to the work of the Wildfowl Trust, considerably more is known about the migratory behaviour of these birds than that of any other group found in Gloucestershire.

The spring migration route used by White-fronted Geese leaving the Severn was mentioned on page 56. Their autumn journey from north Russian breeding grounds to winter quarters in north-west Europe follows a more direct route,[51] but the birds break their journey in East Germany and the Netherlands, as also do some of the Bewick's Swans which travel the same course; even the earliest Gloucestershire arrivals have taken at least a month to come here.

Several thousand wild White-fronted Geese gather at the New Grounds in winter, returning in spring to their north Russian breeding grounds. The view is from a Wildfowl Trust observation tower. (Photo: Wildfowl Trust)

The great flocks of White-fronts approaching north-west Europe in autumn may contain small numbers of other goose species. The scarce Lesser White-fronted and even rarer Red-breasted Geese which reach the Severn estuary may have come all the way from northern Russia with their larger and more numerous companions, while the very small numbers of Barnacle, Greylag and Bean Geese on the Severn are most likely to have joined those White-fronts which, in late autumn, move onwards from Germany and Holland and cross England to reach Gloucestershire.

The Severn estuary is also approached in autumn by small numbers of geese from the north-west. These include members of the Greenland race of the White-fronted Goose, *A.a. flavirostris*, and very occasional light-bellied Brent Geese, *B.b.hrota*, which have overshot their more usual wintering grounds in Ireland. The dark-bellied Brents, *B.b.bernicla*, which occur more frequently, are "overshoots" in the opposite direction, from the Wash-Essex population or perhaps from the south coast.

Pink-footed Geese present a more complex picture. Large numbers used to visit the estuary, but a decline set in from the 1930s. Ringing showed that those still coming between 1950 and 1960 were of Icelandic origin as, presumably, were those of earlier years. The Icelandic population wintering in Britain, however, has retreated northwards into Scotland, and any Pink-feet now appearing in Gloucestershire are more likely to be of continental origin.

Many ducks also winter in the Severn estuary and increasingly in the Cotswold Water Park, or pass through the county on passage. The local populations of Mallard are relatively sedentary, but autumn influxes from north-west Russia and the Baltic are usual. Other surface-feeding ducks, the Pintail, Teal, Wigeon and Shoveler, have breeding populations extending far to the east across Russia, and are regular migrants in large numbers into Britain. No doubt most Gloucestershire birds come in more or less directly from the east coast to both the Water Park and the Severn estuary, and the same applies to diving ducks such as Pochard, Tufted Duck and Goldeneye which have similarly wide breeding distributions in the north and east. Ringing results indicate that many of the ducks already in Gloucestershire tend to move away in autumn to Ireland, France and Iberia, being replaced by the long-distance migrants from Europe and the USSR.[50][51]

Other movements

All migratory movements exhibit some degree of irregularity, if only in the numbers of individuals involved. In some species, however, these numerical variations are very marked giving rise to "irregular migrations" or "irruptions". The British species chiefly concerned are birds of the Eurasian coniferous forest belt, notably the Crossbill and Waxwing, both of these appearing in Gloucestershire more or less regularly but in very variable numbers. Pallas's Sandgrouse, an inhabitant of arid steppe-lands and formerly an irruptive migrant to this country, appeared in Gloucestershire in small numbers during the invasion years of 1863 and 1888, but has not been noted subsequently. All such birds have specialised winter food requirements, and irruptions tend to occur when a rise in the homeland population of birds coincides with developing food-shortages in the same areas.

The availability of food is a major factor also in causing "weather movements" of birds. The most conspicuous examples of these are those associated with very cold and snowy weather from January to March, which often approaches Gloucestershire gradually from the north and east. At such times large numbers of birds may be seen flying in directions most frequently between west and south over all parts of the county. Many species are involved, notably Redwing, Fieldfare, Meadow Pipit, Skylark,

Fieldfares

Woodpigeon and Lapwing, but sometimes also such birds as Song Thrush, Chaffinch and Greenfinch, and all apparently fleeing before the advance of winter.

As the cold weather arrives, other birds may also leave their accustomed haunts, a departure especially noticeable on the hills of the Cotswolds. Dippers and Grey Wagtails may disappear temproarily; fewer gulls visit their Cotswold feeding grounds, and the Thames Area gravel-pits, so richly populated at other times, become virtually birdless when their waters are iced over. In the Severn Vale, on the other hand, bird populations may increase dramatically, for the estuary and adjacent low-lying flood-plain areas are less affected by frost and snow than are the hills. The importance of the Wildfowl Trust's enclosures, with their free supply of food, should not be overlooked in this context (page 81).

Under the severest conditions, however, even the Severn Vale may lose a considerable proportion of its winter birds. In February 1963, for example, the numbers of Lapwing, Curlew, Meadow Pipit and many other species were greatly depleted, while most of the wild geese moved away to the south and west. Ringing studies showed that Teal and, to a lesser extent, Wigeon went first to Ireland and then south to France and the Iberian peninsula. Tufted Duck deserted ice-bound gravel-pits in favour of coastal and estuarine habitats, and many of them later crossed the Channel to France.[50]

No doubt the approach of rough weather from the sea in the west also induces appropriate avoidance movements among birds, but these are seldom noted except for the so-called "wrecks" of sea-birds which occur from time to time. These are the result of prolonged periods of high on-shore winds or sudden changes of wind-direction during gales, which drive tired and hungry birds on to the land, where many are found dead or exhausted. A few wind-blown individuals of several species, however, notably Manx Shearwater, Leach's Petrel, Gannet and Little Auk, are found fairly frequently in Vale and Cotswold localities and also on gravel-pits in the Cotswold Water Park. These are most frequent in autumn and the majority are young birds. The Bristol Channel appears to act as a kind of funnel-shaped trap for inexperienced birds caught in windy weather, and these events are distinct from the major "wrecks" noted above.

Autumn and winter feeding flocks of many terrestrial species are to be found all over Gloucestershire as in most parts of Britain. Those composed of tits, finches, buntings, Lapwings, Woodpigeons, Rooks, Jackdaws and other birds are familiar sights every year, but a particular type of social gathering exhibited by some bird species is of more local nature, although often quite spectacular. This is the habit of communal roosting in huge numbers, the birds dispersing in all directions at dawn to feed in the surrounding countryside, and returning to roost at dusk.

Starling roosts numbering several hundred thousand birds are reported from time to time in the county, and Mellersh[41] gives a graphic description of one near Gloucester at the turn of the century which is said to have contained a million birds or more. The locations of Starling roosts frequently change, but the two large gull roosts in Gloucestershire are much more stable. One is on the Severn near Slimbridge; the other at a large gravel-pit close to South Cerney in the Thames Area (pages 30, 50).

The seasonal nature of Starling and gull roosts is seen also in the large nocturnal gatherings of Pied Wagtails which have been reported from autumn to spring or early summer at Cheltenham, Gloucester, Frampton-on-Severn and elsewhere. Some of these wagtails are known to originate in northern England and Scotland, the birds joining our more local and perhaps less migratory individuals for roosting purposes (*Brit. Birds*, 72, p. 299; Severn Vale Ringing Group[61]). The summer invasion of the Forest of Dean woodlands by Rooks and Jackdaws to feed on caterpillars has already been mentioned (pages 19, 202).

Migratory and other movements 63

The picture of migratory and other movements in and around Gloucestershire is clearly very far from complete. Perhaps the best reason for attempting such an account is that it may stimulate further studies of bird movements at different vantage points in the region. Co-ordinated programmes of observations in spring and from August to October would be particularly valuable in confirming or modifying some of the hypotheses outlined here, and in providing evidence to back up that from ringing studies.

Geese in flight

Selected references pertaining to migratory movements in and around Gloucestershire

(References are to *British Birds* unless otherwise stated).

Vol. 4, pp. 104–112: Jourdain, F.C.R. and Witherby, H.F.: *Recent records from Staffordshire, Warwickshire and Worcestershire.*

Vol. 17, pp. 139–142: Boyd, A.W.: *Notes from Staffordshire.*

Vol. 32, pp. 34–37 and 64–77: Hollom, P.A.D.: *Summaries of inland occurrences of some waterfowl and waders 1924–1936.*

Vol. 42, pp. 308–319: Hinde, R.A. and Harrison, J.G.: *Inland migration of waders and terns.*

Vol. 42, pp. 320–326: Lack, D. and Lack, E.: *Passerine migration through England.*

Vol. 43, pp. 97–112: Raines, R.J.H.: *Observations on passage migration in the Trent valley and inland migration.*

Vol. 43, pp. 241–250: Simms, E.: *Autumn bird-migration across the south midlands of England.*
Vol. 43, pp. 271–278: Holt, E.G.: *Autumn migration along the Bristol Channel.*
Vol. 44, pp. 329–346: Hinde, R.A.: *Further report on the inland migration of waders and terns.*
Vol. 46, pp. 238–252: Barnes, J.A.G.: *The migrations of the Lesser Black-backed Gull.*
Vol. 48, pp. 148–169: Dickens, R.F.: *The passage of Black Terns through Britain in spring 1954.*
Vol. 56, pp. 433–444: Eltringham, S.K. and Boyd, H.: *The moult migration of the Shelduck to Bridgwater Bay, Somerset.*
Vol. 59, pp. 141–147: Morley, J.V.: *The moult migration of Shelducks from Bridgwater Bay.*
Vol. 62, pp. 523–533: Mason, C.F.: *Waders and terns in Leicestershire and an index of relative abundance.*
Vol. 63, pp. 81–83: Morley, J.V. and Cook, R.S.: *Moult migration of Bridgwater Bay Shelduck and migration routes from south-west and southern England.*
Vol. 69, pp. 62–63: Hume, R.A.: *Inland records of Kittiwakes.*
Alexander, H.G.: *Proc. Birmingham Nat. Hist. Soc.,* Vol. XV, part iii, pp. 197–212.
Ferns, P.N. *et al.: The Birds of Gwent* (Gwent Ornith. Soc., 1977), Chapter 7, and references pp. 150–152.
Mellersh, W.L.: *A Treatise on the Birds of Gloucestershire* (1902).
Ogilvie, M.A.: *Ducks of Britain and Europe* (Poyser, 1975).
Ogilvie, M.A.: *Wild Geese* (Poyser, 1978).
Sainsbury, M.: *Bristol Ornithology,* 5, pp. 195– 200 (1972): *Visible migration along the south-east shores of the Severn estuary.*

CHAPTER SIX
Ornithology in Gloucestershire: A Brief History

The early years up to 1900

"Jan. 1683. Next Hosbury Bridge . . . four miles from Gloucester. Here Thomas Stevenson did kill a strange bird, which none in the country hereabout or elsewhere had seen before. This strange bird, having another by it on the tree where we killed it, is near upon as big as a Wind-thrush; upon the head and bill, which something resembles that of a Bull-finch, it hath a fine tuft of feathers of a cinnamon colour; the feathers of the neck, breast, back and part of the wings, something darker; the upper part of the tail where the feathers join the body is ash-coloured, then a ring of black, and on the extreme part of the tail-feathers a ring of aurora flame, or gold colour, but under the tail a perfect cinnamon. The prime flying feathers of the wings are curiously diversified, for upon each wing, whose feathers are for the most part black, are white spots, answerable to each other. Then the extreme points of nine of the longest pinion-feathers are tipped with white and lemon or gold colour; the lesser pinion-feathers, which are seven in number, are tipped with white and the extreme part of these seven feathers on each side are of a pure vermillion colour, but these vermillion tips are no feather, but of the nature of the stem of the feather, though dilated broader at the ends."

Journeys of Thomas Baskerville, 1683[5]

This remarkably detailed and accurate account was written almost 300 years ago by a man who had no idea that the bird was a Waxwing, and long before the "original description", under the name *Lanius garrulus,* appeared in the tenth edition of Linnaeus' *Systema naturae,* in 1758. The passage quoted above is a model of precision and clarity even by present day standards, and must be one of the earliest bird records for Gloucestershire. Unfortunately the care and attention to detail shown by Thomas Baskerville was quite exceptional in the early days of bird recording, and is by no means universal even now. Indeed a notable feature of most accounts of birds seen in this county during the nineteenth century and earlier is the almost total lack of descriptive evidence of identification, even for rarities.

Books on British birds in the first half of the last century contain few references to Gloucestershire. On looking through those written by Bewick,[7] Montagu[42] and Yarrell,[82] all of which first appeared between 1797 and 1843, one feels obliged to conclude that Gloucestershire was not yet on the ornithological map. Later editions of Montagu and Yarrell, edited respectively by Newman and Lankester, and also Howard Saunders' *Manual*,[60] contributed a little more to our knowledge, but real progress was not made until the later part of the century and then only gradually.

Berkeley[6] in 1854, and Payne-Gallwey[54] in 1896, refer to the various kinds of geese to be found on the Severn estuary, and during the same period three papers of interest were produced, two dealing with birds of restricted areas in Gloucestershire, the third with the county as a whole.

Bowly[10] lived at Siddington, near Cirencester, and his *List of Birds* in 1856 applies to his local Parish. Probably it presents quite a good picture of the bird-life of the 1850s, permitting some comparison to be made with the present time. This is the more interesting because Siddington lies close to the recently established Cotswold Water Park with its extensive new aquatic habitats which were not there in Bowly's day.

Wheeler[75] wrote in 1862 on the birds found within a radius of five to seven miles of the centre of Cheltenham, and this likewise helps considerably to convey a picture of the local avifauna of that district.

Evans[26] attempted an account of the birds of the whole county. It took the form of an essay followed by a list of 170 species. Both the account and the list contain many inaccuracies and no evidence of any importance is given to substantiate the reports of scarce species which are included. Great Grey Shrike, Fieldfare, Redwing and Common Gull are indicated as breeding in the county, and he also makes the following extraordinary statement: "Passanger Pigeons, which we read of as occurring in myriads in America . . . sometimes also pass over Stroud in immense flocks."!

Other books, quite delightful to read, which appeared during the nineteenth century, and which contain passing references to the birds of the county, include Mary Roberts' *Annals of my Village*[59] (Sheepscombe), published in 1831 and J.A. Gibbs' *A Cotswold Village*,[29] in 1898, where the subject is Ablington, near Bibury. Of greater significance from the present viewpoint is *The Forest of Dean* by H.G. Nicholls,[47] which appeared in 1858. This fascinating account of an important area of Gloucestershire contains valuable information about the bird-life of the Forest 130 years ago, or more. It includes observations by Edward Machen, Deputy Surveyor of the Forest in the early part of the nineteenth century and a keen observer of wild life.[39]

Formal reporting of rare and unusual species in Britain really began with the publication of *Zoologist*[83] in 1843, a periodical which was eventually incorporated in *British Birds Magazine* (now *British Birds*)[12] in 1917. *Ibis*,[37] the organ of the British Ornithologists' Union, was established shortly afterwards, in 1859. A number of Gloucestershire records of scarce birds are to be found in the pages of these publications, particularly in *Zoologist*, and from 1853 the magazine *Field* also printed some records, although not always in a form which could readily be verified or acepted today.[28]

In 1892 Witchell and Strugnell published *The Fauna and Flora of Gloucestershire*,[80] the only book of the nineteenth century which attempted a comprehensive survey of the birds of this county. Two hundred and fourteen species are listed in the section "Aves". Some of the accounts digress into a variety of topics, but the usual approach is to list brief statements, sometimes conflicting, from a variety of sources. The result is a somewhat confused picture of status and distribution. Records of rarities are not substantiated, some are undated and a few even lack localities.

During the closing years of the century, W.L. Mellersh was busy collecting ideas and data for a much more satisfactory account of Gloucestershire's birds. This was published in 1902 and deserves special consideration.

W.L. Mellersh: "A Treatise on the Birds of Gloucestershire"
The *Treatise*[41] provides an interesting descriptive account of Gloucestershire and a commentary on its bird-life. Mellersh also left an extensive collection of manuscript notes,[40] gathered during the preparation of his book, and later. Together the two form a major source of data and are particularly valuable in setting the late nineteenth century background against which the present state of the county's avifauna can be studied. This importance is reflected in the frequent references to Mellersh which appear in the Systematic Section of the present work.

The check-list in the *Treatise* enumerates 270 "species", including several now regarded as geographical races, and six presented in square brackets. Of the latter, only one, the Crested Tit, now claims a place on the Gloucestershire list on the strength of a subsequent record.

Reference has already been made to the lack of descriptive evidence for records of rarities during the last century, and this problem continued into the twentieth century. Details of identification are not to be expected in county avifaunas, but it is disappointing that Mellersh's manuscripts contain almost nothing of value in this sphere. He gathered much information from local taxidermists and from the shooting fraternity of the day. He also saw a number of scarce birds either in the flesh or mounted, but for the most part he had to be content with rather meagre data attached to the specimens, or provided by the taxidermists' records and recollections. It is surprising how many stuffed birds of this period, privately owned or even in museums, now lack data of any kind. This situation has presented considerable difficulties in evaluating old records, as it may have done also for Mellersh, 80 years ago.

The spectre of the "Hastings Rarities"* will no doubt haunt the writers of county avifaunas for some years to come, and it is possible that some degree

---

* An ornithological scandal involving records of many rare birds reputed to have been taken in a region of east Sussex and west Kent in the period 1894–1924. (For a full account see *Brit. Birds*: LV, pp. 281–384; and LVI, pp. 33–38).

of deception could have occurred in Gloucestershire and elsewhere in Britain.[33] The only evidence to hand of dishonesty of this kind in Gloucestershire is contained in a letter, dated 1 October 1912, from F.C.R. Jourdain to W.L. Mellersh: "Lots of frozen skins are imported by unscrupulous dealers, set up and sold as British . . . One dealer in your county is known to have perpetrated frauds of this kind". There is no reason to suppose that any of the principal taxidermists of Cheltenham and Gloucester were implicated, but it is possible that they were themselves misled on occasion. The following extract from Mellersh's manuscripts demonstrates this possibility: "Dartford Warbler . . . Two were brought to Mr. T. White . . . stated as having been killed the day before being brought, but this statement . . . incorrect owing to the birds being dried up . . ." The locality was said to be near Cheltenham, and T. White was a Cheltenham taxidermist. Mellersh received much useful information from him and from his son, J.T. White, concerning the period from the 1840s to 1900, but the Gloucestershire origins of some of the rarities are open to doubt.

In 1893 the *Naturalists' Journal*[46] published a short article entitled *Rarae Aves that have passed through the hands of T. White and Son*. Among the unusual birds mentioned here are a Golden Eagle near Painswick, a Spotted Eagle at Rendcombe, two Black-winged Kites also near Painswick and two other singles at Cheltenham and Sherborne, a Swallow-tailed Kite near Cleeve Hill, six Scops Owls from various places and a Tengmalm's Owl in Miserdon Park. For once a description is supplied: the two "Black-winged" (Black-shouldered) Kites near Painswick were apparently correctly identified, but the specimens have not been traced and one cannot be sure of their origin. Two Scops Owls were preserved for many years at Parkend, but their history has not been uncovered.

Mellersh, in writing his book, wisely ignored some of these reports, but he included the Golden Eagle and Tengmalm's Owl, and his total of Scops Owls rose to "8 shot since 1865". Other rare birds listed by Mellersh, but omitted for various reasons from the present work, are mentioned under "Reputed Gloucestershire Birds" on page 213. The *Treatise* also includes a number of breeding records some, at least, of which are unsatisfactory: Wigeon, Merlin, Common Sandpiper, "Scandinavian" Rock Pipit, Ring Ouzel, Dartford Warbler and Ortolan Bunting.

One puzzling passage in the *Treatise* is neatly solved on reference to the manuscript notes. On page 76 we read: "In the autumn Curlews would regularly visit the high land between Puesdown and Northleach . . . Strange to relate the rare Avocets would do the same, and were known as 'Black and White Curlews'. Until about 1870 six or seven Avocets were periodically killed . . .". This passage stems from data given in the manuscripts and originally came from J.T. White, the Cheltenham taxidermist. Another manuscript entry, still referring to Avocets, solves the mystery: "Over 60 years ago these as 'Black-and-White Curlews' frequented some light barley fallow above Sezincote . . . they made a great noise at night and cried out as near as possible like 'Curlew' (Akerman k. 1900)." The Northleach "Avocets", in their unwonted habitat, were undoubtedly Stone-curlews in typical habitat!

As a conclusion to this account of Mellersh's work, the reader is invited to make what he will of the following extracts from the manuscripts:

Great Northern Diver: "J.T.W. had one from Toddington floods . . . it had a human back tooth in its crop".

"In 1884 an old woman at Northleach complained of the ghost of a drowned man coming up every night in the reeds of a pond near her house . . . Mr. White . . . stopped the noise by shooting a Bittern."

Woodchat Shrike: "One was killed in Dowdeswell Wood . . . which J.T.W. unwillingly stuffed for a lady's hat."

Stone-curlews

From 1900 to the 1940s

The interval between the publication of Mellersh's *Treatise* in 1902 and 1950 was a slack period in the history of Gloucestershire ornithology. There was as yet no overall repository for records, the collection of which seems to

Ringing Pied Flycatchers in the Forest of Dean: Dr. Bruce Campbell on the ladder.

have depended upon the energy and initiative of a few individuals in widely separated parts of the county.

Chief among these was undoubtedly G.L. Charteris who produced in the early 1950s a very large contribution to the mass of data upon which the Systematic Section of the present work is based. His knowledge of the county extended through several decades, enabling him to make balanced judgements upon many matters of local ornithological importance.

During the same period, from the 1920s to the 1940s, O.H. Wild collected data from various sources and his manuscripts[77] constitute an important fund of information on the status of birds in the county during these lean years. Many entries, however, refer to the area which is now part of the county of Avon.

In the latter part of this period, Dr. Bruce Campbell[13] started his work with the Nagshead nest-box scheme in the Forest of Dean (see Pied Flycatcher, page 195). During the seventeen years from 1948 to 1964 he paid no less than 146 visits to the study area furnishing a remarkably good example of intensive work in a narrow field of study.

Before the turn of the century the Britsol Naturalists' Society had already published, in 1875-76 and 1899, lists of birds of the Bristol area. In 1947 these were revised by H.H. Davis.[21] The "Bristol District" included the southern part of the old county of Gloucester as far north as a line drawn from Tetbury to the northern end of the New Grounds near Slimbridge. Davis's list therefore includes numerous records from the New Grounds and adjacent areas which are still in Gloucestershire in its new (1974) boundaries (see page 7). It is fortunate that the Bristol Naturalists kept such good records of this area during the first half of the present century.[11]

The Cotteswold Naturalists' Field Club, founded in 1846, included some bird notes over the years in its annual *Proceedings*[18] right up to the early 1950s, but these were few in number. Meanwhile *British Birds Magazine* (later *British Birds*[12]) began its long and distinguished life in 1907 and thereafter became the main vehicle for publishing, among other things, reports of rare birds in Britain. Numerous Gloucestershire records have appeared in its pages.

It was not until 1948, however, that real progress began to be made towards effective coverage of the whole county for the collection, storage and evaluation of records. In the immediate post-war years two very significant events occurred in the ornithological history of Gloucestershire. The first was the establishment in 1946 of the Severn Wildfowl Trust (now the Wildfowl Trust) on the New Grounds near Slimbridge; the second was the formation in 1948 of the Cheltenham and District Naturalists' Society, which included an Ornithological Section from its foundation.

From 1950 to the present

The Wildfowl Trust has already been mentioned in connection with the "decoy effect" which the collection of waterfowl has on wild birds in the vicinity (page 31), and an outline of its work is given on pages 80–82.

The Cheltenham and District Naturalists' Society started in a small way but developed quickly, the Ornithological Section producing its first printed *Notes* for the years 1951 and 1952. About this time there was some overlap between this Society and the Cotteswold Naturalists' Field Club in the production of Ornithological Notes, but this was soon resolved, and a Bird Report has been published in every subsequent year (see Table below).

From March 1950 the Society also provided a monthly duplicated *Journal*[31] of general natural history interest, which still continues and now includes articles, notes and regular lists of current bird records. The Society's name was changed in November 1956 to the North Gloucestershire Naturalists' Society.

Up to the end of 1962 the southern boundary for bird recording purposes was the arbitrary line from Tetbury to the northern end of the New Grounds mentioned on page 71, the Bristol Naturalists covering the area to the south of this. In 1963, however, a general agreement was reached between this Society, the Bristol Naturalists' Society, the Dursley Birdwatching and Preservation Society (page 78) and the Wildfowl Trust on the production of an annual *Gloucestershire Bird Report* to cover the whole county as then defined. In effect this was a direct continuation of the annual reports already in production. A County Advisory Committee (Records Committee) was set up to deal with critical records and other matters requiring specialist opinion. When the new county boundaries became operative in 1974, the Society again changed its name appropriately to the Gloucestershire Naturalists' Society. Its interests continue to range over the whole field of natural history, and an account of its work for local ornithology will be found on page 75.

TABLE OF ANNUAL PUBLICATIONS

Summary of the principal annual ornithological Lists and Reports of Gloucestershire birds published since 1948

Year	List	Source	Edited by
1948–49	Ornithological Records	Duplicated, CDNS	L.W. Hayward
1948–50	Ornithological Report	Duplicated, CDNS	L.W. Hayward
1951–52	Ornithological Notes	*Report*, CDNS	L.W. Hayward
1951	Ornithological Notes	*Proc.*, CNFC	G.L. Charteris
1952–53	Ornithological Notes	*Proc.*, CNFC; *Report*, CDNS	G.L. Charteris
1954–1956	Ornithological Notes	*Proc.*, CNFC; *Report* CDNS	G.L. Charteris and C.M. Swaine
1957–1962	Ornithological Notes/Report	*Proc.*, CNFC; *Report*, NGNS	G.L. Charteris and C.M. Swaine
1963–1967	Gloucestershire Bird Report	NGNS	C.M. Swaine and Advisory Committee

1968–1972	Gloucestershire Bird Report	NGNS	M.A. Ogilvie, C.M. Swaine and Advisory Committee
1973–1978	Gloucestershire Bird Report	GNS	M.A. Ogilvie, C.M. Swaine and Advisory Committee
From 1979	Gloucestershire Bird Report	GNS	J.D. Sanders and Advisory Committee

CNFC: Cotteswold Naturalists' Field Club
CDNS: Cheltenham and District Naturalists' Society
NGNS: North Gloucestershire Naturalists' Society
GNS: Gloucestershire Naturalists' Society

(The last three are consecutive names of the same organisation — see text).

The Severn Vale Ringing Group was founded in 1966 to promote work and interest in bird-ringing. It operates under the auspices of the British Trust for Ornithology and receives an annual grant from the Gloucestershire Naturalists' Society to assist with expenses, especially for the production of an annual *Report*.[61] An outline of its work appears on page 77.

Throughout this period of development of local bird studies, the natural history movement has received increasing help and co-operation from the Wildfowl Trust, whose headquarters at Slimbridge fortunately remain firmly within Gloucestershire in spite of the changed county boundary.

The decision to set up a Gloucestershire Trust for Nature Conservation was taken in April 1961. The Trust's work covers many aspects of natural history and that part relating to bird-life is described on page 79. The Trust co-operates closely with the Gloucestershire Naturalists' Society and, indeed, the two organisations are largely complementary in their activities.

During the post-1950 period four booklets have appeared which deal with aspects of the county's ornithology. *Birds of the Dean Forest Park*[49] (Niles and Cooper, 1969) provides a very useful account at a time when the birds of that area were not generally well known. *Birds and Bird Watching in Gloucestershire*[66] (Swaine, 1969) includes short descriptions of the more productive ornithological areas of the county, together with a check-list of species (now out of date; and Great Black-backed Gull was inadvertently omitted). *A Guide to Birds in Gloucestershire with part of Avon*[74] (Webster and Wood, 1976) presents an annotated check-list (duplicated) of the county's birds, but suffers from numerous omissions, misplaced emphasis and uncriticl acceptance of old reports of rarities. *Birdwatching in the Cotswold Water Park*[35] (Holland and Mardle, 1977) is a valuable statement of the bird-life of this extensive new wetland area at an important stage in its development.

Ornithology in Gloucestershire has blossomed in the past thirty years and is now on a very sound footing. This success is due in part to the development of methods of collecting, storing and using data, and in larger measure to the rapid expansion of interest in birds which has resulted in an increasing number of people who supply records and who are willing to take part in fieldwork. Without public participation little progress would have been made,

The future is promising. Changes in numbers and status of many species will need to be monitored, and further investigations comparable with those already instigated by the British Trust for Ornithology, and reported in *Bird Study*,[8] will no doubt be planned. There is certainly scope for more local studies relating to this county, perhaps especially in the field of migration (page 63). Birds, like other forms of wild life, are threatened, mostly inadvertently, by many human activities and the work of protection and conservation is of rising importance in Gloucestershire as in other parts of Britain.

CHAPTER SEVEN

The Work of Some Organisations Based in Gloucestershire

In this chapter the work done by five organisations is briefly described. Two of these, the Gloucestershire Naturalists' Society and the Gloucestershire Trust for Nature Conservation, are concerned with different aspects of the general natural history of the county, but have strong ornithological interests. The Severn Vale Ringing Group and the Dursley Birdwatching and Preservation Society have much smaller memberships. The former, as its name indicates, is principally involved in bird-ringing, while the latter restricts its work to the study of birds in a localised area. The fifth organisation, The Wildfowl Trust, has an international reputation and its headquarters are in Gloucestershire.

The Gloucestershire Naturalists' Society

An outline of the history of this organisation in relation to ornithological recording in the county has already been given on pages 71–73.

The Society's interests cover a wide range of natural history topics, with birds and botany claiming most attention. The need in the 1950s for a society of this kind is shown by the subsequent membership. At the end of 1948, the year of foundation, the number was 69. Early in 1978 the thousandth member was enrolled, and numbers are still on the increase.

With an eye to the future, a Junior Section was started in April 1961, and renamed the Gloucestershire Young Naturalists in December 1977. In view of the large number of interested people in the Cirencester district, a branch was established there in 1963.

The Society holds regular indoor meetings throughout the winter months when lectures are arranged, some on ornithological topics. Films are now a regular feature, notably those provided by the Royal Society for the Protection of Birds, and often shown jointly with that Society and the Gloucestershire Trust for Nature Conservation.

Field meetings are held throughout the year and most of these have at least some ornithological interest. Their number is greater than that for most other natural history societies and they are planned for evening, half-day and whole-day duration.

The main concern of the Society's Ornithological Section, however, is the collection and publication of data referring to the many species of birds which are found in Gloucestershire. Records are now stored in an extensive card-index system and are used in the preparation of the Society's monthly *Journal* and the annual *Gloucestershire Bird Report*,[31] referred to on pages 72 and 219. This great fund of information forms a major part of the material upon which the Systematic Section of the present work rests.

Recording work has gone some way towards establishing an effective monitoring system for changes in status and numbers of birds in the county. Some of the changes are of local nature, while others form part of far more extensive trends, and local natural history organisations have a responsibility to collect data in this field. In relation to this, members of the Society have taken part in enquiries and surveys organised by the British Trust for Ornithology. Over the years these have included the "Breeding Season Census of Common Birds", counts of Mute Swans, Great Crested Grebes and rookeries and, more recently, surveys of Nightingales, Golden Plovers and Blackcaps in winter[8]. A major project of the British Trust for Ornithology, launched in 1968, was the collection of data for *The Atlas of Breeding Birds in Britain and Ireland*,[62] and good cover was provided by members of this society and of other bodies, and organised by P.H. Dymott, then Regional Representative of the Trust (see page 95).

During the 1970s the Society also participated in the "Birds of Estuaries Enquiry", run jointly by the Royal Society for the Protection of Birds and the British Trust for Ornithology. The Gloucestershire Naturalists Society also carried out an eighteen-month survey of Crickley Barrow to investigate the effects of farming practice and game conservation on the bird-life of a Cotswold farm.

Since the formation of the Glouceteshire Trust for Nature Conservation in 1962, there has been close co-operation between this Society and the new Trust. Some society members assisted the Trust in surveying various nature reserves and Sites of Special Scientific Interest (SSSIs), including the study of disused railways on the Cotswolds in 1964, when about 60 species of birds were noted, and a survey of the county's rivers, meadows and wetland habitats. The erection of nest-boxes for the Trust in 1964 in Betty Daw's Wood on the fringe of the Forest of Dean was undertaken by the Society's Junior Section. Members of the Society also gave assistance in the Trust's "Ecological Survey of Gloucestershire", carried out in 1976–77, and most of the Trust's Reserve Management Committees include Society members. Some, but not all of the investigations mentioned above have ornithological significance.

Consultations and other work leading to the establishment of the Cotswold Water Park in the early 1960s, however, were of great importance to all those interested in bird-life. The Gloucestershire Naturalists' Society was represented throughout the discussions which were held between the Nature Conservancy, the Gloucestershire and Wiltshire Trusts, and representatives of the two County Councils and of the various natural history societies.

This Society has also played its part in matters of publicity, helping to keep the interests of natural history in general, and ornithology in particular, in the public eye. It has combined with the Gloucestershire Trust on several occasions in the production of exhibitions, film shows and outdoor activities, notably for the National Nature Weeks of 1963 and 1964, and the Forestry Commission's Jubilee Exhibition in 1969, while during the European Conservation year of 1970, the two organisations held a Gloucestershire Nature Week in May, and an appropriate display at Cheltenham in September.

The Gloucestershire Naturalists' Society has one of the finest of local natural history libraries, with excellent management and facilities for its use.

The Severn Vale Ringing Group

Until the late 1950s bird-ringing in Gloucestershire was practised by a small number of individuals using wire traps to catch a very limited variety of species. The introduction of mist-nets, however, revolutionised trapping techniques and ringers were suddenly able to catch even the most elusive and secretive of birds. This new flexibility encouraged more ornithologists to participate, and in 1966 a nucleus of ringers, whose operations centred at Frampton-on-Severn, formed the Severn Vale Ringing Group (and see pages 52, 53, 73).

The main objective was "to make a determined effort to contribute positive information to add to the ornithological knowledge of Gloucestershire". Towards this end the Group has had considerable success. By means of regular Newsletters and Annual Reports interested bodies and individuals have been kept informed of the Group's latest studies and results. To date, some 87,000 birds of about 140 species have been ringed, of which 800 or so have been recovered.[61]

Two major fields of interest are *site studies* and *species studies*. Examples of regularly worked sites are Frampton Pools and Gamage Court Farm, Minsterworth. The old gravel workings at Frampton have long been regarded as one of the prime ornithological sites in the county, and it was early in the 1960s that regular ringing began. A comprehensive programme started in 1966, with several parties of Group ringers operating different sites among the willow scrub and bramble thickets.

Records over the years have enabled some interesting life histories to be compiled, with details such as life expectancy, mortality rate, site preference and arrival and departure dates. A method (the "Frampton Index") of calculating the annual trend in warbler populations has been devised. (*Glos. Bird Report,* 1976, pp. 29–31).

In 1973, as the Group expanded, a new area on the west side of the Severn was explored in the orchards and hedgerows surrounding Walmore Common, at Gamage Court Farm. Work is progressing well and studies complementary to those at Frampton are well established.

Species-studies encourage the ringer to seek his quarry in suitable habitats throughout the county. Examples of current projects in this field involve Pied Wagtails, Reed and Sedge Warblers, and wintering thrushes. At the request of the Edward Grey Institute and, later, of the Royal Society for the Protection of Birds, Pied Flycatchers were ringed in numbers at the Nagshead Reserve in the Forest of Dean, and other examples of special studies have been the ringing of gulls at rubbish-tips and of waders on the Severn estuary.

The original objective in ringing was to obtain recoveries from which information could be gained on migration and other bird movements, and this is still very important in the long term (see Chapter Five). Recoveries, however, account for so low a percentage of birds ringed that ringers are turning more and more to their own retrapped birds for further study. It is in this field of intensive population studies that the Severn Vale Ringing Group may perhaps make its most useful contribution in the future.

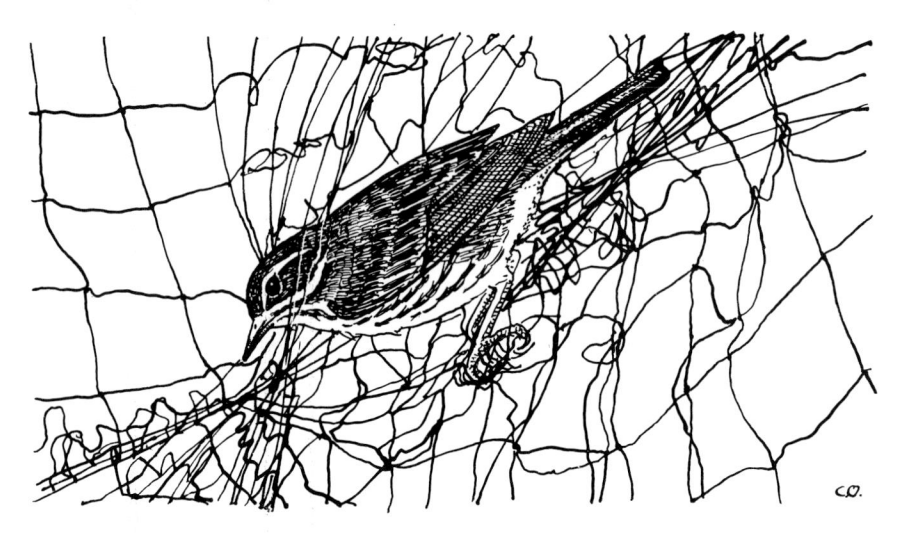

Redwing in mist nest

The Dursley Birdwatching and Preservation Society

This Society was founded in March 1953 by the late T.P. Walsh who was its secretary and guiding light for many years. The functions of the Society are "to promote all aspects of ornithology and to keep accurate records of all birds seen within 16 kilometres radius of St. James' Church, Dursley"; and "to promote conservation of local and national fauna and flora and to stimulate interest in other branches of Natural History".

Lectures and discussions are held throughout the year; also field meetings including spring and autumn weekend gatherings. The Society takes part in the Common Bird Census for the British Trust for Ornithology, and some members participated in surveys for *The Atlas of Breeding Birds in Britain and Ireland*.[62] Sponsored bird-counts for various ornithological projects have been organised and many record cards are supplied annually for the Nest Records Scheme.

The Society produces a regular *Bulletin* which includes lists of current bird records from the district.[24] Membership at the close of 1979 was 114.

The Gloucestershire Trust for Nature Conservation

The Trust was founded in 1962 as part of the movement to establish County Naturalists' Trusts all over Britain. Its headquarters are at Church House, Standish, near Stonehouse, where the Executive and Conservation Officer may be contacted. The Trust's membership at the end of 1979 was over 4,000, but many additional members are needed.

The aims of the Trust, stated briefly are:

(i) To protect and conserve the wild life and wild places of Gloucestershire.
(ii) To establish nature reserves over the range of habitats in the county.
(iii) To promote awareness of the need for nature conservation aesthetically, ethically and scientifically, particularly among those who own, manage and administer land in the county.
(iv) To interest people, and particularly young people, in the countryside and its wild life.

Wise and effective management for conservation purposes requires detailed knowledge, not only of the wild life of the areas concerned, but also of many other aspects of the countryside and its usage. Consequently the Trust spends much time and effort in surveying areas which are of particular interest or which face specific threats in the future. Such studies range from detailed investigations of small areas of land in which, perhaps, a single species requires protection, to county-wide inquiries such as the recent "Habitat Survey of Gloucestershire" and the study of rivers, meadows and wetland habitats recently completed.

In this and other important work, such as that prior to the establishment of the Cotswold Water Park, the Trust works in close co-operation with County Council departments, the Naturalists' Trusts of adjacent counties, the Gloucestershire Naturalists' Society and other organisations. Reference to joint work with the Gloucestershire Naturalists is made in outlining the activities of that Society (page 76).

Most of the Trust's reserves, and other areas of special interest, are on private land and the Trust seeks to maintain good relationships with landowners and tenant farmers, some of whom are Trust members. Satisfactory co-operation has also been achieved with such bodies as the Forestry Commission and gravel extraction companies, the latter having had a major impact on the bird-life of Gloucestershire (see Chapter Four).

In order to advise farmers and land managers on wildlife conservation, the Trust has taken a major role in the County Farming and Wildlife Advisory Group. It funds the services of the County Adviser in this field, and provides office accommodation for him. In this it is helped by the Nature Conservancy Council, the Countryside Commission and the Ministry of Agriculture. The Adviser, who has long experience of both farming and wildlife conservation, may visit a hundred farms a year, or more, at the request of the farmers concerned.

Good public relations are of the greatest importance in the fields of protection and conservation, and these are further enhanced by film shows, lecture, exhibitions and field-occasions (and see page 77).

The Trust now manages some 50 reserves, of which those listed below have specific ornithological interest. They are open to members who may purchase the *Reserve Handbook*. Other intending visitors and all party visitors, should first contact the Trust's headquarters at Standish.

Ashleworth Ham	8326	Wetland; water birds
Betty Daw's Wood	6928	Sessile oakwood; summer birds
Buckholt Wood NNR	8913	Cotswold beechwood
Cokes Pit	0295	Cotswold Water Park; water birds
Dowdeswell Reservoir*	9919	Water birds
Edward Richardson	2100	Gravel pit; water birds
Five Acre Grove*	7904	Breeding birds
Frith Wood	8708	Cotswold beechwood
Guiting Power	0923	Wetland
Lancaut	5496	Wye Valley; hanging woods
Lassington Wood	8020	Breeding birds
Midger (Avon)*	7989	Woodland birds
Mythe Railway	8834	Breeding birds
Popes Wood	8712	Cotswold beechwood
Sandhurst	8123	Severn-side withy-bed
Silk Wood	8389	Breeding birds
Whelford Pools	1799	Water birds
Wetmore (Avon)*	7487	Breeding birds
Witcombe Reservoirs	9014	Water birds

* Guide booklet available

The Royal Society for the Protection of Birds manages the important Nagshead Reserve near Parkend in the Forest of Dean.

The Wildfowl Trust

The Wildfowl Trust was founded in 1946 by Peter Scott, who set up its headquarters at the New Grounds, Slimbridge. Here there was an area of about 988 acres (400 hectares) of low-lying grass fields between the river Severn and the Gloucester–Berkeley Ship Canal, together with a further 3460 acres (1400 hectares) of mudflats. This was the winter home for a large flock of White-fronted Geese which had been protected for centuries by the landowners. In the centre of the New Grounds was a duck decoy, though fallen into disuse. Starting with these existing features, the Wildfowl Trust, over the years, has come to exert a major influence on the wildfowl and other birds of the whole area. This effect can be divided into three main headings: conservation, management and research.

While shooting was strictly controlled before the arrival of the Wildfowl Trust, and other disturbances discouraged, one of the first and very successful aims of the Trust was to rid the refuge area of as much disturbance as was humanly possible. Visitng bird-watchers, while encouraged to come, have been channelled into a gradually extending system of hides with screened approaches, farming activities are reduced to a minimum during the winter months, low-flying aircraft have been banned from the area, and every possible effort is made to prevent the wild geese and other birds from being forced to take flight unnecessarily. The sense of security which the birds gain from living in such a well protected area has an undoubted benefit in terms of the numbers and their duration of stay.

Under the broad heading of management come both deliberate changes to the habitat aimed at improving it for the birds, and more accidental effects which have nontheless made the area more attractive. The first kind is exemplified by the way in which farming activities on the New Grounds are controlled so as to favour the geese. Grazing by sheep and cattle of the most important fields is regulated in such a way that a good sward of grass of suitable length remains when the geese arrive in the autumn. Several fields, in addition, have been ploughed and re-seeded with grass mixtures containing species which the geese are known to prefer. In order to increase the amount of standing water, a tremendous attraction to birds of all kinds, several pools and scrapes have been created on the refuge, and planted with suitable food plants.

The excavation of a series of ponds within the enclosures of the Wildfowl Trust was, of course, originally carried out to provide suitable conditions for the keeping of captive wildfowl. Not surprisingly, however, these pools and the surrounding shrubs and trees form an ideal habitat for a great many birds (see page 31). But it is the provision of food, largely grain, that has attracted the most birds. Regardless of how many wild birds come to live in the enclosures, every single captive bird must be given sufficient to eat. Thus the more birds that come, the more food has to be supplied! The effect in winter is of a giant bird table, with a never failing source of food for all comers. It is hardly surprising, therefore, that on a typical winter's day, wild birds easily outnumber the captive total by nearly 3,000. Ducks, including Mallard, Gadwall, Tufted Duck, Pochard, Shoveler and Pintail are all present in hundreds, while equally numerous are Moorhens, Collared Doves and Coot, with a great variety of finches, not to mention House Sparrows and Starlings.

The research carried out by the Wildfowl Trust has a less direct effect on the birds of the area, although it is as a result of this research that

The Wildfowl Trust: "Swan Lake." The Bewick's Swans and most of the other birds on the water are genuine wild visitors, attracted by food, safety and company.
(Photo: Philippa Scott)

conservation and management techniques are discovered and applied. One of the major research activities of the Trust at Slimbridge has been the catching and ringing of wildfowl. Up to the end of 1979 more than 600 White-fronts, over 1,000 Bewick's Swans, and well in excess of 20,000 ducks have been marked. The last group were predominatly Mallard, but included many hundreds each of Teal, Pintail, Shoveler, Gadwall, Tufted Duck and Pochard. This ringing has produces some 5,000 recoveries, and as many recaptures or resightings. Some of the statements in Chapter Five, on migration in Gloucestershire, and in the Systematic Section, are based upon the results of this extensive marking.

Among other researches carried out upon wildfowl at Slimbridge has been a very detailed study of the wintering Bewick's Swans based upon recognition of the birds as individuals using the yellow and black bill markings. This has provided information on their breeding success, social behaviour, and factors affecting the timing of their migration. Research on the White-fronts has included detailed feeding studies which discovered the main preference of the geese for different fields and food plants, both needed before effective management plans could be implemented, as well as less directly applicable results such as the energy intake and output of the birds. Work on other species has featured a breeding biology study of Mallard nesting within the enclosures, food and feeding behaviour of Wigeon, and territorial behaviour of Moorhens. (See also page 31).[78]

Selected references to Wildfowl Trust research on birds at Slimbridge

Anon. 1958: *Wild Ducks at the New Grounds, 1947–57*. Wildfowl Trust Ann. Rep., 9: pp. 26–32.

Beer, J.V. and Boyd, H., 1963: *Measurements of White-fronted Geese wintering at Slimbridge*. Wildfowl Trust Ann. Rep., 14: pp. 114–8.

Ogilvie, M.A., 1963: *Wild ducks and swans at the New Grounds*. Wildfowl Trust Ann. Rep., 14: pp. 132–6.

Ogilvie, M.A., 1964: *A nesting study of Mallard in Berkeley New Decoy, Slimbridge*. Wildfowl Trust Ann Rep., 15: pp. 84–7.

Scott, P, 1966: *The Bewick's Swans at Slimbridge*. Wildfowl Trust Ann. Rep., 17: pp. 20–6.

Ogilvie, M.A., 1966: *White-fronted Geese at the New Grounds, 1946–47 to 1963–64*. Wildfowl Trust Ann. Rep., 17: pp. 27–30.

Owen, M., 1971: *The selection of feeding site by White-fronted Geese in winter*. J. Appl. Ecol., 8: pp. 905–17.

Wood, N.A., 1974: *The breeding behaviour and biology of the Moorhen*. Brit. Birds, 67: pp. 104–15; 137–58.

Evans, M.E., 1979: *The effects of weather on the wintering of Bewick's Swans at Slimbridge, England*. Ornis Scand., 10: pp. 124–32.

CHAPTER EIGHT
Changes in the Status of Birds in Gloucestershire

Gamekeeper's gibbet

Where sufficient data are available changes in status over the past 100 years or more have been noted under species headings in the Systematic Section (page 101) and the following is a broad discussion of the topic. Much useful information on the subject for Britain as a whole is given by Parslow.[52]

In the early chapters of this book brief reference was made on a number of occasions to the former geographical and climatic conditions of this part of Britain, going back some 10,000 years. No one can doubt that the bird-life of those far off days was very different from anything now to be seen in Gloucestershire. The avifauna has altered gradually over this long period and is still in a state of flux. The forces of change in the early post-glacial days were climatic, but gradually, as our human forbears settled and multiplied, the activities of man in the countryside became more and more important. These two great agents of change, climate and man, still exert their influence today.

Climatic effects since about 1850

Widespread changes in the numbers of individuals and the distribution of species for which no obvious and immediate cause can be recognised are likely to be related to climatic trends affecting important ecological factors such as temperature, rainfall, wind and sunlight. Their precise modes of operation are often complex and obscure.

From about 1850 our climate underwent a gradual warming up, the immediate cause being an increase in the prevalence of warm westerly winds from the Atlantic and the consequent movement of warmer air and water to more northerly latitudes. This has produced a slow withdrawal of the southern fringe of arctic ice and a consequent amelioration of our climate, which became milder in winter and warmer but also wetter in summer. This process lasted until the 1940s since when a reversal appears to have set in.

During this period of 100 years or more, Gloucestershire has been involved in the contraction of the European ranges of several species of bird, and the extension of others. In each case the climatic trend seems to have been the most likely although not necessarily the only causative factor.

The Red-backed Shrike and Wryneck both started to decline in numbers about the turn of the century and are now seldom reported from this county. Both are birds which thrive under conditions of summer warmth and sunshine. Cirl and Corn Buntings in Gloucestershire are similarly on the north-western edge of their European distribution. The former no longer breeds in this county, while the latter has suffered a considerable contraction of range in Britain, although not yet obviously so on the Cotswolds, its main stronghold in this part of the country.

A similar situation applies to the Marsh Warbler and Woodlark, with southern England acting as a western outpost in Europe in each case. Decreases have again occurred in Gloucestershire; the Woodlark appears now to be extinct in the county and the Marsh Warbler very rare. In the cases of these two species other contributary causes have been suggested.

Most of the Marsh Warblers used to nest at the turn of the century in managed withy-beds in the Severn Vale, and it has been claimed that destruction or alteration of this habitat is the primary cause of the birds' disappearance. Marsh Warblers, however, continued to breed in osiers and a variety of other marsh habitats until well into the second half of this century, and many apparently suitable areas still exist in this county, although very few birds are now reported. According to Voous[72] the Marsh Warbler's northern limit of distribution is determined by the July isotherm of 62°F. This passes through the Gloucester–Cheltenham–Tewkesbury area, and a very small climatic shift, therefore, might be all that was necessary to cause a contraction of range into the marginally more sheltered and favourable Avon valley, where the bird still occurs in some numbers.

Marsh Warbler. Once well established in the Severn Vale, this bird is now of rare occurrence and no longer nests annually in Gloucestershire.

The disappearance of the Woodlark is sometimes attributed to the severe winters of 1962 and (especially) 1963, but the decrease started in the late 1950s. A more plausible suggestion is that the virtual elimination of rabbits from the county, as a result of myxomatosis virus in 1954, permitted growth of coarse grasses and scrub to destroy the former habitats of the Woodlark. This, however, cannot explain earlier variations in distribution, and the Woodlark has a history of fluctuation in Britain. Slow climatic changes remain the most likely underlying cuase, with alteration of habitat and severe winters playing contributory roles.

Some birds, however, have extended their ranges in Europe, spreading westwards and north-westwards to reach parts of Britain where previously unknown or merely rare visitors. The striking colonisation of this country between 1940 and 1960 by the Little Ringed Plover and the Collared Dove suggests that habitats suitable in most respects were already present in Britain, and that climate was previously limiting distribution. Details for Gloucestershire are given in the Systematic Section, but it is perhaps worth pointing out here that an additional factor necessary for the establishment of the Little Ringed Plover in this county was the extensive extraction of

Collared Dove

gravel in the Thames Area which, quite unintentionally, provided the right habitat. The occasional occurrence in Gloucestershire of the Serin, Firecrest and Great Reed Warbler are probably a result of the same climatic trend, and both Cetti's and Savi's Warblers may yet appear in the county, having already colonised parts of southern England.

The westward spread in Europe of the Little Gull, Gadwall and Redcrested Pochard appears to be the result of a combination of factors: the gradual shrinkage of their wetland home habitats in the east, coupled with climatic amelioration in the north-west, has allowed spread in that direction. In Gloucestershire there has been a striking increase in the number of reports of Little Gulls, while the two ducks are colonising the area in part as a result of escape from collections.

The importance of severe winters

The hard winter of early 1963 has already been mentioned (page 86). In January and February of that year scores of dead or dying passerines were picked up in various parts of the county; sixteen dead Barn Owls were found on a single Cotswold estate; Moorhens of half normal weight were collected, and 27 species of birds were noted at a single Cheltenham birdtable. Observations such as these encourage the view that exceptionally harsh winters may exterminate susceptible species. In fact this seldom happens except over small areas. Gloucestershire, for example, lost virtually all its Stonechats as a result of winter extremes in 1940 and 1947, but in spite of this the species is now recolonising.

The 1940 and 1947 winters were poorly documented in this county so far as ornithology is concerned; early 1963 was better covered. Fifteen to twenty species were then badly affected, the most vulnerable being the Heron, Moorhen, Woodpigeon, Barn Owl, Little Owl, Kingfisher, Green Woodpecker, Wren, Song Thrush, Mistle Thrush, Goldcrest and Longtailed Tit. Many of these made good recoveries within two to four years, but the Heron, Barn Owl, Little Owl and Green Woodpecker were much slower to build up their numbers (see *Journal*, Glos. Nat. Soc., March and April 1963; May 1964; Jan. and May 1965).

The general effect of very extreme weather conditions such as cold, drought, or wet and chilly breeding seasons is to provide a kind of evolutionary pruning system which reduces numbers but leaves the population better adapted, genetically speaking, after the event than before. The most dangerous situation occurs when several bad winters follow each other without sufficient recovery-time between. If the trend is towards later springs and cool, wet summers, the effect on bird numbers may be just as deleterious, with natural selection operating directly against reproductive success. Matters are then made much worse in all such situations if subsidiary factors also happen to act in the same direction. These additional pressures on birds are mostly induced by man.

The human influence: persecution of birds

Man's most obvious interference with Gloucestershire's bird-life in former years lay in direct persecution by shooting, trapping, egg-collecting and live-bird catching.

Game rearing and gamekeepers probably date from the latter part of the eighteenth century, and the double-barrelled shotgun came into prominence at about the same time. Geese and ducks have long been prime targets as a source of both food and sport. The two duck-decoys near Berkeley in the Severn Vale provided a total of over 70,000 ducks in the period 1845 to 1910, an average of about 1,100 a year. The largest kill was in the season 1846–7 when 3,205 ducks were taken, almost all Mallard, Teal and Wigeon in that order of abundance (M.A. Ogilvie[1]). Such figures give some idea of the destruction which these birds experienced during the last century, but help little in elucidating the effects of such predation upon population sizes.

Other birds, notably the larger waders such as Knot, Golden Plover and Curlew were regularly shot along the Severn for the table during the second half of the last century. Nor were smaller birds immune, and as late as 1902 Mellersh wrote of the Corn Bunting: "It certainly has become an uncommon bird, and poorer country-people can no longer indulge in puddings made of it".[41]

The spread of game-preservation throughout the country estates of Gloucestershire during the nineteenth century was accompanied by a rapid decline in the numbers of Raven, Buzzard and Red Kite, all of which disappeared from the Cotswolds and the Severn Vale, if not from the entire county, during the second half of that century. Keepers' gibbets regularly also carried corpses of Kestrels, Sparrowhawks, Tawny Owls and Barn Owls, and these species are still not entirely free from persecution to this day.

The gamekeepers were not solely to blame for the destruction of Kites and other larger raptors, because the farmers of the day also regarded most of these birds as "vermin" and made increasing use of the shotgun, pole-trap and other means of destruction: ". . . between forty and fifty years ago kites were very common in Gloucestershire. Mr. Ellis of Rendcombe shot seventeen of these birds at one shot, feeding on the body of a sheep". (*Country-Side,*[19] Vol. 2, No. 33. Letter dated 1905). Mellersh[40] gives a milder version of (apparently) the same event, and puts the year as "about 1836", a more likely date.

By the 1870s, free-lance shooting of birds was common practice by large numbers of people in the county, especially along the Severn and in various parts of the Cotswolds. The selection of species became more indiscriminate, and many of the more attractive and less common birds acquired considerable monetary value when stuffed and mounted by professional taxidermists in Cheltenham and Gloucester, thereafter finding their way into private collections. Mellersh's book and manuscripts contain references to many such scarce and rare species reputed to have been killed in Gloucestershire and preserved for sale (see Chapter Six, pages 67–68). The following examples give an indication of the pressures to which some species were subjected during the closing decades of the nineteenth century and the early part of the twentieth:

Hawfinch: "In 1874, no less than 23 were killed in one garden in the town" (Wotton-under-Edge)[80]

Barn Owl: "In the winter months of 1901 to 1902, 28 birds were brought in to be stuffed . . .", and: "On 27 Nov. 1905 there were 22 in Challice's shop in various stages of preservation, all shot during the fall".[40]

Kingfisher: "At the trout-hatchery, Syreford, near Andoversford, Glos., Adam, the owner, killed 52 Kingfishers in one year. Hatchery closed down about 1927–28"([77] n.d.).

The effect of shooting on population size is difficult to assess, but it is probably true that killing birds is likely to bring a species to the verge of extinction only if there is a general belief, rightly or wrongly, that conflict exists with human interests, or if the birds develop a scarcity value and are "collected" for that reason, and especially if they have a slow reproductive rate.

Much the same may be said of egg-collecting. The rarer the species and the more handsome or otherwise desirable its eggs, the greater the pressures put upon it by collectors. This may present a serious threat once a bird's population falls below a minimum level. In Gloucestershire the species most at risk in the past were probably the Marsh Warbler, Red-backed Shrike, Stone-curlew and Hobby, but it seems likely that collecting did no more than accelerate a decline of the first three which was already in progress. The Hobby's somewhat elusive nature was perhaps its best protection.

Although much less prevalent than 50 or 100 years ago, egg-collecting is not extinct, as readers of the R.S.P.B. magazine *Birds* will know from its published reports of prosecutions for the taking of eggs and for the removal of young birds of prey from their nests. It is a sobering thought that should Peregrines return to nest in Gloucestershire their only real hope of rearing young would lie in the triumph of human protective measures over human predation.

Live birds in large numbers were also taken during the last century, for a variety of reasons. The chief methods were netting and the use of "bird-lime"; some birds were then killed for one purpose or another, and many more were sold alive as cage-birds.

Thus J.L. Knapp,[38] referring in 1829 to a locality now in Avon, noted that "An item passed in one of our late churchwardens' accounts was, 'for seventeen dozens of tomtits' heads'!" In 1856 E. Bowly of Siddington, wrote that the Nightingale was "Formerly abundant at Furzenlease, where many were snared and kept the winter in cages . . ."[10] And J.A. Gibbs (1898) refers to Bibury Sparrow Club, which paid boys a farthing a head for dead sparrows.[29]

The following longer paragraph, quoting Edwin Burgh of Cheltenham, is taken from Witchell and Strugnell[80] and pertains primarily to the decline of Goldfinches as a result of the activities of bird-catchers during last century:

"I have often seen flocks of five or six hundred, but now twenty is a good number to see together. Dyer, a Cheltenham bird-catcher, informed me yesterday (1891) that thirty years ago he had caught fourteen dozens in a day; now he gets about half-a-dozen birds; and this scarcity arises from there being so many more catchers than formerly. . . . Londoners will buy anything with a beak and wings. Wrens with a tail are worth twopence apiece to the catchers, who pull out the tail, and let the bird go; the tail-feathers being used to make flies for fishing. Thrushes' wings are used for the same purpose, and sell for twopence per pair . . . I may add that women will give a shilling apiece for robins, to be placed in their hats" (and see page 69).

The human influence: changes in the use of land

It seems that in the face of human progress birds have little respite. As the effects of bird-catching, shooting and egg-collecting declined during the first half of the present century, new threats of more subtle nature were developing.

These mostly derived from changes in land utilisation, a proces which, of course, has been in operation even since primitive man spread into this part of the country. In recent decades, however, the rate of change has greatly increased as a result of improved technology in agriculture, forestry and industrialisation.

Reclamation of marginal land on the Cotswolds during the last century appears to have been the main cause of the decline to extinction of the Stone-curlew. Some of the birds gradually shifted to arable land but seemed unable to establish themselves in the face of improving farm machinery and methods. A similar catastrophic decrease eliminated the Corncrake as a Gloucestershire breeding bird, and no nests have been reported since the 1960s. Here also changes in agricultural practice were responsible, affecting upland and lowland habitats alike.

The Wheatear, formerly not uncommon on the Cotswolds, began to decline in the 1920s, with an acceleration during the 1939–45 war due to increased cultivation of marginal land. The original cause of decline is obscure, and the Cleeve Hill area may now be the sole regular breeding ground. In the Forest of Dean, where a few pairs used to nest on old spoil-heaps, the disappearance may have been due to encroachment by coarse vegetation following the removal of rabbits by myxomatosis in 1954.

The history of the Whinchat has something in common with that of the Wheatear, with a gradual disappearance from the Cotswolds and the Severn Vale, probably brought about by conversion of rough or damp ground to agricultural use. An additional factor in this case was the increasing management of roadside verges, where many Whinchats — and also Tree Pipits — used to nest. Stonechats, already mentioned as being very susceptible to severe winters, also lost habitat as gorse-lands were reclaimed.

About 80% of Britain is now agricultural land and therefore mostly open ground. In lowland farm-land, however, at least three-quarters of the bird-species are really woodland or scrub dwellers, and now depend on hedgerows, gardens, orchards and residual tree growth left in the patchwork of fields.

The early 1940s saw great advances in agricultural chemistry, especially in the advent of herbicides and the use of new pesticides. Widespread employment of weed-killers has resulted in extensive changes in the "weed" composition of farm-land vegetation, and consequently of its invertebrate animal life which is so important a source of bird food. In conjunction with a trend towards the removal of hedgerows to form fewer and larger fields, these programmes add up to huge and widespread changes in the conditions of life for birds. These events produced their most noticeable effects in areas where arable farming occurs on a large scale in the eastern, southern and midland counties of England. Gloucestershire appears to have been much less affected.

The use of new pesticides developed over the same period and in the same areas of Britain. By the early 1960s there was widespread concern about the indiscriminate use of these substances, and particularly of the chlorinated hydrocarbon insecticides. These compounds are persistent in the soil and also tend to pass along food-chains to accumulate in the bodies of the longer-lived members, the "terminal carnivores", such as hawks, falcons, owls and predatory mammals. They also cause infertility, thin-shelled eggs and reduced survival rates of embryos and nestlings.[14,20,43,57]

There was some evidence of agricultural poisoning among Gloucestershire birds in the 1950s and early 1960s. Sparrowhawk, Barn Owl, Little Owl, Heron and perhaps other species were to some extent affected, but this county certainly escaped the worst results. It seems that the limited ban of early 1962 on the use of some pesticides may have come just in time to protect our local bird populations. The use of chlorinated hydrocarbons in sheep-dip can have had little effect on Cotswold wild life, for dead sheep are seldom left lying on these well-watched hills and, in any case, potential carrion-feeders such as the Red Kite and Raven had long since disappeared from other causes.

Although so much of Britain is given over to agriculture, Gloucestershire is one of the more heavily wooded counties, for the Forest of Dean, its outliers and several considerable areas of woodland on the Cotswolds lie within its boundaries. In general these forested areas have tended to act as refuges and a buffer against decline in woodland species of birds.

The Forest of Dean held a few pairs of Red Kite, Buzzard and perhaps Honey Buzzard after these birds had ceased to breed, at least temporarily, over the rest of the county in the nineteenth century. A more recent example is that of the Hawfinch, which is thought to have colonised England early in the nineteenth century, and which in Britain is at the fringe of its range. There were signs of a decrease in numbers in west midland counties from the 1950s, and this seems to have extended to the Cotswolds and the Severn Vale, but numbers have been maintained in the Forest.

It is probable that populations of Goldcrest and Coal Tit have risen in the county in proportion to the increase in area under conifers. This perhaps applies more particularly to the Forest of Dean, where Crossbills also seem to nest more regularly, and where Siskins have recently bred. The remarkable colonisation of the Forest by Pied Flycatchers upon the provision of nest-boxes has already been described (pages 17, 71, 195).

Thus Gloucestershire is still very largely a rural county, and the effects of urban and industrial developments on the status of birds are not so extensive as in some other parts of the country. Gravel-working, of course, which is a rural industry, has had an enormous influence on local bird-life by producing an extensive system of water-filled lakes which are very attractive to birds. The history of these, together with the attendant great changes in bird populations, is described in Chapter Four.

Built-up areas in Gloucestershire support the considerable population of House Sparrows, Starlings, Swifts and other species which are to be expected in such districts, but the most obvious effects of urbanisation on birds in and around the larger towns are associated with collection and disposal of refuse. Large gatherings of Carrion Crows are now to be seen at most of the major rubbish-dumps in the Severn Vale, and the use of such food sources in Britain as a whole and especially in coastal areas, has been held to be partly responsible for the great increase in number of some species of gulls. Herring and Lesser Black-backed Gulls have both increased greatly in Gloucestershire, and both have established breeding colonies in recent years on buildings in the City of Gloucester (see page 24).

Although the Great Black-backed Gull does not breed in this county, there has been of late a striking increase in its winter totals along the Severn, again in association with special feeding sites. (See Systematic Section for various species of gulls).

New arrivals

Closing comments on man's influence on the composition of our local avifauna concern the introduction of new species. The Pheasant, Red-legged Partridge and Little Owl are introduced birds which have been with

The Little Ringed Plover nests on open gravel and is a recent addition to British breeding birds. Its continued existence in this county depends upon the provision of suitable man-made habitats.

us for many years, each now having settled into its own ecological niche. The first two still receive increments to their populations in the county as a result of game-rearing. The Little Owl seems to be firmly established in its own right, and in spite of persecution.

Canada Geese commenced regular breeding in Gloucestershire in the 1950s, following the introduction of birds at Frampton-on-Severn, and now also nest annually in the Cotswold Water Park where the Greylag Goose shows signs of doing the same. Most Greylags appearing in the county are of feral origin. The Red-crested Pochard, Ruddy Duck and Mandarin also seem on the point of settling down as regular feral breeders, and the same may soon be true of the Egyptian Goose and the Barnacle Goose.

Little Ringed Plover and Collared Dove, already mentioned, are relatively recent additions to the list of birds which breed regularly in Gloucestershire, and which colonised without having been introduced by man. Within the past few years there have also been isolated instances of breeding, or attempted nesting, by other species, some of which might establish or re-establish themselves if given the opportunity and adequate protection. These include the Shoveler, Pochard, Goshawk, Ringed Plover, Black-headed Gull, Long-eared Owl and Firecrest.

Prospect

In studying the bird-life of a small area such as an English county we are really looking from a particular viewpoint at the inter-relationships which exist between the physical world of air, soil and water and the "biotic" world of plants and animals, of which birds and men are a part. None of the components of this system is static, and it is the extreme complexity of changing relationships which makes it so difficult to visualise future trends in the composition of Gloucestershire's bird populations.

Enough has been said in this chapter to indicate some of the factors which bring about changes in our avifauna. The one thing which seems abundantly clear is that in man's technological age birds cannot be left to look after themselves: the pressures are too great. If we are to keep a large and varied bird community in Gloucestershire, and in Britain as a whole, much more must be done in the fields of protection and conservation. Nowadays a bird in the bush is worth two in the hand. . . .

CHAPTER NINE
The Atlas of Breeding Birds in Britain and Ireland
(British Trust for Ornithology)

The production of the *Atlas*,[62] which was compiled by J.T.R. Sharrock, was a major landmark in the history of British and Irish ornithology. The programme ran from January 1968 to December 1972, thus covering five breeding seasons. The unit area for the survey was the 10- km. square, and species were recorded for "possible", "probable" and "confirmed" breeding. The Regional Atlas Organiser for Gloucestershire was P.H. Dymott, and very satisfactory cover was achieved. The top-scoring cateory given in the *Atlas* is 76 species or more per 10- km. square, and only one square wholly in what is now "new" Gloucestershire fell below that level: SPOO yielded 75 species.

The tabulated data which appear in this account have been extracted by examination of the *Atlas* maps, the first table showing lists of species for which *confirmed breeding* was reported (a) in all squares, (b) in all but from one to four squares and (c) in only one or two squares:

Confirmed breeding, 1968–72

(a) all squares	(b) all but 1–4 squares	(c) only 1 or 2 squares
Moorhen	Mallard	Gadwall
Woodpigeon	Pheasant	Shoveler
Swallow	Coot	Red-crested Pochard*
House Martin	Lapwing	Pochard
Wren	Stock Dove	Ruddy Duck
Dunnock	Tawny Owl	Hobby
Robin	Swift	Quail
Blackbird	Great Spotted	Lesser Black-backed
Song Thrush	Woodpecker	Gull
Mistle Thrush	Skylark	Herring Gull
Whitethroat	Pied Wagtail	Woodlark
Willow Warbler	Redstart	Stonechat

(a) all squares	(b) all but 1–4 squares	(c) only 1 or 2 squares
Spotted Flycatcher	Garden Warbler	Crossbill
Long-tailed Tit	Blackcap	Hawfinch
Blue Tit	Chiffchaff	
Great Tit	Marsh Tit	* *Atlas* appendix
Magpie	Coal Tit	
Jackdaw	Treecreeper	
Rook	Tree Sparrow	
Carrion Crow	Greenfinch	
Starling	Goldfinch	
House Sparrow	Linnet	
Chaffinch	Yellowhammer	
Bullfinch		

The *Atlas* is of special value to those intersted in the distrbution of birds in the British Isles as a whole, but much less helpful in reviewing internal distribution within an area as small as a single county. For this reason it was decided not to include distribution maps for the county in the present *Birds of Gloucestershire*, the data being less than adequate for this purpose.

The *Atlas*, in fact, produced few surprises so far as this county is concerned, but some maps serve to demonstrate or confirm particular aspects of bird distribution in Gloucestershire at that time. Quail and Corn Bunting, for example, are mainly Cotswold birds, while the Kingfisher, Sand Martin, Reed Warbler, Yellow Wagtail and Reed Bunting tend to avoid these hills. The maps for the Tufted Duck, Little Ringed Plover and Collared Dove register stages in the colonisation of the county by these as breeding birds, while the decline towards extinction of the Corncrake, Woodlark, Red-backed Shrike and Cirl Bunting is clearly shown to have been near to its conclusion at that time, in each of these cases.

From the broader point of view, several species which occur in Gloucestershire are seen here at or close to the edge of their British breeding range. This is plainly shown by the maps for the following examples:

Buzzard	Nightingale
Hobby	Pied Flycatcher
Red-legged Partridge	Red-backed Shrike
Little Ringed Plover	Raven
Dipper	Corn Bunting

A major function of the *Atlas* must be to serve as a basis against which future shifts in the distribution of species can be measured. In fact, during the post-*Atlas* years (from 1972), several species have already shown changes which are more or less noticeable in the county even without further surveys having been undertaken. Reference to Chapter Eight on changes of status, and to the Systematic Section of this book will furnish details and amplification of the following list of examples showing recent change.

Great Crested Grebe	Tufted Duck
Greylag Goose	Collared Dove
Canada Goose	Whinchat
Red-crested Pochard	Stonechat

In the Foreword to *The Atlas of Breeding Birds in Britain and Ireland*, James Ferguson-Lees wrote: "It has been long envisaged that, if successful, the present *Atlas* should be the first of a series at intervals of, say, 25 years." Let us hope that Gloucestershire can produce as good coverage towards the close of the century as it did from 1968 to 1972.

"The Barn Owl is getting scarce . . . and it should be better preserved than it has been." W.L. Mellersh, 1902. The bird is still widely distributed in Gloucestershire, but far from common.

SYSTEMATIC SECTION
Introductory Notes

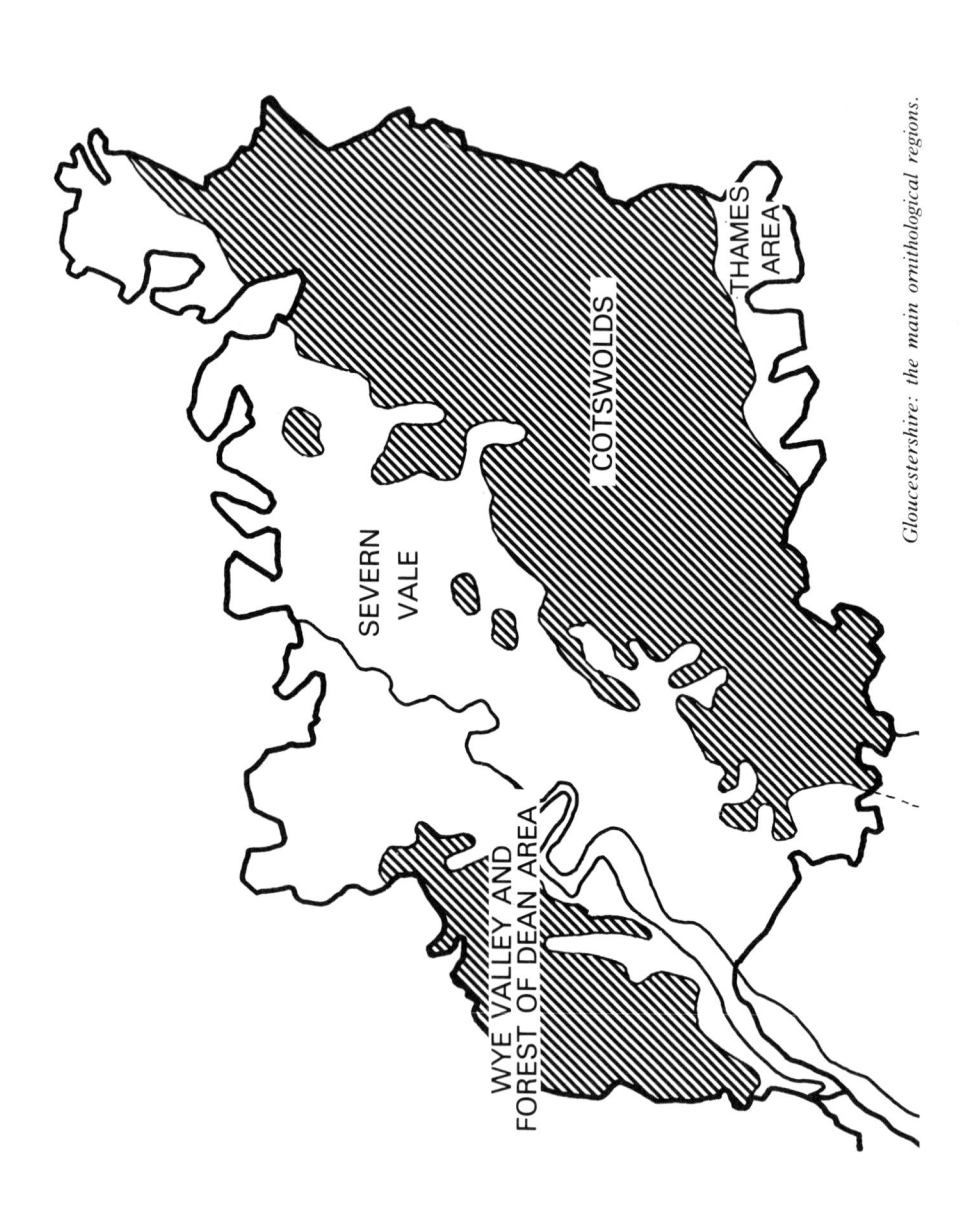

Gloucestershire: the main ornithological regions.

1. The map indicates the main ornithological regions of Gloucestershire as adopted in this book and frequently referred to in the following Systematic Section. An explanatory account will be found on pages 10–11, and in Chapters One to Four where more detail is given.

2. Terminology.

The lower Wye valley is included in the Forest of Dean Region. *The Forest of Dean (the Forest)* refers to the heavily wooded areas of this part of the county, but in certain contexts heathland and other habitats may be included (Chapter One).

The Severn Vale (the Vale) denotes that part of the lower Severn and adjacent ground which occurs in Gloucestershire and is described in Chapter Two. The term *New Grounds* refers to those near Slimbridge unless the Lydney New Grounds are specified.

The *escarpment edge, scarp face* and *scarp edge* are all names for the steep western edge of the Cotswolds facing the Severn Vale, and the *dipslope* is the long, gentle slope of the Cotswolds extending south-eastwards from the escarpment edge towards Oxfordshire and Wiltshire (Chapter Three).

The Thames Area includes the *Cotswold Water Park* (Chapter Four). Gravel extraction commenced long before the nominal establishment of the *Water Park*, but the latter term is used here in connection with all bird records from the district, including those made prior to the late 1960s when the concept of a Water Park developed.

Some Water Park gravel-pits lie just outside the boundary of this county in Wiltshire, but only Gloucestershire records of birds are incorporated in this work. An individual bird seen in both counties is, of course, included here.

Particular gravel pits in the Water Park are not identified in this book, but a system of numbering is included by Holland and Mardle (1977),[35] and these numbers should be employed whenever possible in supplying records to the Gloucestershire Naturalists' Society for use in the *Gloucestershire Bird Report* and in the Society's *Journal*.[31] In view of the continuing excavation of new pits, it is hoped that up-dated maps will appear from time to time.

3. Treatment of species.

The scientific and vernacular names of species, and the sequence followed, are those of *The "British Birds" List of Birds of the Western Palearctic* (1978), based on K.H. Voous' *List of Recent Holarctic Bird Species* (1977). All records refer to Gloucestershire in its new (1974) boundaries (see page 7), and the Systematic Section uses data *up to the end of 1980*. Two hundred and eighty seven species are included.

For each species, with few exceptions, a brief statement of status is given first. This is followed by notes on changes over the past 100 years or so (where these are known), and by some further account of the bird's recent and present situation.

Ringing *details* in general are omitted, but some tentative conclusions based on the work of the Severn Vale Ringing Group[61] (page 77) have been included where appropriate. Descriptive terms such as *resident, summer visitor, winter visitor* and *passage migrant* are used in the Systematic Section in reference to Gloucestershire rather than to the country as a whole, unless the context indicates otherwise.

The month and year are given for the majority of important records, actual dates being furnished only in the case of rarities and other notable occurrences (see *Gloucestershire Bird Report* etc.,[31] and other publications for further details in all such cases.

4. Sources of data (see Chapter Six).

Most of the data used in compiling the Systematic Section have been collected from sources numbered 11, 21, 31, 35, 40, 41, 49, 52 and 61 in the Bibliography (page 217). For purposes of smooth reading most of these sources are not indicated repetitively in the body of the text. Reference to one or other of the above numbered works (for the year in question where appropriate) will usually provide the origin of information if required. This applies especially to records in recent years to be found in the annual Bird Reports, etc. Other references may be identified from the numerical indices in the text, which refer to corresponding numbers in the Bibliography.

The following abbreviations have also been used for two important periodicals: *Brit. Birds* = *British Birds*[12]; *Zool.* = *Zoologist*[83].

In considering data presented or summarised in the Systematic Section of this book, it should be realised that the *apparent* increases in numbers and occurrences of birds of many species which seem to have taken place in the 1950s are, at least in part, distortions due to the remarkable increase in observer activity during that decade. The dearth of Gloucestershire records between the early 1900s and the mid-twentieth century is very marked (pp. 69, 71) and needs to be borne in mind when attempting to assess changes in numbers and status of various species. The Spotted Redshank, Little Tern, Willow Tit and Great Grey Shrike illustrate this point, but many other species might equally well be cited.

Many problems have arisen in connection with evaluating the reliability of old records, and some discussion of this subject will be found in Chapter Six. The introductory comments to Appendix One (*List of birds reputed to have occurred in Gloucestershire. . .*) should also be consulted in this context (page 213).

Great Crested Grebes

Annotated List of Species

Based on records up to the end of 1980.

RED-THROATED DIVER, *Gavia stellata*

An uncommon winter visitor and passage migrant from October to early April, most often reported in January and February. One late bird, still in winter plumage, New Grounds, 19 May 1969.

Five occurrences are recorded from last century[40,41,80], the earliest being of one shot on the Thames-Severn Canal near Cirencester, in 1859. Reports from the first sixty years of this century are of one in Gloucester, March 1934, and another at Hempstead, January 1945[77]; a single at Elmore, January 1947 (B.A. Owen[1]), and another near Tewkesbury in April 1952[18]. Three visited Hewletts reservoirs, Cheltenham, in November 1954 and one was seen at Frampton-on-Severn in January 1957.

Since 1960, eight or nine singles have been noted, five from Severn Vale localities and the others in the Cotswold Water Park. The latter reports were from South Cerney area in February 1966 and February to April 1972; and from Fairford and near Poole Keynes, January and February 1974.

BLACK-THROATED DIVER, *Gavia arctica*

A very scarce visitor.

There are two old and inconclusive records: a "remarkably fine specimen was shot on the Severn near Tewkesbury", February 1841[68], and an immature bird was reported from the Severn Vale, undated [40,41]. The only satisfactory report this century prior to 1979 is of an immature killed on the river Windrush near Bourton-on-the-Water on 27 January 1947 (A.G. Tayler[1]; Cott. Nat. Field Club, XXX[18]).

In the winter of early 1979 seven or eight separate birds were noted. Most reports came from gravel pits in the Cotswold Water Park and involved two immature and two adult birds, seen separately on dates between 17 February and 30 April. A third year bird remained on the river Churn at North Cerney from early April until late June.

In the Severn Vale there were two adults at Frampton Pools in February, one later found dead and the other remaining to early March. An immature, possibly one from the Water Park, visited Witcombe reservoirs, late February to late March. (See *Glos. Bird Report*, 1979, pp. 4-6).

GREAT NORTHERN DIVER, *Gavia immer*

A scarce visitor, November to March.

About a dozen are reported as having been killed in Severn Vale localities, and others seen, between 1870 and 1912[40 80], and one was shot near Fairford, 1906 (*Zool.*, 1907, p.72).

Subsequent records are of one on Dowdeswell reservoir, Cheltenham, January 1954; one found alive on a road at Dumbleton, November 1968; one near South Cerney, late February to late March 1972; and singles, also in the Cotswold Water Park, at Lechlade in January 1978 and near Cerney Wick in December of the same year.

LITTLE GREBE, *Tachybaptus ruficollis*

Widely distributed as a breeding species but not abundant.

Uncommon in the Forest of Dean, where breeding has been reported from Cannop, Soudley and Clanna Ponds. Nests in widely scattered localities in the Severn Vale and sparsely at lake and river sites on the Cotswolds, while a dozen or more breeding pairs are now annual in the Cotswold Water Park.

Autumn and winter numbers may reach 50 to 100 birds in the Water Park, with up to fifteen or more reported at any one time from Vale and Cotswold localities also.

GREAT CRESTED GREBE, *Podiceps cristatus*

Formerly regarded as a scarce visitor but, following a long period of increase, is now quite a common breeding species and present at all seasons.

There are few precise records from the nineteenth century. Bowly[10] reports one on the frozen Thames-Severn Canal, Siddington, in the winter of 1854-5; Witchell and Strugnell[80] refer to five occurrences on or near the Severn, and Mellersh[40] mentions others.

Pairs have attempted to breed, often unsuccessfully, at Dowdeswell reservoir, Cheltenham, since 1914, and at gravel-pits near Frampton-on-Severn (Frampton Pools) since 1927 or earlier (*Brit. Birds*, XXVI, p. 73). Breeding also took place, perhaps regularly, on Cirencester Park lake from 1933 or before, and six nests were found there in 1957 and in 1960. Nesting, sometimes successful, has also occurred at Witcombe reservoirs from 1944; irregularly near Bourton-on-the-Water since 1966; and in Woodchester Park from 1969 to the late 1970s.

Breeding in the east Gloucestershire gravel-pit system, now known as the Cotswold Water Park, started near South Cerney, Fairford and Lechlade in 1955. With the increase in the number of suitable pits in this region, the total breeding population in the county rose steadily, and the census of 1975 gave a total of 148 adults, including 30 breeding pairs, the great majority of birds being in the Water Park. This total of adults is more than twice that from the previous full census in 1965, and the number of breeding pairs is three times as great. Numbers in the Water Park are apparently still increasing (*Glos. Bird Report*, 1975, p.24).

Non-breeding birds are now present in all months, the greatest number again being in the Water Park. Peaks tend to occur in March and in September or October. In 1977, for example, the Water Park totals for these three months were 174, 135 and 110 birds respectively and in 1980, 211, 160 and 152.

Numbers of non-breeders have increased also in the Severn Vale, where from 20 to 30 birds or more are now reported from Frampton Pools and Witcombe reservoirs.

There are no Forest of Dean records.

RED-NECKED GREBE, *Podiceps grisegena*

A scarce visitor from September to April, formerly reported at long intervals, but much more frequently since 1965.

An immature bird was shot near Bibury in January 1850 (*Zool.*, 1851, p.3056). Subsequent records are of singles at Frampton Pools, March 1937 (*Brit. Birds*, XXX, p.373); Shurdington, October 1947 (T.O. James[1]); Frampton Pools, March 1950 (I.C.T. Nisbet[1]); and on the Severn near Hempsted, where a male was shot in February 1956.

Since then, single birds have also been reported from Severn Vale localities in November 1966 and 1969, and in September 1971. Another was noted in the South Cerney area in February 1973.

The early months of 1979 saw an unprecedented influx. Single birds were present on the canal near Frampton-on-Severn in late January; at Dowdeswell reservoir, Cheltenham, from mid-February to mid-March; at Frampton Pools, mid-February to early April, and on the Severn near Tirley in late February. Meanwhile several, perhaps seven or eight, appeared in various parts of the Cotswold Water Park, on dates between early January and late April, including three birds on one pit near Lechlade in February. One was present at the New Grounds at the start of November 1979. (See *Glos. Bird Report*, 1979, pp.4, 5 and 10).

SLAVONIAN GREBE, *Podiceps auritus*

A scarce visitor, reported chiefly from November to March. One was shot at Elmore in 1860 and exhibited as a mounted specimen in 1862 at a meeting of the Cotteswold Naturalists' Field Club, and another was killed near Tewkesbury in June 1862 ([18], *Proc.* III, pp. 54, 62). A female was shot at Witcombe reservoirs, January 1883[80], and Mellersh[40] mentions several inconclusive reports of others seen or killed between 1870 and 1911.

A bird was shot at Frampton-on-Severn in December 1935[77], and more recently singles have been observed at South Cerney gravel-pits in November 1960 and February 1966; at Frampton Pools in December 1966 and January 1967; near Somerford Keynes in December 1968 and at Witcombe reservoirs, November 1970.

In the early part of 1979 one was present on Frampton Pools and later found dead on the New Grounds in mid-February. Another visited the Pools in March and April, and two were seen in the Cotswold Water Park in the same months. One was also present there in the winter of 1979–80, and another in December 1980.

BLACK-NECKED GREBE, *Podiceps nigricollis*
A very scarce visitor.

One, undated but probably in 1861, was shot on the Severn[75]; an adult in summer plumage was killed at Framilode, April 1915[77]; one, found alive off Westgate Street, Gloucester, in February 1936, is now in Gloucester Museum; and a pair was present, and breeding suspected, in early summer 1940, "on a secluded pool in the Severn Vale" (*Field*[28], 15 June 1940.

The only reports since then are of singles at Shorncote near South Cerney, November 1969; on the Severn, Longney Point, March 1973; at Walmore Common, January 1978; on Dudgrove gravel pit, Fairford, in May 1978; and another in the Water Park near South Cerney in February 1979.

FULMAR, *Fulmarus glacialis*

A very occasional visitor, recorded about seven times. Mellersh[40] [41], mentions three, two in the vicinity of Gloucester and one "inland", but without further details. The only recent records are of single birds blown ashore at Pighole, Tidenham, May 1965; flying past Frampton breakwater, October 1967; over the river Wye in both Gwent and Gloucestershire, August 1969 (*The Birds of Gwent:* 1977); and one found dead on the Severn tideline at the New Grounds, Slimbridge, in April 1970.

MANX SHEARWATER, *Puffinus puffinus*

A storm-blown visitor, chiefly in autumn (see page 62).

There are various reports from former years of birds recovered alive or dead from such Cotswold localities as Aldsworth, Northleach, Leckhampton Hill, Uley and Cirencester, and from widely separated places in the Severn Vale.[40] [77] [80]

Relatively recent occurrences include one in flight off the New Grounds in September 1950 and one near Tewkesbury in June 1952. Since 1966 records have been received for most years, and almost all refer to the month of September. A small "wreck" resulting from a gale in early September 1967 brought reports of fifteen or more casualties (about twelve near Lydney), and others of birds in flight along the Severn. In most years since then from one to six birds have been noted, chiefly from Vale localities but one in September 1974 from Great Barrington on the east side of the Cotswolds, another found dead at North Cerney, in September 1980. There appear to be no Forest of Dean records.

STORM PETREL, Hydrobates pelagicus

An occasional storm-blown visitor.

Records from last century are largely undated and lacking in detail[40,77,80]. Mellersh mentions a bird shot at Gloucester in the winter of 1832, and one was found at Siddington, near Cirencester, in October 1856[18]. There is a preserved specimen in Gloucester museum from near Witcombe in 1886 (*Zool.*, 1886, p. 488).

More recent records are of one at Brockworth, December 1929[77]; two in flight with Leach's Petrels at the New Grounds, October 1952[11], and singles over the river Severn, New Grounds, in November 1964, May 1967 and October 1980.

LEACH'S PETREL, Oceanodroma leucorhoa

Occurs occasionally as a storm-driven visitor, recorded most often in September and October; rarely in mid-winter (see page 62).

A dozen or more records, chiefly of single birds, between 1865 and 1912 and mostly in the Severn Vale up-stream from Berkeley[40,77,80,83]. There were scarcely any reports between 1912 and 1952, in which year exceptional numbers occurred in the Severn estuary during the disastrous and widespread "wreck" of late October. Many were then seen alive, and some found dead, at Sharpness on 26th and 27th, and at least 260 were noted flying at the New Grounds on the same days. Small numbers, or single birds, were also recorded then and during the following days from many widely separated localities including Dursley, Frampton-on-Severn, Gloucester, Cheltenham, Coombe Hill, Tewkesbury, Cleeve Hill, Colesborne, Cirencester, Lydney, Dymock and Cannop (*Brit. Birds* XLVII, pp.137–163).

Subsequent records are few: one at the New Grounds, September 1955, and a single at Purton, September 1957; one was picked up at Stonehouse in November 1963 (*Brit. Birds*, LVII, p.46), and the New Grounds produced another single in September 1977. A bird was found dead near Eastleach, December 1978, and one was seen near Minsterworth, late 1979.

GANNET, Sula bassana

Occurs fairly frequently in stormy weather (see page 62).

Twelve or more were recorded during the last 40 years of the nineteenth century[40,80]. There were then few occurrences noted until 1935, in which year about 30 birds were reported from scattered localities after south-westerly gales in September (*Brit. Birds*, XXXII, p.310), followed by isolated instances during the next twenty years[77].

Single birds were seen almost annually between 1957 and 1966. Eight were reported in 1967 and from one to seven in almost every year since.

Of nearly 40 birds reported since 1960, some 30 were noted in the Severn Vale, five on the Cotswold dipslope, one (Cotswold Water Park, April 1977) in the Thames Area, and none in the Forest of Dean. There were no reports for the period January to March, and more than twice as many in September as in any other month. May and August produced several each.

Increase in the number of reports may be due in part also to a rise in the number of observers, but the Gannet has increased greatly in its British colonies since the end of last century.

CORMORANT, *Phalacrocorax carbo*

Present in all months and apparently much more numerous than 80 years ago[40,41,80].

A regular visitor as far up the Severn as Tewkesbury and on the Wye to Redbrook and beyond. Numbers on the Wye are usually small, but 34 were present upstream from Lancaut in November 1978, and 50 in February 1979, using a roost on the Gwent side of the river at Piercefield Cliffs.

Most records from the river Severn are from the New Grounds, Berkeley and Aylburton Warth, with up to fifteen birds or more sometimes noted, showing a steady increase since about 1970. Many birds move between the Severn and Frampton Pools, where regular roosting in trees began about 1971. In 1978, twenty-four birds used this roost in April, and up to 36 during the ensuing winter.

Birds are often seen at reservoirs in the Severn Vale and occasionally in other places, including Cotswold localities. On rare occasions a bird may be seen flying over the Forest of Dean.

Reports have come increasingly from gravel-pits in the Thames Area since the early 1950s, when the bird was no more than an occasional visitor. Most of these Water Park records are from September and October, but since the winter of 1976–7 birds have remained through to the spring, and up to three started roosting near South Cerney in 1979, if not earlier. Numbers in general are small, but thirteen were seen at South Cerney, January 1972, and eleven over Somerford Keynes, April 1979 (and see R.M. Sellers: *Glos. Bird Report*, 1979, pp. 56–61).

SHAG, *Phalacrocorax aristotelis*

A scarce visitor, mostly in relation to Atlantic gales. Mellersh[40] refers to several reports from last century including one of about eleven birds found in November 1894. The first record this century appears to be that of a bird (now in Stroud Museum) at Bull Cross, Painswick, in winter, about 1938. One was shot from a party of three in flight to the north-west of Gloucester, October 1945[77]. Singles were found at Stroud and Cheltenham in August 1948, and nine were claimed at the New Grounds, September of that year.[78]

A further nine birds have been recorded since 1956, eight of them in the past twelve years. All were in Severn Vale localities. So far there have been no reports from the Forest of Dean nor from the Thames Area.

BITTERN, *Botaurus stellaris*

A fairly frequent visitor. Nearly all records fall between October and

March, with the majority in January and February.

Some idea of numbers in former years is given by Mellersh[40] who refers to about twenty-five reports between 1860 and 1910, while H.E. Norris, writing in the *Wilts and Gloucestershire Standard* (9 January, 1926), listed the occurrences of over twenty birds between 1831 and 1925. O.H. Wild[77] heard of "at least thirty Bitterns being shot in various parts of the Severn Vale" in the winter of 1925–6, and collected also numerous reports from other years.

Since then there have been about twenty-five further records, mostly from the Severn Vale. There are no recent reports from the Forest of Dean, but Nicholls, in 1858,[47] referred to two shot in the Forest "within the last twenty years". The few Cotswold notices have come from widely separated localities such as Birdlip, Cherington, Ampney St. Peter, Coln St. Aldwyns and Bourton-on-the-Water. The first Water Park record was in August 1980.

LITTLE BITTERN, *Ixobrychus minutus*

Mellersh[40,41] mentions two: singles at Cheltenham in 1872, and Bourton-on-the-Water about 1883, but corroborative evidence is lacking except that the 1883 bird was "seen by Aplin stuffed at Burford in 1888".

The only recent record is of a male at Frampton Pools, seen three times at close range, 31 May 1964 (*Brit. Birds*, LVIII, p.356).(*Glos. Bird Report* gives date incorrectly as 30 May.)

NIGHT HERON, *Nycticorax nycticorax*

One is reputed to have been shot near Colesbourne between 1867 and 1875[40,41].

The only satisfactory records are of a single adult at the New Grounds, Slimbridge, on 4 September 1950[11]; another from 4 to 11 July 1971; and one beside the Severn at Sandhurst, Gloucester, 11 and 12 June 1979.

SQUACCO HERON, *Ardeola ralloides*

One record: an adult shot at the New Grounds, Slimbridge, August 1867, and presented by Lord Ducie to the City Museum, Gloucester, in 1911 ([40,41]; *Brit. Birds*, XLI, p.154).

CATTLE EGRET, *Bubulcus ibis*

Two records, both of adults, one at the New Grounds, Slimbridge, on 20 August 1974, and the second (or perhaps the same bird) in the area of Slimbridge village and also at the New Grounds, 2 to 7 March 1975. (An escaped bird was seen in the same area, and elsewhere, in 1980.)

LITTLE EGRET, *Egretta garzetta*

Four records. An adult at the New Grounds, Slimbridge, from about 6 to 19 April 1955 (*Brit. Birds*, XLVIII, p.320), was also seen near Frampton-on-Severn on 9th[31]. An adult bird visited the Wildfowl Trust enclosures, Slimbridge, on 24 May 1971; another was seen at Witcombe reservoirs on 11 May 1975, and one was present near Slimbridge on 11 June 1979.

GREY HERON, *Ardea cinerea*

Resident, breeding in small numbers, and a winter visitor.

Yarrell[82] (1843, 1885) does not include Gloucestershire in the list of counties with known heronries. Mellersh[41] also refers to the absence of heronries in this county but in his manuscripts[40] mentions numerous instances of isolated pairs or very small groups nesting in widely scattered localities.

A small heronry was in fact present near Frampton-on-Severn prior to 1860, and then deserted until 1899. By 1914 it again held some fifteen nests (M.F. Clifford,[40]) and seems to have been in use from that time onwards, with a maximum of 23 nests in 1959, before declining to extinction about 1965.

Purple and Grey Herons

Meanwhile another heronry developed at Elmore, commencing about 1934[77]. There were six nests here in 1939, ten in 1951 and 28 in 1959. Numbers decreased here also after the severe winter of early 1963, but three or four nests may still be found annually. Single nests, or small groups, are found periodically in other vale localities.

From time to time small, temporary heronries have been found in various Cotswold localities, such as near Oddington, Adlestrop, Siddington, Sherborne Park, Windrush village and Miserden Park. Most Cotswold breeding, however, as Mellersh suggested, is by isolated pairs or small associations of two or three pairs, but the Windrush colony has increased considerably in recent years.

Single non-breeding birds, or small loose groups, are to be seen feeding at all seasons along the rivers Severn and Wye; also at reservoirs and large pools, and along the Cotswold trout-streams. Birds also use streams in the Thames Area, and particularly the gravel-pits of the Cotswold Water Park, where there is a small heronry just over the border with Wiltshire. Herons are uncommon at Forest of Dean waters.

PURPLE HERON, *Ardea purpurea*

The only records are of an immature bird seen at Frampton Pools and Hasfield Ham on 28 April 1968, and then at the Noose, New Grounds, Slimbridge, on 4 May; and a second year bird near Splatt Bridge, Frampton-on-Severn, 2 and 3 May 1980.

WHITE STORK, *Ciconia ciconia*

A single record. Of two birds reported near Ashton Keynes in Wiltshire in early September 1972, one moved into the Gloucestershire part of the Cotswold Water Park, where it was seen near South Cerney and Cerney Wick on 20 and 22 September 1972.

This bird bore a ring and is considered by the *British Birds* Rarities Committee to have been the Danish-ringed bird captured in Somerset in 1971, and later released in August 1972.

GLOSSY IBIS, *Plegadis falcinellus*

The only satisfactory record is of one at a sewage-farm near Cheltenham for at least a fortnight in October 1943 (*Brit. Birds*, XXXVII, p.158). Wild[77] gives the locality as "Barn Farm, Elmstone Hardwicke".

A report of one shot at Arlingham about 1909 is not supported by further data[77].

SPOONBILL, *Platalea leucorodia*

An infrequent visitor, almost all records coming from Severn Vale localities.

An early report of one "shot in a meadow on the banks of the Avon" near Tewkesbury, June 1838[68], is probably referable to Gloucestershire but the exact locality is not given. A small party of six or seven is recorded by Mellersh[40] as having been seen flying up the Severn about 1878. A bird was shot at Newnham, February 1919[77], and another was killed at Framilode, February 1920 (*Brit. Birds*, XIV, p.234). Single birds visited the New Grounds, Slimbridge in September 1945[21], October 1949[11] and October 1953.[11]

There have been eight records since 1960, two in March and the others from July to August. All but two were from the New Grounds area, the exceptions referring to a bird flying up the river Windrush from Oxfordshire into Gloucestershire, March 1964, and another on the Gloucestershire-Wiltshire border near Ashton Keynes, in the Cotswold Water Park, July 1978.

MUTE SWAN, *Cygnus olor*

Resident and not uncommon in suitable areas.

The Mute Swan is scarcely mentioned by nineteenth-century writers on the birds of the county, and Mellersh (1902)[41] describes it as a winter straggler to the Severn, and makes no other comment. Since then there has been a steady increase up to the 1950s with some later decline in numbers.

The chief breeding areas are in the valleys of the Severn and Frome, along the Cotswold streams and, increasingly, in the gravel pits of the Water Park. It is uncommon over the rest of the Cotswolds, in the Forest of Dean and in the north-west of the county, where suitable habitats are few.

British censuses were carried out in 1955-6, 1961 and 1978, but the Gloucestershire results are not strictly comparable. In 1955-6, 114 birds were found nesting and 247 were non-breeders (some holding territories). In 1978 the corresponding figures were 88 and 177. This decline in numbers is in spite of the extension of apparently suitable habitats in the Water Park, and is most marked in streams and canals of the Severn Vale (Ogilvie M.A.: *Glos. Bird Report*, 1978, pp. 27-28).

The main area now occupied from September to March is the Cotswold Water Park, where totals from 120 to 160 birds may be noted. Colour-ringing shows that some of these have moved into the area from Oxfordshire, although not necessarily from far afield. Other wintering sites are at gravel-pits near Bourton-on-the-Water, where up to 35 birds have been seen, and in the Severn Vale, notably at the New Grounds, Frampton Pools and Coombe Canal, where flocks of 40 or 50 swans are sometimes reported.

Ringing recoveries have come from as far afield as Glamorgan, Shropshire and Staffordshire. An adult female, ringed at Saul, was retrapped at the Wildfowl Trust fifteen years later.

An important cause of mortality and reduction in breeding success of Mute Swans is lead poisoning resulting from the ingestion of discarded fishing equipment, and this may apply to the Gloucestershire populations (see Birkhead, M: *New Scientist*, 2 April 1981).

BEWICK'S SWAN, *Cygnus columbianus*

Formerly a rare winter visitor. Now occurs annually in considerable numbers.

Mellersh[41], in 1902, described it as a "very rare straggler to the Severn. No records since 1861" (but see Whooper Swan). There appear to be no certain records this century prior to December 1938, when twelve were seen near Tewkesbury;[77] nineteen were present at the New Grounds near Frampton-on-Severn in February 1939 (*Brit. Birds,* XXXII, p.380). At least one bird appeared in the Wildfowl Trust enclosures in November 1948;[11] five were seen at Tewkesbury, January 1951; three at the Wildfowl Trust, January and February 1953, and up to nine at Coombe Canal and elsewhere in the early months of 1955.

Thereafter birds appeared annually in the Severn Vale, gradually building up a large winter population, at first chiefly near Elmore and at Coombe Canal, but since the early 1960s, based increasingly upon the Wildfowl Trust enclosures, where food and safety are to be found, and on the adjacent pastures of the New Grounds.

In 1964 up to 35 birds visited the New Grounds and the Trust enclosures, while in December 1966 over 160 birds were seen together there. From 1969 onwards, the maximum number of birds seen on any one occasion in most winters has been between 300 and 400 or even more, but during cold weather in early 1979, 620 were recorded on one occasion.

A technique, developed at the Wildfowl Trust by Sir Peter Scott, for identifying individual swans has shown that these maxima do not represent totals for the whole region. For example, in 1971, when the largest number seen on one occasion (in January) was 412, a total of 626 different birds were recognised for the whole winter.

First autumn arrivals are usually in the second half of October, and as the winter advances birds tend to come and go according to weather conditions: cold weather prolongs their stay well into March; mild conditions may result in fewer birds and an early departure[27]. There is also much movement between the New Grounds, the Wildfowl Trust, Walmore Common, Ashleworth and Hasfield Hams, Coombe Canal and occasionally elsewhere.

The first report from the Thames Area gravel-pits (the Cotswold Water Park) was of two birds at South Cerney, February and March 1956; fifteen were noted near Fairford in November 1961 and two, again at South Cerney, in February 1962. From 1969 birds have been reported in every year in the Thames Area, sometimes at Water Park pits but most frequently at the South Cerney sewage-farm. Numbers have mostly been from one to ten, but nineteen were seen near South Cerney in December 1975, and 23 at the sewage-farm, January 1977. There are also two reports from further up the Cotswold dipslope, at Bourton-on-the-Water, November 1976, and near Bibury, November and December 1978.

There is a single record from the Forest of Dean area: five birds at Noxon Pond, January and February 1973. (See also pages 30, 56, 59, 82).

WHOOPER SWAN, *Cygnus cygnus*

A winter visitor in small numbers.

Mellersh[41], (1902) stated that small flocks appeared in both Severn Vale and Cotswolds in some winters. He also gives a few instances in his manuscripts[40] of up to 30 birds at a time being seen since 1860, but confusion with Bewick's Swans (*q.v.*) is a possibility. Two Whoopers were reported in the Vale in December 1890 (*Zool.*, 1891).

Reports from the first half of the present century are of five near Tewkesbury, April 1927 (*Brit. Birds*, XXI, p.21); about twenty, same place, December 1938 (*Brit. Birds*, XXXII, p.381), and two at the New Grounds in December 1946. The 1950s brought several records of from one to fourteen birds, all in Vale localities, and throughout the following decade reports become more frequent. Five birds appeared on Noxon Pond near the Forest of Dean in October 1960[49], and up to fourteen have spent much of the winter there almost every year since then. Two visited Cannop Ponds in the Forest in January 1979.

In the Severn Vale most reports during the past twenty years have been from the New Grounds and the Wildfowl Trust enclosures: fourteen different birds were noted at the latter place in 1969. From one to seven have been seen also at Walmore Common, Coombe Canal and elsewhere.

The only reports from the Thames Area are of three at South Cerney sewage-farm, January 1970, one at Dudgrove gravel-pit, March 1975, and three near Poole Keynes in January 1979.

BEAN GOOSE, *Anser fabalis*

A winter visitor, perhaps more numerous formerly, but now occurring only in very small numbers.

Owing to confusion between Bean, Pink-footed and other "grey" geese, references by early writers to Bean Geese should be treated with caution, and Mellersh's statement[41] (1902) that by the end of September there were "from two to three thousand" of them at the New Grounds is surely incorrect.

Records made since about 1940 show the bird to be more or less regular at the New Grounds, from one to six being reported almost every year, usually in company with White-fronted Geese. Birds have been seen in all months from September to March, the majority in January and February.

Geographical races of the Bean Goose are ill-defined[51]. Most of the birds reported on the Severn probably come from the Scandinavian population, *A. f. fabalis*, but since 1962 from one to four birds showing characters of the Russian group known as *A. f. rossicus*, or some intermediate form, have been reported at irregular intervals. There is also an old report (*Ibis*, 1940, p. 136)[21] of two unusually large birds killed between Berkeley and Arlingham about 1912, which may have stemmed from a population still farther to the east. (See also page 60).

PINK-FOOTED GOOSE, *Anser brachyrhynchus*

A winter visitor in small numbers to the Severn estuary, formerly more numerous (but see Bean Goose).

Payne-Gallwey's remarks in 1896[54] about large numbers seen on the banks of the Severn probably refer to the New Grounds, where totals of 500 to 1,200 birds or more were still to be seen in the 1930s (Blathwayte, in *Glos. Countryside*, 1932;[9] H.G. Alexander, H.H. Davis, H. Tetley[1]).

Then followed a steady decline to flocks of 50 to 130 birds in most years between the late 1940s and the early 1960s. Ringing showed that during this period the birds belonged to the Icelandic population, and their subsequent disappearance seems to have been part of the general retreat northwards of communities wintering in Britain.

Since the early 1960s parties have continued to arrive very occasionally in September and early October, and these also are presumed to be from Iceland. The stragglers found among White-fronts on the New Grounds in recent years, however, are thought to be of Continental origin, probably from the Netherlands. The largest flock reported in the county since 1963 was of 30 birds near Lydney, January 1979 (see page 60).

WHITE-FRONTED GOOSE, *Anser albifrons*

A winter visitor in large numbers to the Severn estuary.

Reports from the New Grounds early this century vary considerably[70,71], but Mellersh's statement[41] that numbers lay between 3000 and 4000 is probably reliable. These totals have frequently been attained since then and were exceeded in several years between 1966 and 1979, with a maximum of 7600 birds in January 1970.

Birds were formerly to be seen in some seasons early in September, and a few may still stay until the end of March, but main arrivals are now in October and November, peak numbers are reached in the second half of January or in February, and the spring departure is completed, more or less, in the first half of March. Numbers tend to be low and exodus early in mild winters, the converse being the case in severe seasons.

The New Grounds near Slimbridge form the winter quarters of virtually all these birds, but small numbers appear at times at Coombe Canal, Walmore Common, Elmore and elsewhere. Since 1969 small flocks have occasionally visited the South Cerney sewage-farm and have been seen also in the Cotswold Water Park.

The vast majority of White-fronts visiting Gloucestershire are of the nominate race *A. a. albifrons*, but nine dark, yellow-billed birds seen at the New Grounds in November 1945 undoubtedly belonged to the Greenland form, *A. a. flavirostris*,[21] and from one to six or more birds of this race have been noted at the same locality in numerous subsequent winters (and see pages 28, 59, 60, 82).

LESSER WHITE-FRONTED GOOSE, *Anser erythropus*

An uncommon, but now almost annual visitor to the New Grounds. Former status unknown.

The first Gloucestershire record was on 16 December 1945, when two adults were recognised at the New Grounds, one remaining into February 1946 (*Brit. Birds*, XXXIX, pp. 77–9), but it is highly probable that birds were overlooked among common White-fronts (*A. albifrons*) in earlier years.

Between 1945 and the end of 1980 about 65 birds have been recorded, all at the New Grounds, Slimbridge, and almost without exception in the months December to March, with most being noted in February. From one to three birds are usual, but six were identified in the early months of 1951 and 1956, and five in February 1966 (see page 60).

GREYLAG GOOSE, *Anser anser*

A very scarce winter visitor to the Severn. Small breeding populations of feral birds are now established in the county.

Berkeley, in 1854[6], referred to this bird as being among the geese killed on the Severn, but gave no details, and in 1902 Mellersh[41] stated that "The Grey Lag-Goose of ancient England is exceedingly rare about the Severn".

Birds were seen, usually singly, at the New Grounds on about ten occasions, 1933 to 1956. Since then occurrences have been somewhat more frequent, but it is often impossible to decide if a bird is a genuine wild migrant. Indeed, most of these occasional visitors to Gloucestershire are likely to have had feral origins. It is probable also that stragglers are picked up by the flocks of White-fronts moving in from the Netherlands or East Germany, where many thousands of Greylags may be seen in autumn and winter, having bred in Scandinavia. Three Greylags seen at the New Grounds, December 1953, showed characters suggestive of a Russian origin (Wildfowl Trust *Ann. Rep.*, 1953–4 p. 13). (See also page 60).

The Wildfowl Trust collection includes free-flying birds (at least six, unringed, escaped in 1964), and a semi-domesticated flock has developed at Frampton Pools, with sixty birds counted in 1979, and with much movement between these and the Wildfowl Trust enclosures. Feral breeding has been reported at Frampton and in the Cotswold Water Park since 1976, but numbers in the Park are still relatively low. Two were seen flying over the Forest of Dean in June 1980.

SNOW GOOSE, *Anser caerulescens*

A rare visitor to the Severn estuary.

Mellersh records three "near Berkeley before 1885", but these are not included by Witherby in the *Handbook*[81]. Three were present at the New Grounds in the severe winter weather of 1890–1; a party of three adults and five immature birds was seen there in October 1901, and three adults also appeared in November 1906 (Mellersh[40, 41]; *Brit. Birds* VI, p.191). In no case was the race determined, but a Lesser Snow Goose (*A. c. caerulescens*) was shot from a party of three adults at the New Grounds in the hard winter of 1916–7, and is preserved at Berkeley Castle.

Snow Geese were being kept in captivity in Britain and Europe in the last century, and this seems as likely a source of these Gloucestershire birds as genuine trans-Atlantic wandering.

CANADA GOOSE, *Branta canadensis*

A scarce visitor prior to 1953, when over 40 were released at Frampton Pools. Now established as a feral breeding species.

Early records are of single birds at the New Grounds in the winter of 1939–40 and in February 1941. Four were present at Walmore Common in February 1940 and ten at the New Grounds, March 1947.

Following the 1953 introduction at Frampton, breeding commenced and up to fourteen pairs nested there annually during the early 1970s, the winter flock sometimes exceeding 100 individuals. Removal of birds at the owner's request then reduced the breeding stock, but winter numbers remained high, with much commuting between Frampton Pools, the New Grounds and the Wildfowl Trust enclosures. Small numbers are often seen elsewhere in the Severn Vale and also at Cannop Ponds in the Forest of Dean, where an attempted introduction in 1962 failed.

Meanwhile birds began to appear with increasing regularity at the gravel-pits and streams of the Thames Area, and for some distance up the Cotswold rivers. Breeding commenced at Fairford Broadwater in 1955 and at gravel-pits in the Water Park in the early 1960s. Increase was slow, and in 1977 the number of breeding pairs was still no more than eight, rising to twelve in 1979. Counts of non-breeders in the area, however, have shown a considerable rise in population to over 100 birds in 1978 and almost 200 in 1979. Birds are now seen increasingly in scattered Cotswold localities, and nesting occurred at Bourton-on-the-Water in 1978 and 1979.

Further increase and spread seems inevitable.

BARNACLE GOOSE, *Branta leucopsis*

Formerly very rarely seen; now a winter visitor occurring in very small numbers on the Severn in most years.

Mellersh[40] records one shot at Stratton, Cirencester, in 1847, and also refers to an undated record "from Berkeley". From the 1930s, one to four or five birds have been seen at the New Grounds with "grey" geese in most winters; seven were present in February 1962, up to nine in the winter of 1963–4, and ten in February 1976. Nearly all records are from the period December to March, with the majority of birds seen in January and February. These are unringed birds regarded as probably genuine wild migrants. Barnacle Geese of the Russian breeding population winter in the Netherlands alongside European White-fronts. The birds which reach the Severn valley come with flocks of the latter species.

During the past two or three years feral birds have been noted in the

Cotswold Water Park and in the Severn Vale. A feral pair bred at Frampton Pools in 1979 (see page 60).

BRENT GOOSE, *Branta bernicla*

Formerly very scarce, but now occurring annually in winter in the Severn estuary.

Mellersh[41], in 1902, described it as "but a passing visitor in small numbers". Very few were recorded in the earlier years of the present century, but from one to three birds were noted among "grey" geese at the New Grounds on various occasions between 1934 and the early 1960s. Since 1964 birds have been observed every year. Numbers are usually between one and four, but up to sixteen have been reported from the New Grounds, and fifteen were seen at Witcombe reservoirs in January 1951.[18] Almost all reports are from the New Grounds and birds have been noted in all months from October to April, with most records for December and January.

The great majority of birds are of the dark-bellied race, *B. b. bernicla*, but single pale-bellied *B. b. hrota* were seen at the New Grounds, February and March 1941, and from September to November 1946[21]; and two adults were present from late December 1976 to mid-January 1977. (See also page 60).

RED-BREASTED GOOSE, *Branta ruficollis*

Eight records, all between late December and mid-March.

Single immature birds were present at the New Grounds in February 1941 (*Brit. Birds*, XXXV, p.83), and from January to March 1954; another was shot at Hasfield, near Gloucester, in December 1954. An adult stayed at the New Grounds from late January to mid-March 1959, and another from the end of December 1963 to March 1964. In 1967, an immature was there in January (and seen also over Frampton Pools), and then an adult in February. The most recent record is of an adult, also on the New Grounds, in January 1969 (see page 60).

SHELDUCK, *Tadorna tadorna*

A well known species in the Severn estuary, breeding in small numbers and numerous at certain seasons.

The main non-breeding concentration is at the New Grounds, Slimbridge, with some birds on the opposite side of the Severn, chiefly near Aylburton. Following the moult-migration in July and August (see page 56), when few birds are present, the New Grounds population builds up from September throughout the winter and spring to early July, when maxima usually lie between 100 and 200 birds, but are occasionally in the region of 400. Numbers drop sharply later in July leaving, in some summers, fewer than twenty birds in charge of the year's ducklings. The number of young thus left in creche varies from less than 20 to 140 or more, depending on breeding success.

Regular breeding (ten to twenty pairs) occurs along the Severn at least as far upstream as Frampton-on-Severn, a few pairs nesting also along the lower Wye and sometimes (but not recently) on Walmore Common. Nests are occasionally found far from water: Mellersh[41] records one at the top of Stinchcombe Hill, four and a half miles from the Severn and at an altitude of 700 feet above sea-level.

Birds have been reported from Thames Area gravel-pits since the early 1950s, regularly in recent years, and most frequently from January to May. Occasional birds have been noted also at scattered localities on the Cotswold dipslope.

MANDARIN, *Aix galericulata*

This species, often kept in captivity, is showing signs of developing a feral breeding population in the county.

A single male was seen at Cannop Ponds in the Forest of Dean, January to April 1965[49]. Breeding was reported at Frampton Pools and Uley in 1978, the birds almost certainly originating at the Wildfowl Trust; and at Stowell Park near Yanworth, Cotswolds, in the same year. Non-breeders were reported in 1979 from several Severn Vale localities, including a maximum of 22 birds at Frampton Pools in July. Up to 50 were seen there in 1980, and at least six pairs bred in the Frampton–Slimbridge area. Birds were also noted in several Cotswold localities in 1980, when ten were shot near Withington in autumn.

WIGEON, *Anas penelope*

A winter visitor from September to April, maxima occurring December to February.

Totals of between 2,000 and 3,000 birds are reported fairly often from the New Grounds and much less frequently on the opposite bank of the Severn and at Coombe Canal. Considerable populations of 500 to 1,000 birds or more may also be found at Ashleworth and Hasfield Hams and on Walmore Common, with smaller numbers elsewhere in the Vale. Some movement between the New Grounds and these other localities is usual. In 1979 numbers were much larger than usual, probably in relation to the severe weather: a maximum in excess of 8,000 birds was recorded in Severn Vale localities in February, and over 5,000 early in 1980.

Many Wigeon winter also on the gravel-pits of the Cotswold Water Park in the Thames Area, where some increase has been observed since the 1950s owing to the rise in the number of waters and in the availability of suitable grazing ground. From 300 to 500 birds are usual in mid-winter, and counts approaching 1,000 have been made.

No evidence has come to light in support of Mellersh's assertion[41] that the bird "formerly nested" near Sharpness, but occasional Wigeon remain into early summer in various localities. (See also pages 60, 62).

AMERICAN WIGEON, *Anas americana*

Recorded once.

A male was present with Wigeon and Teal on the Severn between the New Grounds, Slimbridge, and Frampton-on-Severn, 9 March 1946.[11] This was probably a wild bird, but the possibility that it had escaped from captivity cannot be ignored (*Brit. Birds*, XXXIX, p.219–220).

GADWALL, *Anas strepera*

Present at all seasons and now breeding regularly in one part of the county.

Regarded by Mellersh in 1902[41] as an uncommon winter visitor to the Severn Vale, and this was probably its status until after the formation of the Wildfowl Trust in 1946. During the 1950s birds were noted increasingly in the New Grounds and Frampton area, some being wild migrants, others derived directly or indirectly from the Trust collection. Ringing at the Wildfowl Trust has confirmed the wild origin of many of the birds, with recoveries as far afield as Scandinavia, eastern Europe and southern France.

A nest was found at Frampton Pools in 1956. The growing resident population in and around the Trust enclosures was augmented in 1967 by release of twenty captive birds, and by 1969 some twenty pairs were breeding in the neighbourhood, the winter population by then numbering between 150 and 200 birds. Nesting occurred also near Aylburton in 1978 and Awre in 1979.

By 1974 the Wildfowl Trust population exceeded 250, and was then deliberately reduced and maintained at less than 150 birds. By this time up to 100 were visiting Frampton Pools and small numbers had been noted in many other Vale localities, notably at Ashleworth Ham, Coombe Canal and Walmore Common. Two pairs were seen on Noxon Pool in the Forest of Dean in March 1976, and 70 birds were present on Flaxley Pool, near Blaisdon, in December 1980.

In December 1965 a bird was seen at Great Barrington on the Cotswolds, and in the following May a male appeared at a Lechlade gravel-pit. From then onwards birds have been noted at various other Water Park localities, and in increasing numbers, with about 40 present in the early months of 1977 and 1980. Breeding in the Water Park has not yet been proved. (See also pages 31, 49, 87, 95).

TEAL, *Anas crecca*

Best known as a passage migrant and winter visitor in considerable numbers from August to March or April, but present at all seasons.

The highest totals, from 600 to 1,000 birds or more are noted in various localities, most often in the periods September-October and January-February, preceded by a gradual build-up in August and followed by a sharp decline in late March as spring passage is completed.

The most favoured localities are the New Grounds, Frampton Pools, Ashleworth and Hasfield Hams, Coombe Canal and Walmore Common, all in the vicinity of the Severn; and also at the gravel-pits of the Water Park on the far side of the Cotswolds. Smaller numbers, however, may be met in many other places away from the Severn, including the ponds, lakes and streams of the Forest of Dean and the Cotswold dipslope. (See also pages 60, 62).

There is no fully satisfactory evidence of breeding in the county, but Mellersh[41] states that "As late as 1862 Teal and Wigeon were supposed to breed occasionally. . . near Sharpness", and, in manuscript[40], he quotes Purcell (1905) as "finding one or two nests about the Lydney marshes in a season"; also that the bird is said to have bred near Tewkesbury. Breeding was reported at Highnam in the 1940s (F.W. Baty[1]) and on Sherborne Brook on the Cotswolds in 1951[18] (W. .Hill[1]), but without detail, and has been suspected elsewhere in the lower Windrush system, and also at Walmore Common in the Severn Vale. A female and young were said to be present on the The Churn at Colesbourne on 13 June 1953, but details were not supplied.

A male showing characters of the American race, *A. c. carolinensis*, was present near and in the Wildfowl Trust enclosures on 3 and 4 May 1964, and another visited Dowdeswell reservoir, Cheltenham, on 13 January 1979.

MALLARD, *Anas platyrhynchos*

Resident and winter visitor in large numbers.

Breeds in most suitable localities throughout the county, particularly in the Severn Vale, beside Cotswold rivers and lakes and in the Water Park. It is less plentiful, but not rare, along the lower Wye and in the Forest of Dean.

At the New Grounds a sedentary breeding population, which has increased to several hundred birds since the formation of the Wildfowl Trust, receives large additions in the autumn, some birds coming from the Continent. Totals of 1,000 to 2,000 birds are not unusual between September and early February, and up to 3,000 have been noted occasionally. Much smaller numbers are usual in many other places in the Vale. (See also page 60).

On the east side of the Cotswolds, winter populations in the Water Park have grown considerably in recent years, and totals in excess of 1,000 birds have been noted from time to time since 1975.

PINTAIL, *Anas acuta*

A winter visitor chiefly to the Severn Vale where numbers have increased considerably during the past thirty years.

The New Grounds and Wildfowl Trust enclosures form the main winter resort in the county, peak numbers usually being reached in January. From 100 to 200 birds are quite usual, up to 300 are occasionally recorded, and 400 were noted in December 1957 and again in December 1976, rising to 600 in the following month.

Pintails

Large numbers are also reported less regularly at Coombe Canal, Ashleworth Ham and Walmore Common, depending upon levels of floodwater. Totals in excess of 100 birds are not uncommon; 200 have been seen at Coombe Canal and 300 near Ashleworth. Smaller parties may be found at other sites in the Vale.

The Pintail is virtually unknown in the Forest of Dean and on the Cotswold dipslope, but from one to three birds were noted occasionally at Thames Area gravel-pits between 1952 and 1968. Since 1969 reports from these waters have been much more frequent, involving from one to twelve birds.

GARGANEY, *Anas querquedula*

Chiefly a passage migrant in small numbers in spring and autumn. Much more frequent recently than at the close of last century[40][41], although apparently in decline since about 1970: in the period 1958–68, about 165 birds were reported; only 100 or so in the following decade.

Reports of birds on spring passage from March to early May are about three times as numerous as those in August and September (but autumn males are less conspicuous than those in spring). Birds have been noted in all months, but very few from October to February, and these chiefly in Wildfowl Trust enclosures, presumably because of the favourable conditions there (1953, 1960, 1963[11]).

The great majority of record are from Severn Vale localities, especially at the New Grounds. There are no reports from the Forest of Dean and hardly any from the Cotswold dipslope. The initial Thames Area records were those of a drake at a South Cerney gravel-pit, March 1955, and three reports from the same area during 1958. At least seven were seen at South Cerney in April 1960, and thereafter reports become more frequent, including one of twelve birds at the neighbouring sewage-farm, August 1966. One or two birds have been noted at the sewage-farm, or at Water Park pits, in each year since 1971.

There are no recent breeding records, but nesting was noted near Gloucester in 1928 (*Brit. Birds*, XXII, p.113), and again in 1929[40]. Wild[77] reported seeing single broods on the banks of the Severn in 1930 and 1934, and two in 1937.

BLUE-WINGED TEAL, *Anas discors*

Two records of this North American species.

An adult male visited the Wildfowl Trust enclosures, Slimbridge, on 24 December 1956, and reappeared on successive days until finally caught and feather-cut on 28th (*Brit. Birds*, L, p.349).

An immature male was present at Ashleworth Ham Nature Reserve from 24 April to 1 May 1979, and in the Wildfowl Trust enclosures on 2nd May.

SHOVELER, *Anas clypeata*

Present in all months, but chiefly an autumn and winter visitor. Has bred occasionally.

The largest populations are found in the Severn Vale, notably at the New Grounds and in the Wildfowl Trust enclosures. Numbers have increased considerably since the 1950s: 200 birds are now reported fairly often, and totals approaching 400 have been recorded occasionally. Up to 100 or more may be seen at times at Coombe Canal, Ashleworth Ham and Frampton Pools, while smaller numbers occur in many other Vale localities.

Shovelers are scarcely known in the Forest of Dean and are seldom seen on the Cotswolds, but very small numbers have been noted at Thames Area gravel-pits since about 1950, increasing in recent years at these Water Park sites, and at South Cerney sewage-farm, to maximum totals around 30 birds. Most are reported between September and March.

The earliest confirmed breeding record is of a nest at Elmore Back, near Gloucester, in April 1937 (W.C. Taunton[1]), and pairs bred at Frampton Pools in 1966 and 1967 (K.J. Grearson[1]). A female and brood, seen at the north end of the New Grounds, May 1969,[62] may have come from the Wildfowl Trust enclosures, but at the time this was considered unlikely. A male, female and small young were present on a gravel-pit just in Gloucestershire, near Ashton Keynes, in June 1972.

RED-CRESTED POCHARD, *Netta rufina*

At best a scarce vagrant. Most birds are likely to be of captive origin, and a feral breeding population is becoming established.

Mellersh[40,41] mentions a bird shot last century at Woodchester Park, later preserved and seen by H.C. Playne, and another said to have been shot near Coombe Canal in January 1907. A female seen on gravel-pits near Fairford, January 1960, and a male at Thornhill Waters, Fairford, in March 1965, may have been wild birds, but at that time full-winged birds from the Wildfowl Trust were already visiting Frampton Pools in the Severn Vale.

Birds at Frampton are usually regarded as of Trust origin. The first nest was found there in 1964, and one or two pairs have attempted to breed, but with little success, on numerous subsequent occasions. Three young fledged in 1969, six were seen in 1977 and at least one was reared in 1978. Up to ten birds may now be seen at the Pools outside the breeding season.

Meanwhile records came more frequently from the Cotswold Water Park. Breeding was reported in 1975 and in each of the two following summers. 1978 produced no breeding reports but up to 13 birds were present. One pair bred in 1979 and one in 1980. Since 1974 birds have been seen at Bourton-on-the-Water, and a pair hatched at least two young there in 1976 (see also page 87 and *Glos. Bird Report*, 1975, p. 28).

POCHARD, *Aythya ferina*

An autumn and winter visitor, now much more numerous than formerly. Reported in all months and has bred.

Comments by earlier writers[40,41,75,80] suggest that the Pochard was not particularly common, but a record of "70 or 80, Frampton-on-Severn, Dec. 1910" is mentioned[40]. Since the late 1940s, when records have been kept in some detail, there has been a steady increase in winter totals at the New Grounds and Frampton Pools, reaching 150 to 300 birds in most winters during the 1960s (500, January 1966), and maintained at these or higher levels to the present. In the hard weather of 1979, over 1,000 birds were counted in that district in mid-February. There is much commuting between the two sites. Elsewhere in the Severn Vale smaller numbers may be seen, notably at Ashleworth Ham. Relatively few visit pools in the Forest of Dean.

A spectacular increase has occurred in the Thames Area gravel-pits (Cotswold Water Park). In January 1954, 120 birds at South Cerney was regarded as an unusually high total. In October 1973 nearly 3,000 Pochard were present in the Water Park as a whole, and since that time totals between 1,500 and 2,500 birds have been noted on numerous occasions. Up to 180 birds, or more, have been seen in recent years at Bourton-on-the-Water in the Windrush Valley, but numbers elsewhere on the Cotswold dipslope are usually very small.

The winter population in the county builds up from September and peak totals are usually reached between November and February. In recent years small but increasing numbers have remained throughout the summer, and there have been two breeding reports: a duck with two small young was seen at Frampton Pools in June 1971, and another with four ducklings was found at a gravel-pit near Fairford in July 1977.

RING-NECKED DUCK, *Aythya collaris*

An accidental visitor from North America.

An adult male visited the Wildfowl Trust enclosures from 12 to 14 March 1955. This was the first accepted occurrence for Europe (but see *Brit. Birds*, XLVIII, p.377). The second Gloucestershire record was of another male caught and ringed, again at the Wildfowl Trust, on 1 March 1977. This bird was later shot in south-east Greenland on 23rd May of the same year.

A male was present in the Cotswold Water Park near Ashton Keynes from 8 April to 3 May 1978, and seen in both Gloucestershire and Wiltshire. (*Brit. Birds*, 72, p.514, gives the dates as 8 to 30 April, and also mentions a bird, believed to have been a hybrid with Tufted Duck, seen in the same area in April 1978 and again in February 1979.)

A male was present in the Poole Keynes-Somerford Keynes area, 21 January to 18 March 1979, and another at Lechlade on 20 February of the same year.

FERRUGINOUS DUCK, *Aythya nyroca*

An accidental visitor.

An adult male was observed closely on a gravel-pit near South Cerney on 21 December 1955, and another at an old pit near Fairford, 21 February 1957. An immature male was identified at Frampton Pools on 23 December 1978, and a male was present on Dowdeswell reservoir, Cheltenham, from 6 to 14 January 1979.

There is no evidence that these birds were other than genuinely wild, but the possibility of escape from confinement cannot be ruled out. A male in the Water Park in 1980 was regarded as an escaped bird.

TUFTED DUCK, *Aythya fuligula*

Primarily a well known autumn and winter visitor, but now found at all seasons, and breeding in increasing numbers.

The main winter locality in the Severn Vale is provided by Frampton Pools and the New Grounds area, including the enclosures of the Wildfowl Trust to which wild birds frequently resort. There is much movement between the sites. In the 1950s totals in the region of 100 birds were noteworthy, but by 1969 counts of 300 were sometimes made. Four hundred birds have been seen together in several winters since then; 625 were present at the Pools and New Grounds in February 1979 and over 700 in December 1980. Smaller numbers are to be found in various other Vale localities, but very seldom in the Forest of Dean.

Tufted Ducks are not numerous over most of the Cotswolds, although

100 or more may be seen at times near Bourton-on-the-Water, and 190 were present there in September 1979. Since the late 1940s, the gravel-pit system in the Thames Area has expanded steadily, and the winter population of Tufted Duck has risen accordingly from a few dozen birds in the early 1950s to the recent totals for the Water Park as a whole, which have come close to or exceeded 1,000 birds on several occasions.

Mellersh[41], in 1902, mentioned a single instance of breeding on the Cotswolds. The first report for the present century was of a duck with six ducklings near Frampton-on-Severn in 1959 (erroneously first reported as Scaup — *Glos. Bird Report*, 1959). A pair bred at a gravel-pit near Fairford in the following year (Glos. Nat. Soc.,[31] 1961), and a female with seven young was seen at Lechlade in 1963.

An extensive colonisation by breeding birds then developed throughout the Cotswold Water Park from Lechlade and Fairford to South Cerney and Poole Keynes. Thirty-three broods at least were hatched in 1974, nearly 80 in 1976, but fewer from 1978 to 1980. A pair bred on Sherborne Brook in the Windrush system in 1976 and again in 1979.

Meanwhile breeding continued in the Frampton Pools area. Following the 1959 hatch (see above), the next report was in 1964, and from one to eight pairs have nested there almost every year since, but with rather low breeding success. Three broods were seen on the Stroudwater Canal, Wheatenhurst, in August 1980.

SCAUP, *Aythya marila*

A winter visitor occurring almost annually in small numbers.

The majority of records are from October to April, and particularly during the first three months of the year, but birds have been seen at all seasons, even occasionally from May to August. Most reports have been of one to three birds at Frampton Pools or the New Grounds, and less often elsewhere in the Severn Vale. Eleven were present on Frampton Pools in February 1980.

One was seen on Rendcomb Lake in 1963 and another at Bourton-on-the-Water in 1973, both Cotswold dipslope localities. Early notices from the Thames Area gravel-pits were at South Cerney and Fairford in 1955 and 1956, and reports from these and other Water Park localities have become relatively frequent since 1973, involving from one to three birds. (Reports of *Aythya* hybrids have been made in both Severn Vale and Water Park localities in recent years and confusion between some of these and genuine Scaup cannot wholly be discounted.[31] [78] The report of feral breeding in 1959, mentioned in the *Glos. Bird Report* for that year, was in error: see Tufted Duck).

EIDER, *Somateria mollissima*

Three records.

Two males were shot at Witcombe reservoirs, 12 February 1896, and until recently were preserved in the Cheltenham College Museum (*Zool.*, 1896, p. 101). A female or immature male was present on a gravel-pit at Bourton-on-the-Water from 28 November to 5 December 1965, and another was seen on the river Severn, New Grounds, 28 April 1969.

LONG-TAILED DUCK, *Clangula hyemalis*

An occasional winter visitor of somewhat irregular but, in recent years, fairly frequent occurrence.

Mellersh[40] listed a number of reports, but with little detail, including one of a bird shot at Elmore in November 1882[18]. Two (perhaps four) were seen on the Severn, New Grounds, in November 1948[11]; one was seen, and later shot, on the canal at Slimbridge, November and December 1954; a female remained in the Frampton-on-Severn area from December 1955 until the following April, and another was present at Frampton Pools in November 1957.

From 1965, records came more frequently, with several from the vicinity of the Severn, including one at Walmore Common in November 1967, and others, from 1969 onwards, from gravel-pits in the Cotswold Water Park.

In all there have been reports of about twenty birds since 1950, noted from October to May, but most often in November and December.

COMMON SCOTER, *Melanitta nigra*

An uncommon visitor recorded irregularly in former years but now occurring almost annually.

Writers referring to the last century[40][80] mentioned a number of birds seen along the Severn as far as Tewkesbury, and one or two inland occurrences. There are also about a dozen dated records in the twenty years following 1937.

Since 1958 birds have been noted almost every year and in all months except January, but with a slight preponderance of spring reports. Most observations are from Severn Vale localities, including Frampton Pools, Hewletts reservoirs near Cheltenham, Witcombe reservoirs and the river itself. There were six or seven records during this period from Water Park gravel-pits, one (Coln St. Aldwyns, 1958) from the Cotswolds, and none from the Forest of Dean.

The majority of reports refer to single birds, but from two to five are not uncommonly noted; eight were seen off the New Grounds in May 1966, and 13 in October 1978.

GOLDENEYE, *Bucephala clangula*

A winter visitor in small numbers.

Early reports[40][41][80] suggest that Goldeneye occurred in very small numbers in the Severn Vale, but seldom elsewhere. Since the early 1950s, when recording was put on a sound basis, reports have been received every year from the Vale and, increasingly, from the Thames Area gravel-pits. A majority of Vale reports refer to Frampton Pools, but birds are often noted also on the river Severn, at local reservoirs and on flood waters near the river.

Up to eight or even ten birds at a time are not unusual in Vale localities, but these numbers were not equalled in the pits of the Water Park until the early 1970s. From about 1973, however, there has been a striking increase from that area, and winter counts for the whole Water Park produced maximum annual totals of 40 to 50 birds during the past five years. There are a very few records from the Cotswold dipslope and also from Cannop Ponds in the Forest of Dean.

In the county as a whole, few birds have been seen in October, but November reports are numerous. The main period is from December to March, with many birds staying into April, when a rapid departure follows.

SMEW, *Mergus albellus*

A scarce and irregular winter visitor, often associated with hard weather.

Witchell and Strugnell[80] give records of two at Rendcombe, 1886, and one at Gloucester in 1891; Mellersh[40][41] mentions more than a dozen reports, and Wild[77] lists birds for various occasions up to 1938 (see also *Brit. Birds*, XXXII, p. 399; *Zool.,* 1891).

Since 1954, when Smew were seen near Coombe Canal and Tewkesbury, reports have been much more frequent, chiefly from Frampton Pools and localities along the river Severn, where up to 14 birds were seen together on dates in February 1956, and at least five early in 1963. Other Vale reports have come from the Wildfowl Trust enclosures and the Gloucester-Berkeley Canal.

Three birds were seen at Thames Area pits early in 1956, and singles were present at Kempsford in October 1961 and at Fairford in February 1962. A male was seen at Dudgrove pit in January 1976, and two females or immature males elsewhere in the Water Park in February and March of the same year. Several were found in the same area in 1979, and one in autumn 1980.

RED-BREASTED MERGANSER, *Mergus serrator*

A scarce autumn and winter visitor.

Early writers, notably Mellersh[40][41] recorded about a dozen occurrences in the latter part of last century; also one at Colesbourne Lake, October 1927. One was noted at Tewkesbury in November 1938 (*Brit. Birds*, XXXII, p.399), and Wild[77] mentioned a male at Slimbridge, February 1940. Single birds were seen near the New Grounds in February 1952 and at South Cerney in the same month of 1956.

Since 1960, birds have occurred in most years, chiefly on the Severn and at Frampton Pools; also on gravel-pits in the Cotswold Water Park almost annually from 1974.

Most reports are of singles, but occasionally of two or three together.

Birds have been noted in every month, from August to May (except January), with perhaps a slight preponderance in October-November and in February. There is one August record and several for May.

GOOSANDER, *Mergus merganser*

A winter visitor, usually in small numbers, reported irregularly in former years but annually since 1956.

There were numerous records prior to 1900[40][41][80], but many with inadequate data. Early reports in this century include those of several near Tewkesbury, December 1938 (*Brit. Birds,* XXXII, p.399); up to five off Minsterworth and the New Grounds in February 1942,[21] and several in Vale localities in 1956.

Since then from one to five birds, occasionally more, have been seen together in the Severn Vale in every year except 1975, usually on the river or at Frampton Pools, and sometimes on the reservoirs at Witcombe and Dowdeswell. The hard weather early in 1963 produced unusual numbers, up to 14 birds being seen together on the river Severn, while the early months of 1979 also brought reports from many Vale localities, including one of 18 birds on Dowdeswell reservoir, and up to 16 seen together on the river Severn.

The first report for the Thames Area gravel-pits was of a female at South Cerney, January 1961, followed by that of three birds in the same locality in March 1963, and a single at Fairford, February 1967. March 1969 saw six birds at Horcott pit, Fairford, and in the following year there were no fewer than sixteen there, and twenty at Dudgrove pit in February. From one to nine birds have been seen at these or other Water Park pits in each subsequent year to 1978. The large influx of early 1979 brought many reports from Water Park localities, with up to thirteen birds being seen together. Eleven were present near Lechlade in November 1980.

The only reports from the Cotswold dipslope are two records from Bourton-on-the-Water in the Windrush valley, where two birds were seen in November 1976 and four in January 1979. A bird was seen on the Wye near Bigsweir, January 1963, and the only report from the Forest of Dean is of two birds at Cannop Ponds in November 1973.

The great majority of all records in the county are from November to March, with most between December and February, and very few in October and April.

RUDDY DUCK, *Oxyura jamaicensis*

A feral population is showing some signs of becoming established in the county.

Birds escaping from the Wildfowl Trust collection at Slimbridge since 1952 soon started to appear at Frampton Pools, where pairs have bred, or attempted to do so more or less regularly from about 1959. Few young are reared, probably because of predation by pike (*Esox lucius*). Fourteen birds were reported there, November 1969, but numbers are usually much lower.

Single females were seen at Witcombe reservoirs in 1976.

Since 1973, from one to three birds have been noted annually at gravel-pits in the Cotswold Water Park, but as yet there is no sign of breeding there. (See *Glos. Bird Report*, 1975, p. 28).

HONEY BUZZARD, *Pernis apivorus*

Appears to have been a scarce summer visitor in the nineteenth century, breeding in small or very small numbers, and perhaps not regularly. Now seldom reported.

References in several early books and manuscripts mention specimens obtained, birds seen and some breeding reports, chiefly from the Forest of Dean but also at Tibberton and Michael Wood in the Severn Vale, and from several Cotswold localities, including Woodchester Park, Birdlip, Farmington and in Oakley and Hailey Woods near Cirencester ([40, 41, 46, 75, 80]; and *Zool.*, 1871, p.2520). Details are lacking.

The only subsequent reports are of a bird seen at Belas Knap, October 1951[18]; and one in display flight in an area of woodland in August 1976.

RED KITE, *Milvus milvus*

Well known formerly as a resident in the Forest of Dean and on the Cotswolds. In recent years reported only as an infrequent visitor.

There was a considerable decrease prior to 1850, and no clear evidence of breeding on the Cotswolds after about 1860, nor in the Forest area subsequent to 1875[39, 40, 41, 46, 47, 77, 80], (and see pages 89, 92).

Records this century are of two birds over Seven Springs near Coberley, in May 1955, and of singles in flight as follows: Sherborne, September 1962; Cheltenham, March 1964; Chipping Campden, April 1972; Cleeve Hill, July 1976; one bird seen in three places in the Severn Vale on the same day in December 1978, and one over Stroud, April 1979.

MARSH HARRIER, *Circus aeruginosus*

A scarce visitor, with most reports in spring and autumn.

There are four or five notices, none with adequate detail, for the period 1870 to 1910[40, 41, 80], and fourteen satisfactory records subsequent to 1946.

Single birds were seen at Frampton-on-Severn in autumn 1947[21, 78] (*Brit. Birds*, XLI, p.120); Dixton Hill near Cheltenham, September 1953; on the Severn Ham at Tewkesbury, May 1954, and at the New Grounds, April 1963. A bird, long dead, found at Snowshill in May 1964 had been ringed in Germany in June 1963 (record not included in the *Glos. Bird Report*). Subsequent occurrences are of singles near Frampton-on-Severn, May 1966; Aylburton, April 1967; flying over the Severn towards Blakeney, August 1969 and another found injured near Nailsworth in autumn of the same year; at the New Grounds in October 1971, and at Frampton Pools, April 1978. Three were seen in 1980: New Grounds in April; Frampton area in May, and near Bibury in June.

HEN HARRIER, *Circus cyaneus*

Reputed to have bred in the past. Now an occasional visitor.

Yarrell[82] included Gloucestershire in the list of counties in which it formerly bred, and Mellersh[40][41] described the bird as a former resident on open ground in the Forest of Dean "before the re-planting of the forest" about 1800; also on the Cotswolds where "it was still frequent about 1850", although perhaps not still nesting there. It appears to have been quite a well known visitor early in the present century, thereafter becoming much scarcer.

Wild[77] mentions a bird at Bourton-on-the-Water in October 1930, and since 1950 there have been reports of fifteen to twenty birds or more (some "ring-tails" not being specifically identified). The majority of these records have come from Cotswold localities, but several are from the Severn Vale. A "ring-tail", thought to be a Hen Harrier, on May Hill, October 1974, and another on Tidenham Chase, September 1980, provide the only recent records from the Forest of Dean area, and an adult male near South Cerney, December 1977, is the sole Thames Area occurrence on record.

MONTAGU'S HARRIER, *Circus pygargus*

A rare visitor on migration.

About six reports from last century, but none is convincing[40][41][80]. More recent records, apparently reliable, are of a late bird, "Nov. 17, 1922, Gloucester" (*Handbook*[81]); a juvenile shot near Northleach, August 1923, and now in the Cheltenham Museum[77], and of single males at Broadwell Hill near Moreton-in-Marsh, June 1958, and near Colesbourne in April 1963.

Some "ring-tailed" harriers, not specifically identified, may have been of this species.

GOSHAWK, *Accipiter gentilis*

Reported at considerable intervals in the past but with greater frequency during the past decade or so. Has bred.

Mellersh[40][41] mentions one seen pursuing a pheasant in Cirencester Park in 1831, and also a pair which were shot by a keeper in the same locality in 1878. He also gives a circumstantial account[40] of the breeding of a pair in the Crippets Wood above Shurdington in 1903 and 1904. Eggs were reported to have been taken in both years, the identity of those from the 1903 nest being confirmed by Ogilvie Grant at the British Museum (Nat. Hist.). In 1904 both birds were shot at the nest and later preserved as mounted specimens, but neither these nor the eggs have been traced. (See also *Field*, May 28th 1904, and Wild[77]). A pair is reported to have attempted to breed at Longhope, near May Hill, about 1926. Two eggs were laid (C.G. Grosvenor[1]).

More recent reports are of single birds seen near Withington in April 1968; at the New Grounds in September 1969; over Frampton Pools in April 1978 and in May 1979, and at Churchdown in July 1979.

Recent breeding has been proved in one locality (some Goshawk records may refer to escaped birds, or to birds deliberately released into the wild state).

SPARROWHAWK, *Accipiter nisus*
Present at all seasons and occurring in most parts of the county.

Probably most numerous in the Forest of Dean and in the wooded parts of the Cotswold river valleys; less so in the Cotswold Water Park, where more often seen in winter, and scarcest on the higher open ground of the Cotswolds.

The widespread and conspicuous decline in eastern England from the late 1950s was less noticeable in Gloucestershire, and the bird has increased again in this county, even where game is preserved, during the past decade (see page 92).

BUZZARD, *Buteo buteo*
At present a scarce and local breeding species.

Bred quite commonly over much of the county prior to about 1850, after which numbers diminished rapidly and the species probably ceased to breed regularly on the Cotswolds in the 1860s and in the Forest of Dean about 1880. Nests were still to be found in the Wye valley near Newland as late as 1890[40,41,80].

Throughout the earlier part of the present century the Buzzard appears to have been no more than a scarce visitor to the Dean and eastwards on to the Cotswold Hills. Visits become more frequent from about 1940 and breeding again occurred in the Forest, the Severn Vale and on parts of the Cotswolds in 1948 or perhaps earlier.

The virtual disappearance of rabbits in 1954 as a result of myxomatosis provided a temporary set-back on the Cotswolds but apparently not in the Forest. Numbers recovered, more or less, within the next few years, and several pairs now breed annually in the Forest, the Wye valley and in the central Cotswolds, particularly near the escarpment edge and down the main river valleys. Breeding is unusual in the Severn Vale and there are no Water Park reports.

ROUGH-LEGGED BUZZARD, *Buteo lagopus*
A rare visitor. Several old records are without convincing evidence[40,41,75,77].

A bird was trapped in Guiting Wood on the Cotswolds on 30 March 1907, and the preserved specimen is now in Gloucester Museum ([77]; J.D. Sanders[1]). Another was killed at Dumbleton, 17 November 1920 (G.L. Charteris[1]). The only recent report is of one seen perched and in flight at Aylburton Warth, 7 April 1969.

OSPREY, *Pandion haliaetus*

A scarce passage migrant.

The majority of records are in May, June and October, and fairly evenly distributed between the Severn Vale, the Cotswold dipslope and the Cotswold Water Park. In all about 30 post-1850 records have been traced, almost all at lakes, reservoirs and gravel-pits, and more than half of them since 1960. Most birds soon move on, but one stayed at Colesbourne Lake through most of October 1957, and another may have remained in a Cotswold edge locality for three weeks or more in June 1977. The only reports from the Forest of Dean area are of two birds in 1979 and one in 1980 (J.D. Sanders[1]).

The post-1960 increase in reports of Ospreys may be due in part to greater observer activity, but it may also reflect the population increase in Scandinavia in the 1940s and the recolonisation of Scotland in the following decade.

KESTREL, *Falco tinnunculus*

Quite a common breeding species throughout the county and present at all seasons.

Most nests are in trees, but Niles and Cooper[49] imply that quarries are the usual Forest of Dean sites. Cliff-nesting also occurs in the Wye valley and sometimes on the Cotswold escarpment, while buildings are occasionally used. A pair nested on Gloucester Cathedral in 1976 and perhaps in other years.

The decline in eastern England from about 1959, attributed to toxic chemicals, was not noticeable in this county.

RED-FOOTED FALCON, *Falco vespertinus*

Two old and three recent records.

Mellersh[40][41] refers to one killed near Colesbourne about 1870, and another said to have been shot at Duntisbourne "possibly in the same summer".

A male was seen at the New Grounds, Slimbridge, on 25 May 1973, and a female visited a gravel-pit in the Cotswold Water Park, near South Cerney, on the 30th. An adult male was seen flying across the Avon-Gloucestershire border near Severn House Farm, south-west of Berkeley, on 16 September 1974.

MERLIN, *Falco columbarius*

A scarce but fairly regular visitor from autumn to spring.

The Merlin is said to have nested, a hundred years ago or more, on heathlands in the Forest of Dean area[41], and Mellersh[40] also mentions two nests from unlikely Cotswold habitats at Colesbourne and Bagendon. There is no such report from Cleeve Hill, which appears much the most likely locality. No doubt this bird has always been a more or less regular passage and winter visitor. During the past 25 years, from one to four or more reports have been received almost annually, nearly all from October to April. The great majority of birds have been seen at the New Grounds and other localities along the margins of the Severn, but there have also been scattered records from places on the Cotswolds. Birds were seen in the Cotswold Water Park in March and October 1976.

HOBBY, *Falco subbuteo*

A summer visitor breeding in small numbers.

Mellersh, at the end of last century, could find little evidence of the Hobby occurring in the Forest of Dean area, and remarked that "Two or three pairs. . . still nest in certain woods on the (Cotswold) hills"[41]. Hobby occurring in the Forest of Dean area, and remarked that "Two or three pairs. . . still nest in certain woods on the (Cotswold) hills"[41].

The bird is now said to nest, perhaps annually, to the west of the river Severn[1] and, although proved breeding is not often reported, there are frequent records of suspected nesting from certain localities in the Severn Vale and from quite widely separated places on the Cotswolds. Brown's comment in 1957 (*Brit. Birds*, L, p.149) that Gloucestershire is "unlikely to have more than 5 pairs" is probably an understatement.

Birds on passage, or moving to and from favoured feeding areas, are reported more widely, and in recent years there have been annual records, sometimes numerous, from the Cotswold Water Park, a region which may be attracting the birds to an increasing source of insect and avian food.

GYRFALCON, *Falco rusticolus*

The only acceptable record appears to be of one seen at the New Grounds, Slimbridge, on 26 January 15 February and 11 March 1964.

Mellersh[41] appears to have accepted a somewhat extraordinary account given by Witchell and Strugnell[80] of an immature bird caught near Cheltenham about 1885. It is said to have hit the ground while in pursuit of finches, and was then caught by W.B. Strugnell, who "seized it in his soft felt hat".

PEREGRINE, *Falco peregrinus*

Chiefly an autumn and winter visitor, but has been noted in all months, and has bred in the past.

An early breeding record is of a pair which nested on the old Severn Railway Bridge near Sharpness, before construction was finished in 1878. Four eggs could be seen from the track in a recess in one of the pillars[77]. Mellersh does not mention this, but refers to breeding on a Wye valley cliff in 1929[40]. Birds bred or attempted to do so on the lower Wye in several years between 1937 and 1960. A food-pass was observed between a pair over the New Grounds in 1976, but there has been no other indication of possible breeding in recent years.

In 1902, Mellersh[41] regarded the Peregrine as a "straggler" to the Severn Vale and the Cotswolds. There is little information on wintering birds between then and the 1950s, but during the past 25 years, up to three or four birds have been noted annually in Severn Vale localities between autumn and spring, chiefly near the river and notably at the New Grounds. Wintering in this area continued in spite of the severe decline in Peregrine numbers in Britain in the late 1950s.

There have been very few reports from the Cotswold dipslope and the Thames Area during the same period, except for the winter of 1978–9, when birds were seen in the Water Park and elsewhere on a number of occasions.

BLACK GROUSE, *Tetrao tetrix*

Probably not uncommon in the Forest of Dean during the first 60 years or more of the nineteenth century, but there have been no satisfactory records for more than 100 years.

Mellersh[41], in 1902, described it as a rare straggler from adjacent counties and refers in manuscript[40] to a nest said to have been found about 1900 near Berkeley. Gladstone, in 1924, also states that the bird has been recorded only as "a rare straggler to... Gloucester...," a statement probably taken from Mellersh (*Brit. Birds*, XVIII, pp.66–8).

There seems no reason, however, to doubt Machen's comment[39] of October 1859, in reference to lekking grounds, that "There are 4 or 5 of these in different parts of the Forest, and early in the morning and again about sunset the birds from all quarters to the number of 30 or 40 assemble and make a kind of crowing and stalk about like pigeons and then fly away to their respective places" (extracted from Wild mss.[77]).

The report ([19]*Country-Side*, Vol.8, No.186) of a bird seen on Brockeridge Common, Tewkesbury, 20 November 1908, provides no evidence of identification, and may in any case refer to Worcestershire. (Introductions of Black Grouse have been made in various parts of the country, but none appears to have been recorded for this county.)

RED-LEGGED PARTRIDGE, *Alectoris rufa*

An introduced resident, locally quite numerous, especially on the Cotswolds.

The earliest reports for the county appear to be those of single birds shot at Corse Hill in September 1828 (*Bath and Cheltenham Gazette*) and at Leckhampton in the same month in 1829 (*Cheltenham Chronicle*). Wheeler (1862)[75] described it as local and rare, mentioning Cleeve and Corndean on the Cotswolds. An increase on these hills towards the end of the century was attributed by Mellersh[41] to the release, about 1865, of some twenty brace near Chipping Norton in Oxfordshire (and see[44] More, A.G: *Ibis*, 1865). In the closing years of the nineteenth century the Red-legged Partridge had barely crossed the Severn in its westward spread in this county, but by 1907 it was reported as numerous round Newent[70].

Work prior to publication of the *B.T.O. Atlas*[62] in 1976 confirmed that the bird is now widespread over most of the northern part of the Cotswolds, but apparently scarce or absent to the south of a line drawn approximately from South Cerney and Kemble through the Stroud area to Slimbridge. It is local but not uncommon in the Severn Vale south to Slimbridge, but now evidently scarce in the region around Newent and Redmarley, and not to be found in the Forest of Dean. Birds are still reared in captivity and released in the county in moderate numbers (I. Dennis[1]).

GREY PARTRIDGE, *Perdix perdix*

A common resident and distributed over most of the county.

Scarce in the Forest of Dean proper, but present in the larger open areas and in surrounding marginal and agricultural land. Nicholls[47], in 1858, wrote that Partridges became plentiful in the Forest in the early nineteenth century "when the plantations were first made", but that they then disappeared as the woods grew up. Many Hungarian birds are reported to have been turned loose in the county about 1904, and a record bag of 126½ brace is noted in the *Victoria History*[70].

The bird is still quite common in much of the Severn Vale, and all over the Cotswolds and Thames Area, but there appears to have been a gradual decline in numbers, considerable in some places, during the present century, and perhaps due chiefly to changes in agricultural methods. Small numbers are still reared and released in Gloucestershire (I. Dennis[1]).

QUAIL, *Coturnix coturnix*

An uncommon summer resident, but showing considerable fluctuations and not reported every year.

According to More's questionnaire[44] in 1865 Quail were breeding regularly in Gloucestershire and were probably quite common in some years on the Cotswolds but unusual in the Severn Vale. Mellersh[40,41] mentioned 1916 and 1924 as good Quail years; Wild[77] listed numerous records up to the 1940s, and A.G. Tayler[1] stated that the birds were to be heard near Bourton-on-the-Water almost every year from 1924 to the 1960s.

During the past 30 years numbers have varied considerably. There were no reports for 1955–60 and 1973–4. Almost all records are from widely separated localities on the limestone of the Cotswolds, with very few from the Severn Vale, only one from the Forest of Dean (Coleford, 1962), and none in the Cotswold Water Park. (See also *Brit. Birds*, XLIV, pp.257–276; and British Trust for Ornithology records).

PHEASANT, *Phasianus colchicus*

A common and widespread introduced resident. Numbers are still reared in captivity and released.

It seems probable that the bird was not plentiful in Gloucestershire until well into the nineteenth century. Nicholls, in 1858, quoting Machen[47,39], referred to the introduction of some Pheasants at Whitemead in the Forest of Dean, and remarked that they "soon spread over the whole Forest". The bird was also well known on the Cotswolds and elsewhere in the county by the end of the century, and there has been a gradual increase in population ever since. Most plentiful in wooded areas on or near large estates, but birds may sometimes be found even on the high, open ground of the Cotswolds.

WATER RAIL, *Rallus aquaticus*

Mainly an autumn to spring visitor in rather small numbers, but reported in all months and breeding is occasionally noted.

In earlier years the situation was probably much the same as now[10,40,41,75,80], although there is evidence of greater abundance in some winters. Due to its elusive habits, however, this is undoubtedly an under-recorded species and the picture is not clear.

Since 1950 more detailed records have been kept, and small numbers of birds have been reported annually, mostly from October to March and April. The majority are from sites in the Severn Vale and the Stroud valley, but Cotswold records are also frequent and from widely scattered localities. There were six reports at gravel-pits near South Cerney from 1957 to 1970, and breeding may have occurred in 1966. Subsequently there have been further Water Park records from the same general area and from near Lechlade, with several of single birds in 1979 at a number of pits.

On the far side of the county, the Forest of Dean has produced a small number of reports, including that of a pair in the breeding season of 1956.

Breeding is seldom proved in the county, but certainly occurs, at least occasionally, in the Severn Vale and perhaps elsewhere. The most recent confirmed cases were at Over Ponds, Gloucester, 1975, and Frampton-on-Severn (unsuccessful), in 1980.

SPOTTED CRAKE, *Porzana porzana*

Now seldom reported, but the bird seems to have been more numerous prior to about 1915[40,41,75,77,80].

Mellersh, in his manuscripts[40], lists about fourteen instances of birds seen or killed, including a note of "some 30 or 40 about Coombe Hill Canal, Autumn 1904. . .", and mentions also that ten eggs were taken in the same locality.

A bird was seen at Netherswell, Stow-on-the-Wold, 28 January 1914 (*Brit. Birds*, VII, p. 348). Another, shot at Bourton-on-the-Water, September 1916, is now in Gloucester Museum; a third was reported at Minsterworth, August 1920, and one was seen at Walham Pools in December 1925[77]. Wild also mentions three others, but with little detail.

Since 1940 there have been only six reports, all of single birds: Ebley, near Stroud, April 1942 (R.H. Casson,[1]); Bisley, near Stroud, autumn 1949 ([18]; 1951); Wildfowl Trust enclosures, December 1959; Splatt Bridge, near Frampton-on-Severn, April 1964; one caught and ringed at the

Wildfowl Trust in October of the same year, and one at Sandhurst, September 1977 (J. Rowe[1]).

LITTLE CRAKE, *Porzana parva*

One is said to have been obtained near Deerhurst about 1876[40][41]. The only subsequent record is of a bird at the New Grounds decoy-pool, Slimbridge, from 22 to 29 April, 1951. It was finally found dead in one of the decoy-pipes and is now in the British Museum (Nat. Hist.)[11][78].

BAILLON'S CRAKE, *Porzana pusilla*

The only record is of one killed at Over, near Gloucester, in 1882[40][41][81]. The bird was presumably shot at one of the ponds still present near the bridge over the Severn.

CORNCRAKE, *Crex crex*

Formerly a widespread and plentiful summer resident; now no more than one or two are reported in most years. Has been recorded at least twice in mid-winter, in 1867[28] and 1903[77].

The long decline of the Corncrake in Britain began to affect Gloucestershire late in the nineteenth century. By 1914 the bird was becoming scarce, but some still bred, "chiefly in the river flats" (*Brit. Birds*, VIII, p.84)[40][41][80]. The decrease was very marked by 1930[77].

Nesting ceased in southern areas first and on the Cotswolds earlier than in the Severn Vale, where breeding continued into the 1950s. A nest of broken eggs was found on Tidenham Chase near the Wye valley in 1964, and a pair probably bred there in 1968. These are the latest breeding records.

In recent years single birds, and sometimes pairs, have been reported from a variety of Cotswold and Vale localities, some birds remaining for up to a week or more. (See also *Brit. Birds*, XXXVIII, pp.145, 148, 278; B.T.O. *Atlas* records[62]).

MOORHEN, *Gallinula chloropus*

A common breeding bird, present at all seasons.

It occurs in all the main areas of the county, and there is no evidence of major change in population since last century, other than an increase in the Thames Area where a steady rise in the number of gravel-pits has created more breeding sites.

The winter population in the county may be increased by autumn immigration, with considerable numbers gathering in suitable places such as Coombe Canal, where over a 100 birds were seen in February 1959, the Wildfowl Trust enclosures, which held a total of at least 355 birds in

January 1980, and Sandhurst near Gloucester where a winter population of 100 to 150 is usual. Numbers may be much reduced in hard winters, and between 60 and 70 Moorhens were found dead in Stowell Park, near Chedworth, in the severe weather of early 1963 (see page 88).

COOT, *Fulica atra*

Resident and winter visitor, with considerable increase this century.

Apparently rather uncommon in the latter part of the nineteenth century: Mellersh wrote that it is "remarkable how scarce the Coot is in the county generally".[10,40,41,75,80]. It appears to have been quite widely distributed by the 1930s, but still by no means abundant[77]. The breeding population has increased considerably during the past 30 years, especially in the Thames Area, where the Water Park gravel-pits provide a whole range of new nesting sites. Here the breeding population probably exceeded 100 pairs by 1978. The bird now breeds throughout the county wherever there are large ponds, lakes and other waters, with some pairs also on slow-flowing reaches of rivers.

There has been also a huge increase in the autumn and winter population since the 1950s, very large numbers now being found in the Water Park, at Frampton Pools and Bourton-on-the-Water, with smaller (but still considerable) gatherings elsewhere. The December counts in the Cotswold Water Park for the years 1977–79 gave maxima of 4,382, 5,873 and 5,570 birds respectively. The corresponding figures for Frampton Pools in the Vale were 500, 700 and 390, and at Bourton, 302, 307 and 330 birds.

When waters are frozen over the birds tend to move elsewhere. This was especially noticeable in early 1963, when Frampton Pools and the Water Park gravel-pits were largely deserted. At such times, Coot may appear on the Severn mud-banks, or leave the county altogether.

Ringing results suggest that most Coot visiting Gloucestershire in autumn and winter come from as far afield as eastern Europe, even as far as Moscow[61].

CRANE, *Grus grus*

A young male was shot at Fiddington, near Tewkesbury, on 17 May 1869 (*Zool.*, 1869;[40,41,80]). The only recent records are of one at Aylburton Warth, near Lydney, 2 April 1976 (*Glos. Bird Report*, 1977); one at the New Grounds, Slimbridge, 13 November 1979; and an adult in the Frampton-on-Severn and New Grounds area from 31 August to 5 September 1980, in flight over Frampton on 25 September and over Cheltenham on 26th, then returning to the New Grounds on 29th and 30th.

A specimen, now in Gloucester museum bearing the label "Minsterworth, Glos., August 1914", and previously stated to be of this species, has been identified as an example of the White-naped Crane, *Grus vipio* (J.D. Saunders,[1] 1980).

LITTLE BUSTARD, *Tetrax tetrax*

One was seen near Rectory Farm, Turkdean, Northleach, on 20 May 1946, and remained in the neighbourhood for several weeks[77]. The bird, apparently an adult female, was then shot on 30th July, and is preserved in the farm-house. Subspecific identification was not made at the time, and the late B.W. Tucker subsequently considered it impossible to do so after comparison with skins in the British Museum (Nat. Hist.).

GREAT BUSTARD, *Otis tarda*

This bird may have bred on the Cotswolds in the past, but records appear to be lacking. The only recent report is of one flying south over Leckhampton Hill, near Cheltenham, on 24 May 1977. (The birds released at Porton Down, Wiltshire, were all pinioned).

OYSTERCATCHER, *Haematopus ostralegus*

An annual visitor to the Severn estuary and occasionally elsewhere, noted in all months but mostly from March to October.

The majority of birds are seen in the New Grounds area, but reports come from both sides of the river, and sometimes in Vale localities away from the Severn and as far up-stream as Tewkesbury, while a few birds visit the lower Wye. Along the Severn they are usually seen in ones and twos, but parties of up to six are not rare, and from twelve to sixteen birds have been noted together, chiefly in July.

Birds are reported very occasionally flying over the Cotswolds, probably passing between the Severn and the Thames Area gravel-pits of the Cotswold Water Park. About a dozen Water Park reports of from one to five birds have been received since 1958, all so far between March and September.

Very rarely reported from the Forest of Dean area.

AVOCET, *Recurvirostra avosetta*

A scarce visitor to the margins of the Severn.

Pennant's record in 1768 referring to these birds as occurring "in Gloucestershire at the Severn mouth" probably belongs to Avon. Most records prior to the early 1900s are confused and none is fully satisfactory. Mellersh's statements about Avocets formerly resting in arable fields on the Cotswolds near Northleach were not founded on his own observations, and clearly referred to Stone-curlews[40,41] (pages 68–69).

Four birds "seen together at Stonehouse, on the Severn", March 1913 (*Brit. Birds*, VII, p.235), were presumably at the New Grounds where all subsequent records have been made. Five were seen there in August 1954, and one in December of the following year. Two were present in mid-winter, 1959–60, followed by a single in May 1960.

One or two appeared in June 1965 and 1966, and no less than fifteen were seen at the end of May 1969, with one bird in mid-June. In 1974, seventeen arrived in early May. Several remained for a few days, two were seen in June and singles in July and September. Solitary birds were subsequently reported in April 1975, May 1977, February 1978 and March 1980.

STONE-CURLEW, *Burhinus oedicnemus*

Formerly a not uncommon summer resident on the higher Cotswolds.

According to Mellersh[40][41], this species was well known until about 1860, after which there was a rapid decline. His statements about Avocets on the Cotswolds near Northleach ("Black and White Curlews") around the middle of last century must be regarded as referable to Stone-curlews (see pages 68–69). A few pairs were still to be found, and eggs were taken, in the 1890s and perhaps into the early years of the present century[77]. The latest reference in Mellersh's manuscripts is to a bird shot at Shipton Oliffe in April 1923.

A nest was found near Aldsworth in June 1953, and birds were present in the same locality in 1950, 1952 and 1954, when breeding was also suspected near Turkdean (*Proc.* Cott. Nat. Field Club[18], 1953; A.G. Taylor[1]). There have been no other breeding reports, and the only recent record of any kind is of one bird at a gravel-pit to the west of Ashton Keynes, 27 July and 3 August 1980.

COLLARED PRATINCOLE, *Glareola pratincola*

Mellersh mentions an unconfirmed report of one killed at Paradise, near Painswick. Different dates are given: "May 1876"[41], and "about July 9 1882"[40]. This record does not appear in the *Handbook*[81].

The only satisfactory report is of a bird seen near Cricklade, Wiltshire, on 30 May 1968, which then flew across the county boundary into Gloucestershire.

LITTLE RINGED PLOVER, *Charadrius dubius*

A very local summer visitor.

First reported in the county in 1953 when three pairs bred near South Cerney. Two pairs nested in the same place in 1954; in 1955 there was an unsuccessful attempt there and breeding was suspected at another site.

The next confirmed breeding was in 1961, again in a Thames Area gravel-pit, and birds have nested or attempted to do so in the Water Park in every year since then, with numbers gradually increasing as new pits were opened up. The highest number of breeding pairs so far recorded is 25 in 1978, when 48 young from eighteen broods were counted. Breeding has also been noted from two localities outside the Cotswold Water Park (see also pages 47, 86, 93).

Reports of wanderers or birds on passage first came from the Severn Vale in 1958, and have been annual since 1965. These birds have been noted chiefly from the New Grounds area, but also from Frampton-on-Severn, Witcombe reservoirs, Ashleworth Ham, Walmore Common and Aylburton Warth.

RINGED PLOVER, *Charadrius hiaticula*

Chiefly a passage migrant, but present in all months.

The spring and autumn passage movements are quite extended, peak numbers being attained in May and in August or early September. The localities along the Severn where most birds are seen are the New Grounds and the Aylburton-Guscar Rocks areas where, in the 1960s, totals well in excess of 1,000 birds were occasionally reached. In recent years, however, maximum numbers have been much lower than this.

Small numbers of Ringed Plover have been noted in the Thames Area gravel-pits since the early 1950s, mostly from March to October. These are usually birds on passage, but an unattached male made a "scrape" at one Water Park pit in 1977, and the following year a pair had a nest with eggs which was unfortunately flooded before hatching-time. Breeding was suspected, but not proved, in 1979, and territorial behaviour noted in 1980.

Gloucestershire-caught birds in autumn are not in moult and this, together with the meagre ringing data, suggests that those which pass through the county breed in Iceland and Greenland, and migrate up and down the west coast of Britain. There is no evidence that birds of the British breeding population occur on the estuary, although the few that winter at Guscar Rocks may belong to this group[61].

KENTISH PLOVER, *Charadrius alexandrinus*

A scarce visitor, chiefly on spring passage and noted only during the past twenty years.

The first report was from the New Grounds, Slimbridge, 4 April 1960, and there have been about eighteen records since then, all from March to September, and the majority in April and May. Most reports are from the New Grounds and near Frampton-on-Severn, but birds have been seen recently at gravel-pits in the western part of the Cotswold Water Park in May 1975, in May and August 1977, and in May 1980.

DOTTEREL, *Charadrius morinellus*

Formerly known as a passage migrant in spring and autumn on the Cotswolds. Now apparently much less frequent.

Mellersh[40][41] refers to small parties on high ground above Sherborne Park about 1850, and records that seventeen were killed on Cleeve Hill about 1870. Of other occurrences given by Mellersh, only one is dated: a party of fourteen birds on Cleeve Hill, 8 to 10 May 1909, three or four remaining for a week.

Subsequent records are of two, also on Cleeve Hill, May 1934[77], and one at Hewlett's reservoirs, Cheltenham, in April 1953 (not 1952 as stated in *Ornith. Notes for 1952 and 1953*[18][31]). None was reported thereafter until 1969, when a bird was shot near Aylburton on the west bank of the Severn in September; another was seen in the same area in May 1973. The most recent record is of five in a field beside the Severn at the New Grounds, April 1975.

LESSER GOLDEN PLOVER, *Pluvialis dominica*

One record. A bird was seen with Golden Plovers and Lapwings on salt-marsh and wet pasture beside the river Severn, near Frampton-on-Severn, on 4 October 1967. (The thirteenth bird reported for Britain and Ireland).

GOLDEN PLOVER, *Pluvialis apricaria*

A passage migrant and winter visitor.

Flocks of 100 to 200 birds on passage are frequent in favoured localities in spring and autumn, and much larger numbers are by no means rare: 300 have been noted at Redmarley, 400 at Maisemore, up to 500 near Hawling and over 600 in the South Cerney area. Passage movement occurs over most of the county, with regular feeding grounds along the Severn and elsewhere in the Vale, on various parts of the Cotswolds and in the Water Park. There are few reports from the Forest of Dean area.

Winter flocks, from November to February, are also widespread. One of 750 birds was seen near South Cerney in December 1973, but most flocks are much smaller than this. In severe winter weather birds may feed on the mud-flats of the Severn estuary, and many leave the county for the south and west.

Birds showing characters of the northern race, *P. a. altrifrons*, have occasionally been identified from April to July.

GREY PLOVER, *Pluvialis squatarola*

Chiefly a passage migrant, but noted in all months. A few remain as winter visitors in Severn estuary localities.

Apparently much less well known at the end of last century than now: Mellersh[41] described the birds as rare, even along the Severn, ". . .mere stragglers".

Both spring and autumn passage periods are long-continued, and even July is not without records. Small peak numbers are now noted in April and May, with up to twenty birds sometimes seen, and as many as 40 have occasionally been reported in the period from August to November.

A few birds have been noted at gravel-pits in the Cotswold Water Park since 1974, and at various times of the year.

LAPWING, *Vanellus vanellus*

Chiefly a resident and winter visitor. Numbers are much affected locally by weather-related movements.

Breeding occurs sparingly in open country around the Forest of Dean; more plentifully in the Severn Vale and towards Newent and Redmarley; widely but somewhat thinly over the Cotswolds and throughout the Thames Area, including some unflooded gravel-pits.

Internal flocking of Lapwings in Britain begins soon after the breeding season. Immigration to the country extends from early June to December; emigration from January to late spring. This explains the occurrence of large flocks of 2,000 birds or more in Gloucestershire as early in the summer as June and July, and thereafter throughout the autumn and winter, in various parts of the county.

In recent years considerably larger flocks have been reported of from 4,000 to 5,000 birds at South Cerney sewage-farm in December and at the New Grounds in November and December. Some 6,000 Lapwings, in four flocks, were in the South Cerney area of the Water Park in December 1974, and an estimated total of 7,000 were feeding to the east of Tewkesbury in February 1978. These numbers are reminiscent of Mellersh's reference in 1902[41] to a flock of "not less than ten thousand" on Cleeve Common, at a time when the Lapwing was probably more abundant, at least as a breeding bird, than it is today.

Ringing data show that many birds move south for the winter as far as the Iberian peninsula, and suggest also that a proportion of birds in the big flocks from late June onwards may originate in Germany and the Netherlands[61].

KNOT, *Calidris canutus*

Chiefly a passage migrant, most numerous in autumn, but birds may be seen in all months.

Totals occasionally reaching 60 to 90 birds have been noted chiefly in August and September: the maximum so far is an exceptional 400 off the New Grounds, August 1946[11]. Spring numbers are considerably less and few are noted from December to February, an exception being a flock of 60 at the New Grounds in February 1968.

Nearly all records come from localities along the river Severn, chiefly at the New Grounds, but there are a few reports from Walmore Common, and three or four of single birds in autumn at Thames Area gravel pits since 1954.

SANDERLING, *Calidris alba*

A passage migrant in spring and autumn, chiefly in the Severn estuary.

Spring passage is from March to June, with flocks of 40 to 60 birds not infrequent. Small numbers are then present in July and August in most years, followed by a second and much smaller peak in late August, September and early October. The report of 120 birds seen off the New Grounds, 26 October 1959 is surprising at this season. There are few records for November and only two in mid-winter: three birds at South Cerney, January 1954, and one at the New Grounds, January 1972.

Most records come from the New Grounds and other localities along the river Severn, while reports of one or more birds at gravel-pits in the Cotswold Water Park are now almost regular. Eleven were present at

Dudgrove pit, near Fairford, in May 1973, and six birds paid visits to wet tarmac at Little Rissington airfield for a week in September 1974.

LITTLE STINT, *Calidris minuta*

An uncommon passage migrant on the Severn estuary and occasionally elsewhere; recorded in most months.Considerably more numerous in autumn than in spring, with flocks of 20 to 30 birds not infrequently noted in September and October; nearly 100 were present at the New Grounds in October 1966, and 80 in September 1967. Very few birds have been seen in mid-winter.

Most records are from the Severn estuary, with occasional notices from elsewhere in the Vale, but there are also reports, almost annually of recent years, from Thames Area gravel-pits, single birds being noted from May to August, and up to eight in the autumn.

TEMMINCK'S STINT, *Calidris temminckii*

A very scarce visitor.

There is one early record[40][41][80] of a bird said to have been "shot at the Dark Mill, Bourne, near Stroud", 1878, but no details of identification are given.

There have been seven recent records, all of single birds. Five are from the Severn Vale: Frampton Pools, August 1965; Frampton Marsh, May 1966; Frampton Pools again, August 1976, the New Grounds, May 1977, and Wildfowl Trust enclosures, November 1980. The other two reports come from the Cotswold Water Park, of a bird near Cerney Wick, May 1975, and one near Somerford Keynes, May 1977.

WHITE-RUMPED SANDPIPER, *Calidris fuscicollis*

A bird at the New Grounds, near Frampton-on-Severn, on 14 November 1976, provides the only Gloucestershire record of this northern Nearctic species.

BAIRD'S SANDPIPER, *Calidris bairdii*

The sixteenth British record of this species, and the first for Gloucestershire, was of a bird seen on mud near the breakwater, Frampton-on-Severn, on 30 and 31 August 1966. Another (or perhaps the same bird) appeared at the same spot on 18 October 1967.

PECTORAL SANDPIPER, *Calidris melanotos*

One seen at the New Grounds, Slimbridge, 6 to 14 August 1975, was found at the time of an influx to Britain of Siberian waders and may have originated from that region. Two birds were present in the same area, 15 and 16 September 1977, and one on the 17th.

A Pectoral Sandpiper near Ashton Keynes in Wiltshire, early October 1977, was seen at an adjacent gravel-pit in Gloucestershire from 11th to

16th, and one was present in the same part of the Cotswold Water Park on 29 and 30 September 1979.

CURLEW SANDPIPER, *Calidris ferruginea*

A passage migrant, usually in small numbers, and more frequent in autumn than in spring.

The spring movement is very sparse, usually of birds seen singly in May and June, and not every year. Autumn passage is largely completed between August and October, with occasional birds seen in July and a very few in November. Largest numbers are reported in August and September, notably 40 birds in early September 1963, up to 100 (mostly juveniles) at the end of August 1969, and about 140 adults, 5 August 1975. Such numbers are somewhat exceptional (see page 55).

These, and indeed nearly all reports, come from the Severn estuary and mostly from the New Grounds and the Aylburton-Guscar Rocks area. Records of from one to three birds have also been made recently at gravel-pits in the Cotswold Water Park: November 1973, September 1976 and August-September 1978.

PURPLE SANDPIPER, *Calidris maritima*

The only satisfactory record is of a single bird seen on 10 and 18 April 1971 at Guscar Rocks, a stony patch on the edge of the Severn near Woolaston, and almost the only suitable habitat in the county. (The report of another, 11 January 1981, was included in error in *Glos. Bird Report,* 1980).

Mellersh's manuscripts contain the statement that "J.T.W. had one about 1877 in the autumn from Tewkesbury", but this record is not included in his book[40][41].

DUNLIN, *Calidris alpina*

A winter visitor and passage migrant, but some are present in all months. The most abundant wader on the Severn estuary.

The largest numbers are to be found in the Aylburton-Guscar Rocks area, and at the New Grounds near Frampton-on-Severn. Flocks at these localities frequently consist of between 1,000 and 2,000 birds, and sometimes more. Up to 600 have been seen at Walmore Common, and smaller numbers in other localities.

The highest totals are from January to March, declining and fluctuating through April and May, before rising again as the return migration develops. Ringing and biometric data suggest that July and August flocks consist of *C. a. schinzii*, and perhaps *C. a. arctica*, migrating south to West Africa (returning in April and May); and that after a September lull, *C. a. alpina* birds arrive from about mid-October as winter visitors from the north-east. There are several controls of Gloucestershire-ringed birds in the Wash area, indicating the most likely route from the continent[61].

Small numbers of Dunlin have been noted in the Thames Area ever since the start of gravel excavation, and the Water Park now sees a few birds in most months.

BROAD-BILLED SANDPIPER, *Limicola falcinellus*

A bird was seen at the New Grounds, Slimbridge, from 6 to 9 May 1976, and presumably the same bird on 2nd June (see Glos. Nat. Soc. *Journal*, July 1976[31]). Another was present near Aylburton, 15 May 1980.

BUFF-BREASTED SANDPIPER, *Tryngites subruficollis*

A vagrant from arctic North America.

There are four records, all of single birds, and three of them in September, the month of most British occurrences: one at the New Grounds, Slimbridge, 17 September 1961[11]; another on the opposite side of the Severn, near Lydney, 20 to 22 September 1970; a third was reported from a Wiltshire gravel-pit near South Cerney on 9 September 1975, and then flew into Gloucestershire; and the fourth report, again from the New Grounds, was for 9 and 10 May 1977.

RUFF, *Philomachus pugnax*

Reported in all months, but chiefly a passage migrant from March to May and, somewhat more plentifully, from July to October. Small or moderate numbers now visit the county irregularly during winter months.

Formerly regarded as an occasional visitor[40,41], but now much more numerous and regular. The majority of birds appear in Severn Vale localities, mainly at the New Grounds but also at Walmore Common, Aylburton, Ashleworth, Coombe Canal and elsewhere. Smaller numbers are reported annually from Thames Area gravel-pits and South Cerney sewage-farm.

67 birds were counted at the New Grounds in March 1976, but spring maxima are usually much lower than this, with flocks of twenty or more being unusual, and most birds occurring singly or in small groups. Up to 40 birds at a time have been noted at the New Grounds in September, however, and totals of up to twenty are not uncommon in autumn. Birds in the Cotswold Water Park are seldom numerous, but up to eighteen have been seen in March.

The number of Ruffs visiting the county in winter has increased in recent years, with flocks of up to 44 noted at the New Grounds in February and 24 at Walmore Common, but fewer than ten together in the Water Park. Winter visits to the Severn Vale seem to be related to river flooding, which determines the suitability of feeding sites.

JACK SNIPE, *Lymnocryptes minimus*

A winter visitor from September to April.

Occurs annually in small numbers in the Severn Vale, where reported from many localities, and in the Thames Area where it is found chiefly at gravel-pit sites. There are relatively few records from the main part of the Cotswold dipslope (although Mellersh[41] thought it more common than the Snipe on the higher hills), and only three or four from the Forest of Dean and adjacent ground.

Much less numerous in the county as a whole than the Snipe, and usually flushed singly, but from eight to sixteen have sometimes been disturbed at a single site.

The majority of records are from October to March, with a few in September and April, and two in August.

SNIPE, *Gallinago gallinago*

An autumn to spring visitor in considerable numbers. A few probably breed every year.

There are numerous reports of from 100 to 200 birds, sometimes more, at favoured localities in the Severn Vale and the Thames Area gravel-pits. Notable places are Walmore Common, Ashleworth Ham, South Cerney sewage-farm and Lechlade pits, while smaller numbers are usual at many other sites. Snipe are uncommon in the Forest of Dean; also over most of the Cotswold dipslope, where they are found chiefly in the broader parts of the main river valleys.

Records of proven breeding are rather few. Mellersh[40] mentions several, and others have come from the New Grounds and other places along the Severn, from Walmore Common, St. Briavels and from the Windrush valley on the Cotswolds. Display-flight is now reported almost annually from Vale localities and elsewhere. Ringing recoveries in Gloucestershire include birds from Germany and Finland.[61]

GREAT SNIPE, *Gallinago media*

The only satisfactory record of this north-western Palaearctic species is of one flushed several times at the New Grounds, Slimbridge, on 28 January 1958[11]. (Mellersh[40,41] mentions several from last century, but without any evidence of identification.)

WOODCOCK, *Scolopax rusticola*

A regular winter visitor in modest numbers from October to April, and also a local breeding species.

Nicholls[47] refers to it as breeding in the Forest of Dean in the mid-nineteenth century, and Mellersh mentions the report of a dozen nests there annually in 3,300 acres of woodland. He also records three or four isolated breeding occurrences on the Cotswolds ([40,41]; and see Alexander: *The Woodcock in the British Isles*, *Ibis*, Vols 87–89).

The Forest is still the main breeding stronghold today, but since 1960,

Cotswold breeding has become more firmly established, with nests or breeding behaviour reported regularly and widely.

Woodcock are more widespread in the county as winter visitors, although not abundant.

BLACK-TAILED GODWIT, Limosa limosa

Formerly of rare occurrence; now a regular passage migrant in spring and autumn, and recorded in all months.

The bird was not included by Witchell and Strugnell[80] in 1892, and Mellersh[40,41] scarcely mentions it (1902). There are few reports this century prior to the 1930s ([21,77]; *Brit. Birds*, XXXI, p.30: XXXIX, p.192), but since then there has been a gradual increase on passage, especially in autumn, when 20 or 30 birds are not infrequently reported, and occasionally more than 40. The heaviest movement is from July to September. Spring numbers are much lower, but 24 were seen together in April 1977. There have also been a few reports of one or two birds in January and February during the past twenty years, and ten were seen at the New Grounds, February 1980.

The great majority of records come from the Severn Vale, chiefly from the New Grounds area, but also from Aylburton, Elmore, Walmore Common, Hasfield Ham, Coombe Canal etc. Since 1970, from one to five birds have been reported almost every year from gravel-pits in the Cotswold Water Park, and from the South Cerney sewage-farm.

There was a report of territorial behaviour in the Severn Vale in 1967, and breeding was suspected in the same locality in 1969[62] (not included in *Glos. Bird Report*).

BAR-TAILED GODWIT, Limosa lapponica

Chiefly a spring and autumn passage migrant, but recorded in all months.

The peak spring movement is in April and early May, when up to 50 or more birds are frequently reported, and many more occasionally. 167 were counted in the New Grounds area, late April 1962, and 300 in the same period of 1976. Autumn maxima, usually in September, have been lower than those in spring, seldom reaching 40 birds together. Winter reports of singles or very small groups from December to February are unusual.

Almost all records are from the river Severn in the Frampton-New Grounds area, and from the west shore near Aylburton. There have also been a few reports since 1975 of from one to three birds in spring and autumn in the Cotswold Water Park gravel-pits.

WHIMBREL, Numenius phaeopus

Not uncommon as a passage migrant, chiefly on the Severn estuary where it is regular in both spring and late summer.

Numbers reported in spring are considerably higher than on return passage. The chief movement is in late April and early May, when up to 40 birds, occasionally more, are noted fairly frequently. An exceptional flock of about 150 was seen (and some birds caught and ringed) near Aylburton in May 1968[49]. There are no March reports and few in June.

Return passage begins in July and is usually completed before the end of August. Up to 30 birds have been seen together, but numbers are normally much lower.

The majority of all records are from the Severn Vale, mostly at Aylburton Warth and at the New Grounds, Slimbridge, on the opposite side of the river. Birds are very occasionally seen in flight over the Forest of Dean and, more frequently, while crossing the Cotswolds.

The first report from a gravel-pit in the Thames Area was in July 1955. From one to three were present at South Cerney sewage-farm in April 1969, and birds have been seen almost annually in the Water Park since 1974.

CURLEW, *Numenius arquata*

Chiefly a passage migrant and winter visitor in considerable numbers, but present throughout the year. A few pairs breed.

Many hundreds are now present in almost all months. Maximum numbers are reached in some years during passage, in others in mid-winter, but totals are difficult to calculate. The two main feeding areas are at the New Grounds and from Aylburton to Guscar Rocks. Counts from these, taken together, have given maximum totals of from 1,200 to 1,800 birds.

Smaller numbers are regular elsewhere in the Severn Vale, but Curlews are not common passing over the Cotswolds and seldom noted flying above the Forest of Dean. Visits to Cotswold Water Park gravel-pits, however, have increased in recent years.

Mellersh's book[41] gives no case of breeding, but in his manuscripts[40] he refers to a nest at Tirley in 1922. Several pairs were breeding by 1930, and nesting in the low-lying ground of the Severn Vale appears to date from that period[77]. In recent years, nests have been found, or breeding strongly suspected, from Moreton Valence northwards on both sides of the Severn to Tewkesbury, and eastwards to Alderton. Only a few pairs are present, however. Nesting probably occurred at Walmore Common at least in the late 1960s and early 1970s, and a bird was seen to make a "scrape" near St. Briavels in 1955, where breeding may have occurred on other occasions. In 1980 a nest was found at Dymock and breeding may have taken place at Coleford.

Nesting has been suspected also in the Thames Area at various times since the 1950s in localities as far apart as Poole Keynes and Lechlade. Proved breeding was reported in 1961 and 1968[35].

Ringing details show that some birds wintering in Gloucestershire come from as far to the north-east as Finland. All adults caught in August and September have been in moult, suggesting that the Severn estuary may be important for this purpose[61].

SPOTTED REDSHANK, *Tringa erythropus*

A passage migrant in small or moderate numbers, chiefly to the river Severn.

Formerly very scarce: Mellersh[41] refers to one shot near Tewkesbury about 1872, and Morris[45] mentions two. The next report seems to have been of a bird at Frampton-on-Severn in September 1938 (*Brit. Birds*, XXXII, p.240;[21]). It seems likely that birds had been overlooked in former years, for reports have come annually, and in increasing numbers since 1953, to some extent reflecting increase in observer activity.

Most birds are now reported from the New Gronds and elsewhere along the estuary, and autumn passage is heavier than that in spring. Between 20 and 30 birds are noted fairly frequently from July to October, but most often in August and September. Spring records, from March to May, are mostly of single birds or small parties, while the variable numbers in June suggest an overlap between the main periods of passage. November reports are not infrequent, but mid-winter birds are rare.

There were isolated records from the Thames Area gravel-pits in 1953 and 1954. Such reports became gradually more frequent and then almost annual from 1972, up to three birds at a time being noted in the Water Park and at South Cerney sewage-farm.

REDSHANK, *Tringa totanus*

Chiefly a passage migrant in spring and autumn and a winter visitor. Small numbers breed annually.

Non-breeding birds are present in all months along the Severn estuary, with numbers between 50 and 100 frequently reported. There are some indications of a slight peak in March and a larger rise between July and September. Smaller numbers are also noted in the Vale at localities away from the river, and along the lower Wye. A few non-breeders are also to be seen at gravel-pits in the Cotswold Water Park at various times of the year.

Four ringing recoveries seem to suggest that most wintering birds on the Severn come from northern England. There are no foreign ringing data in relation to Gloucestershire, but the Icelandic race, *T. t. robusta*, has been identified on the estuary in winter[61].

Mellersh[40] mentions breeding records between 1900 and 1923 from Lydney, Elmore, Gloucester and Coombe Canal. Birds bred in the Windrush valley below Bourton-on-the-Water in 1914 (*Brit. Birds*, XXXVI, p.14; A.G. Tayler,[1]) or perhaps earlier, and by 1928 about 25 pairs were nesting there, with others in neighbouring areas. Breeding appears to have continued also in the Severn Vale during this period, notably at Coombe Canal.

The Windrush valley population has since declined, but during the past 30 years a small population has built up around the gravel-pits of the Water Park, and breeding has continued more or less regularly along the Severn Vale from Aylburton and the New Grounds northwards.

GREENSHANK, *Tringa nebularia*

A passage migrant reported in all months from March to November.

Spring birds, chiefly in April and May, tend to be fewer in number than those in late summer, when from ten to twenty are noted quite often on dates in July, August and September. Visits become irregular in November; there are usually none in mid-winter and very few in March.

Most reports are from the New Grounds and other places along and near to the Severn, but birds have been noted at Thames Area gravel pits since the early 1950s, and almost annually since 1965. From one to five are usual at these Water Park pools, but sometimes higher numbers are present there, and also at the South Cerney sewage-farm. There are very few reports from the main Cotswold dipslope and only one from the Forest of Dean (October 1976).

LESSER YELLOWLEGS, *Tringa flavipes*

The only satisfactory record is of a bird at Frampton Marsh, at the north end of the New Grounds, from 2 to 26 April 1970. During much of this time it frequented flooded marsh-land and wet fields.

(A "Yellowshank" was reported in flooded fields near Calmsden, Cirencester, in autumn 1918 (J.H. Purvis, *Field*, 9 November 1918) but there are no other details).

GREEN SANDPIPER, *Tringa ochropus*

A passage migrant in moderate numbers and a rather scarce winter visitor, but noted in all seasons.

Frequently reported from many localities in the Severn Vale, from scattered places all over the Cotswolds where pools and streams provide suitable habitats, and from the Thames Area gravel-pits where the number of records has increased greatly since the 1950s. There appear to be hardly any records from the Forest of Dean, but the bird does occur in the Wye valley.

Birds are much less regular and numerous on spring passage from March to May than in summer, when many pass along the Severn Vale and through the Cotswold Water Park. Up to twenty or more have been seen in August at South Cerney sewage-farm.

Wintering in the county seems to be on the increase. One or more birds have been reported in mid-winter in almost every year since 1950 in Severn Vale localities, the Water Park and occasionally from the Cotswold hills. Several individuals may now be found at favoured Vale and Thames Area localities in January and February of most years.

WOOD SANDPIPER, *Tringa glareola*

An uncommon passage migrant.

Early records are of birds at Shipton Oliffe, September 1874 and 1892[41]; near Gloucester about 1880[80], and at Uckington, September 1903[40]. One was seen at Frampton-on-Severn in August 1949 (*Brit. Birds*, XLIV, p.110), and a great increase in the number of records then commenced in the early 1950s. Of more than 60 birds reported since then, almost two thirds were seen along the Severn and in adjacent localities, the remainder at the Thames Area gravel-pits and South Cerney sewage-farm.

All reports are for the period April to October, with about a dozen each for May and September, and twice that number in August.

COMMON SANDPIPER, *Actitis hypoleucos*

A regular spring and autumn migrant, and occasionally reported in winter.

Considerable numbers pass through the Severn estuary and adjacent ground in spring and autumn, especially in late April-May and in July-August. Much smaller numbers follow the Wye valley, and few are seen at Forest of Dean waters. The Cotswold Water Park also attracts many birds on passage, and a few are observed moving along the Cotswold river valleys.

There are about fifteen winter records of one to four birds from December to February (plus a few in November). Most are from Water Park localities, but two from Bourton-on-the-Water and several from the Severn Vale.

Mellersh[40][41] refers briefly to about five instances of supposed breeding but with little evidence. A pair was said to have nested at Rendcomb in 1950 ([18]1951), and possible breeding has been noted elsewhere, but there is no fully satisfactory record[62].

TURNSTONE, *Arenaria interpres*

A passage migrant and winter visitor, but noted in all months.

Amost all reports are from the river Severn and chiefly from Guscar Rocks and Aylburton on the west bank of the river, where parties of 50 to 100 birds, and sometimes more, are not infrequent. Generally smaller numbers may be seen elsewhere, such as at Berkeley and the New Grounds. This pattern reflects the distribution of exposed rocks in the estuary.

The highest numbers are reached in April and in September-October, representing spring and autumn passage movements. Few birds are generally to be seen in June and July, but the winter population, from December to February or March, may occasionally exceed 70 birds.

There have been reports of from one to four birds from Thames Area gravel-pits in 1954, 1958 and almost annually since 1974, all between April and September.

WILSON'S PHALAROPE, *Phalaropus tricolor*

One record of this North American wader: a bird was seen at Frampton Pools, Frampton-on-Severn, on 2 September 1976.

RED-NECKED PHALAROPE, *Phalaropus lobatus*

A very scarce visitor.

One is said to have been shot in autumn at Bibury prior to 1870[40,41], but no other data are given; a single bird visited Hewlett's reservoirs, Cheltenham, 23 to 26 September 1950 ([31], 1948–50), and an immature appeared at the New Grounds, Slimbridge, 2 August 1963.

GREY PHALAROPE, *Phalaropus fulicarius*

An occasional visitor.

The earliest report is probably that of a bird at Tewkesbury in 1832 ([68]; *Cheltenham Chronicle*, 12 January 1832), and another was killed at Mitcheldean in the Forest of Dean in 1847 (*Zool.*, 1847). Mellersh[40] lists about ten occurrences between 1840 and 1900, but details are few. Localities given include the Wye valley, Westbury-on-Severn, Coombe Hill, Bibury and Cirencester. Witchell and Strugnell[80] state that several were killed near Wotton-under-Edge in 1886, and J.A. Gibbs (1898)[29] writes that the Grey Phalarope "occasionally finds its way to the Cotswolds".

Single birds were reported near Tetbury, October 1929 (*Country-Side*[19], Vol. 8), and on the river Windrush near Naunton in November of the same year (A.G. Tayler[1]); at the New Grounds, November 1949[11]; Cheltenham, September–October 1954, and at Frampton Pools, August 1957.

Reports during the past twelve years are of one or two birds at the New Grounds, September 1968; one in the same month, 1974; and one in October 1978.

POMARINE SKUA, *Stercorarius pomarinus*

A very scarce visitor.

There are no satisfactory early reports. Three were seen flying over the River Severn, New Grounds, Slimbridge, on 12 May 1970, and an immature bird was identified in the same area on 13 June 1977.

ARCTIC SKUA, *Stercorarius parasiticus*

Formerly regarded as an occasional visitor, usually in relation to rough weather[40,41]. Now recorded almost annually, chiefly in spring and autumn.

About 32 records since 1960, all but one from Severn localities and mostly at the New Grounds, but one as far upstream as Tewkesbury. There is a single report from the Cotswold Water Park, where a bird was seen at a South Cerney gravel-pit in January 1974.

Almost all birds have been dark-phase adults or immatures, usually seen singly, but up to four have been noted together. There are distinct peaks in their occurrence, in April-May and September-October, and on overland passage between the Severn and the Wash-Humber area seems likely (see page 55).

LONG-TAILED SKUA, *Stercorarius longicaudus*

Mellersh[40][41] mentions one said to have been shot near Badgeworth, Cheltenham, about 1867, but no details of identification are given.

An adult was seen and closely observed down to ten feet at the New Grounds and Frampton Warth on 27 May 1967.

GREAT SKUA, *Stercorarius skua*

A scarce visitor to the Severn estuary.

The only early reports are of single birds at Ullenwood, above Cheltenham, about 1884, and near Sharpness, September 1896[40][41].

One was noted at the New Grounds in November 1938 (*Brit. Birds*, XXXII, p. 278–9); another in September 1968, and three were seen flying over the river there in August 1976. A bird was also found dead on the tideline near Awre in October of the same year.

MEDITERRANEAN GULL, *Larus melanocephalus*

Two records.

A bird in first winter plumage was seen at a gravel-pit near South Cerney, 9 April 1962, and one approaching adult plumage flew over Eastcombe, near Stroud, on 17 April 1968.

LITTLE GULL, *Larus minutus*

Formerly a very scarce visitor; now regular in small numbers.

Witchell and Strugnell[80] note one at Sharpness, 1863, and Mellersh[40] mentions three occurrences but with very little data. An immature bird was seen, and later found dead, at Hewlett's reservoirs, Cheltenham, November 1949 (*Brit. Birds*, XLIII, p. 407), but the report of another there in July 1952 lacks adequate detail (*Brit. Birds*, XLVII, p.356).

There has been a remarkable increase in the number of records since about 1960. Between 100 and 120 birds have been noted during the past twenty years, the great majority in pre-adult plumages. Most reports are from the river Severn and adjoining localities, but birds began to visit the gravel-pits of the Cotswold Water Park in 1971, and have been seen there in most years since then.

May and June are the months in which largest numbers are recorded, including a flock of fourteen birds at the New Grounds in June 1971. April and September have the next highest totals. There are few reports from December to March, (See also page 87).

BLACK-HEADED GULL, *Larus ridibundus*

Chiefly an abundant visitor in late summer, autumn and winter, but present in other months also.

Mellersh, in 1902[41], noted that thousands were sometimes present on winter flood-water in the Severn Vale, but that the bird was scarce on the Cotswolds. During the present century there has been a general increase.

Relatively few birds are now seen in the Severn Vale from April to June, but numbers then rise rapidly to late August, several thousand being noted in some years from then until the late winter, when birds disperse to breeding grounds in northern Europe and perhaps elsewhere in Britain. Numerous ringing recoveries suggest that most birds in the county come from northern parts of Europe and especially from Scandinavia[61]

These Vale birds roost on the Severn near Slimbridge (6,000 to 10,000 estimated in August 1974) and disperse by day to feed in both Vale and Cotswolds. Small numbers began visiting the Thames Area gravel-pits during the early 1950s, and roosting commenced at a pit near South Cerney some ten years later (see under Common Gull, and page 50). By 1970 up to 4,000 birds were gathering there on winter evenings, their numbers increasing to 6,000 in 1974 and 8,000—10,000 in 1978. These birds disperse to feed by day on the Cotswolds and, as in the Severn Vale, the roost breaks up during early spring.

Wild[77] records breeding close to the Severn near Framilode in 1938 and 1939. Attempted nesting was suspected in the Cotswold Water Park in 1970, and in 1979 two pairs built nests, and one egg was laid, at Ashleworth Ham Nature Reserve in the Vale, but both nests were flooded. In 1980 a nest with one young was found in the Cotswold Water Park.

COMMON GULL, *Larus canus*

A visitor in large numbers from late July to April.

Witchell and Strugnell[80], in 1892, described it as "common;. . . and sometimes. . . abundant on the Cotswolds". On the other hand, Mellersh[40] [41], in 1902, made no mention of a roost on the Severn, and provided no clear picture of this bird's numbers and distribution. It seems likely that it was less plentiful than at present.

There is now a very large roost on the Severn sandbanks opposite Slimbridge[8], said to exceed 30,000 birds in some years (much higher and lower estimates have been made). It builds up from July and August to reach peak numbers from November to early March, when the birds disperse rapidly. (See pages 30, 38).

Birds from this roost spread out each morning to feeding grounds chiefly in the Vale and on the Cotswolds, returning to the Severn sandbanks in the late afternoon. Small numbers may feed also in open areas around the Forest of Dean.

Another roost came into use in the 1960s at a gravel-pit near South-Cerney in the Cotswold Water Park (see page 50). Several hundred birds now gather there during the late afternoon, but many then move on to the Severn roost before dark (see Black-headed and Lesser Black-backed Gulls).

Recoveries in Gloucestershire of birds ringed as *pulli* in Denmark, Germany and the Netherlands suggest the origins of our winter visitors. As yet there are no recoveries in the county of Scottish-ringed birds[61]. (See under *Bird Study*[8]).

LESSER BLACK-BACKED GULL, *Larus fuscus*

Now present in all months in considerable numbers, and with an increasing breeding population at Gloucester.

The former status of the British race, *L. f. graellsii*, some 80 to 100 years ago, is not clear, but the bird was certainly much less numerous in the county than now, and none were breeding here[40][41][60][75][80] (see also page 93).

During the first 60 years of the present century the bird increased very gradually, and most of those seen were presumed to be passing through the county to or from north-western and northern breeding grounds, with a few non-breeders remaining for the summer in the Severn Vale. Wintering in the Vale commenced during the late 1940s, and by 1960 the mid-winter population around Gloucester and Cheltenham was about 150 birds.

Numbers at all seasons subsequently increased rapidly, and by the late 1960s gatherings of 100 birds or more were to be found at rubbish-dumps and other places in the Vale at any time between July and February. Eight hundred adults were counted at the Elmstone Hardwicke rubbish-tip, Gloucester, in September 1972, and an exceptional 1,500 in January 1974. Birds also began to use the great gull-roost on the Severn near Slimbridge, and in October 1977 more than 1,000 were counted as they arrived with other gulls (see page 30).

Meanwhile numbers increased also at the Thames Area gravel-pits. Very few were to be seen there in the 1950s, and in some years none. Roosting commenced, with other gulls, on a pit near South Cerney during the 1960s. Two hundred Lesser Black-blacks were noted there in January 1971, and 500 only one year later, while in August 1973, 330 birds were counted at Dudgrove Pit in the eastern part of the Water Park. The numbers seen at the South Cerney roosting-site reached 700 in December 1974 and 800 in the same month, 1979 (page 50). Not all of these birds remain for the night, however, for some move on over the Cotswolds to the Severn roost. Apart from these, very few Lesser Black-backs occur on or over these hills.

Breeding began in the City of Gloucester in 1967, when two pairs nested on buildings in the docks area. Numbers remained low until 1973, when there was a spectacular increase, with 53 nests in various parts of the City. By 1978 the breeding population had risen to 135 pairs, and birds had spread as far south as Quedgeley. In 1980, 206 pairs bred in Gloucester, and a nest was found on the cliffs opposite Chepstow. (See also B.A. Owen: *Journal*, Glos. Nat. Soc., October 1977; and under Herring Gull).

Gulls showing characters of the nominate Scandinavian race, *L. f. fuscus*, have been reported occasionally from the Severn Vale and also from the Cotswold Water Park. Most are seen singly, but ten dark-mantled birds were present with many *L. f. graellsii* at Elmstone Hardwicke, March 1971. (See also *Brit. Birds*, XLV, pp. 3–17; *Bird Study*, 8, pp. 127–147; 14, pp. 104–113).

HERRING GULL, *Larus argentatus*

Present at all seasons and breeding at two localities.

There is said to have been a breeding colony on the cliffs of the Wye valley many years ago (Miss C.A. Shirley[1]), but nesting is not mentioned by Mellersh *et al.*[40][41][80].

The present Wye colony started with a single nest in 1947. There were ten by 1953, rising to 25 or 30 between 1959 and 1965. There followed a further steady increase to about 75 breeding pairs (on the Gloucestershire side of the river) in 1972, and nearly 100 in 1976. In 1980 the number of nests had fallen to 49, a decline thought to be due to the disease botulism (see Mudge, G.P. and Ferns, P.N.: *A Census of Breeding Gulls in the Inner Bristol Channel*, Cardiff, 1980). Most nests in this colony have been on the cliffs in Gloucestershire but some birds are now nesting on the Chepstow side of the Wye in Gwent. Since 1967 a few pairs have bred or attempted to do so, farther upstream in the Pen Moel and Woodcroft district (Lancaut). A few pairs have bred on the rail and road bridges across the Wye valley estuary and, in 1973 a pair nested unsuccessfully on an islet in the Severn estuary off Beachley Point.

Herring Gulls began to breed on buildings in the City of Gloucester from 1971 (five pairs), four years after the Lesser Black-backs' colonisation (*q.v.*). Their numbers soon matched those of the latter species and corresponded approximately in the following years, with at least 107 nests in 1978, extending from the City south to Quedgeley. By 1980, however, with 126 nests, numbers had fallen behind those of Lesser Black-backs (*q.v.*).

Outside the breeding season birds may be found all along the Severn Vale to Tewkesbury, and numbers up to 400 or more sometimes congregate at refuse tips. Small numbers of birds move on to the nearer parts of the Cotswolds to feed by day, returning before dusk to roost along the Severn. The big gull-roost off the New Grounds in some seasons may hold between 1,000 and 2,000 Herring Gulls (see Common Gull, etc., and p. 30).

In the 1950s Herring Gulls were seldom reported from localities far down the Cotswold dipslope, even records from the Thames Area gravel-pits being scarce, but these latter reports increased through the 1960s, and up to 30 or 40 birds or more may now be seen at times in the gull-roost near South Cerney, although some of these usually move on to roost on the river Severn. (See also page 50).

ICELAND GULL, *Larus glaucoides*

A very scarce visitor.

An immature bird at the New Grounds on 16 and 18 January 1947 was identified as this, but "There is some possibility that this may have been a small Glaucous Gull (*L. hyperboreus.*)" (*Ann. Rep.* Wildfowl Trust, 1948, p.50).

An adult was seen over the river Severn at Awre on 16 September 1973.

Another adult bird at a gravel-pit near South Cerney on 30 December 1973 was either this species or a Glaucous Gull.

GLAUCOUS GULL, *Larus hyperboreus*

A very scarce visitor to the Severn.

An adult is recorded as having been shot on the Severn near Fretherne in January 1906 (*Field*, March 1906;[40]). An immature bird was seen on numerous occasions at the New Grounds from February to April 1950, and a fourth-year bird was reported in the same area on 12 February 1952. Two third-year birds (or older) were present, again at the New Grounds, on 17 December 1954. Recent records are of singles at the New Grounds on 24 September 1968 (adult); 9 February 1974 (second winter); and 23 April 1975 (second year). (See also under Iceland Gull.).

GREAT BLACK-BACKED GULL, *Larus marinus*

Present in the Severn estuary at all seasons, but chiefly from October to February.

There appears to have been a big increase during the past 30 years[31 41 77]. Birds may now be seen upstream as far as the county boundary at Tewkesbury, but most occur below Gloucester, and especially at the New Grounds. Up to 40 have been seen together on the west side of the river in the Aylburton-Lydney district, and 50 to 60 are not infrequently noted at the New Grounds, where the highest totals so far reported are 111 birds in December 1972, and 123 in the same month of 1977. The largest flock so far reported for the whole county was stated to contain 260 birds at Stoke Orchard in January 1979. (See also page 93).

There are very few records from the east side of the county. The first concerned a bird at Lechlade in September 1961, and from one to four have been seen occasionally at Water Park gravel pits since then. Two birds appeared at Great Barrington in April 1966. In the summer of 1980 birds were noted over the Forest of Dean on several occasions.

A nest with one egg was found on a rock near the mouth of the Wye in 1955, and another was probably robbed of eggs there in 1957.

KITTIWAKE, *Rissa tridactyla*

A wanderer or storm-blown visitor, but also sometimes occurring in considerable flocks, possibly as part of a spring overland movement (see Hume: *Brit. Birds*, 69, pp. 62–3).

Most reports are of birds seen between mid-March and early May and include the only records of large flocks. About 120 birds were seen off the New Grounds on 17 March 1968, and 100 on 1st April. In 1969 a flock of 270 was seen at the end of March, about 75 on 11th April, and a further 50 to 100 birds were flying in thick mist on 4th May, again off the New Grounds, Slimbridge. Flocks totalling 690 birds were seen flying up the estuary on 28 March 1979, and 180 passed on the following day. About 120 were seen there on 1 April 1980. (See also page 56). There have been few records in late summer and rather more from November to February, mostly of single birds.

Almost all occurrences have been along the river Severn, with none from the Forest of Dean and hardly any from the Cotswolds and Thames Area. Twenty-one, however, mostly adults, were seen at Dudgrove Pit, near Fairford, 31 May 1980.

IVORY GULL, *Pagophila eburnea*

One record of this arctic species: an adult was shot on the river Severn, near Gloucester, in late January 1921 (*Brit. Birds*, XVII, p. 288).

GULL-BILLED TERN, *Gelochelidon nilotica*

One was seen among Black-headed Gulls at the northern end of the New Grounds, near Frampton-on-Severn, on 1 October 1967.

CASPIAN TERN, *Sterna caspia*

A rare visitor, with three records to date.

An adult in summer plumage was seen on the river Severn, New Grounds, and at Frampton Pools, 8 and 11 August 1971. Another adult visited the Pools on 9 July 1976, and an immature bird was observed over the estuary at the New Grounds, Slimbridge on 21 May 1979.

SANDWICH TERN, *Sterna sandvicensis*

Formerly of rare occurrence; now noted almost annually.

Mellersh[40][41] mentions two records from the last century, and there appear to have been no reports this century until the 1950s. Since 1958, records of from one to six birds have come from the Severn Vale almost every year and in each month from April to September, with a slight preponderance in April.

There have been several reports from gravel-pits in the Cotswold Water Park: three birds in April 1956 and one in September of the same year were probably of this species; two in May 1972; two in September 1974; one in May and two in September 1980.

ROSEATE TERN, *Sterna dougallii*

Two records: A bird seen over the river Severn, New Grounds, Slimbridge on 28 September 1968, and another at Frampton Pools on 30 May 1971. (See also *Glos. Bird Report*, 1968, p. 12)[31].

COMMON TERN, *Sterna hirundo*

A passage migrant in spring and autumn.

The problem of assessing the relative abundance of Common and Arctic Terns passing through the county is difficult, for a majority of the records sent in still refer to "commic" terns and do not indicate the species (see Arctic Tern).

Of those birds specifically identified about three-quarters are Common Terns, recognised in all months from April to October, with most appearing in May, and somewhat lower numbers in August and September. Parties of up to 35 birds of this species have been seen occasionally at times of peak passage, but much larger flocks, of 150 to 370 birds, reported in late April and May, have all been described so far as "Common or Arctic Terns".

Reports are mainly from Severn localities and notably from the Severn at the New Grounds, from Frampton Pools and Witcombe reservoirs. Cotswold Water Park records, irregular in the past, have been received annually since about 1970. Most refer to single birds or to small groups, but from ten to 30 are seen occasionally, and 60 were present at Dudgrove Pit in May 1980.

In 1979 a pair was found displaying at a Water Park gravel-pit. The nest was later found just over the county boundary, in Wiltshire, and three young were reared. The family visited feeding grounds in both counties. A pair bred there again in 1980. (See *Journal*, Glos. Nat. Soc., September 1979.)

ARCTIC TERN, *Sterna paradisaea*

A passage migrant in spring and autumn, apparently much scarcer than the Common Tern (*q.v.* for comments).

Of "commic" terns clearly identified since 1950, only about a quarter were Arctic Terns. They have appeared in all months from April to October (chiefly May and August), and have been reported annually since 1966 in the Severn Vale, where up to seven birds have been seen at one time. Records from gravel-pits in the Cotswold Water Park are few and refer to single birds or up to five at a time.

Yarrell[82] records that a great number of Arctic and Common Terns appeared in the Severn in early May 1842, and that many were killed or captured alive as far upstream as Tewkesbury but, in general, early writers provide little help in comparing Gloucestershire occurrences of these two species[40, 41, 75, 80].

LITTLE TERN, *Sterna albifrons*

An uncommon visitor on passage.

Apparently very scarce in former years. The first record seems to be that of a bird shot on the Gloucester-Berkeley Canal on 12 September 1887 (*Zool.*, 1887, p.387). Mellersh[40,41] describes it as an occasional visitor to the Severn in October and November, but birds may have been overlooked. A specimen in Gloucester museum is labelled "Arlingham 1910". Only since about 1950 have records become more or less regular. Since then there have been reports in most years of singles or small parties (occasionally up to twelve or fifteen birds) from localities in the Severn Vale. Most records are in May, but birds are noted in all months from April to October.

The first report from the Thames Area gravel-pits was of two birds at Shorncote, near South Cerney, in August 1953, and recent reports from the Water Park are of one to three birds, April to October, each year since 1975, and ten birds were seen together in August and September 1980.

BLACK TERN, *Chlidonias niger*

An irregular spring and autumn passage migrant in variable numbers from April to June and from July to October (very rarely in November).

Mellersh[41] describes it as occasional in spring and autumn, and in manuscript[40] lists numerous occurrences from 1870 to 1929, but gives no records of large numbers. Birds were seldom reported this century until the late 1940s, but thereafter with increasing frequency, and annually since 1955. In some years passage is sparse; in others considerable flocks are seen, sometimes in excess of 100 birds (as in May 1958; August 1969; May 1978). Most of the bigger flocks are noted in May, sometimes in August, and have been seen at the New Grounds, Frampton Pools and Witcombe reservoirs.

Black Terns

A majority of reports are from the Severn Vale, but birds are now seen annually in the Thames Area gravel-pits, chiefly in the western part of the Water Park and at Dudgrove pit in the east. Numbers are usually small, but flocks totalling 34 birds were present in May 1966, 80 or more were seen together in August 1978, and 50 in July 1980. (See also pages 55–56).

WHITE-WINGED BLACK TERN, *Chlidonias leucopterus*

Four records.

A bird in moult was seen with many Black Terns over the river Severn, New Grounds, on 27 August 1960[11]. An adult was present at Horcott gravel-pit, Fairford, on 23 July 1964, and another was reported and photographed in the Wildfowl Trust enclosures, Slimbridge, on 18 and 19 May 1979[31][78]. A juvenile was seen at Frampton Pools from 26 to 28 September 1980.

GUILLEMOT, *Uria aalge*

A scarce and irregular visitor to the Severn estuary, and occasionally storm-blown to inland localities.

Mellersh[40][41] mentions several early occurrences from last century, but there are very few records from the first half of this. Of nine reports between 1950 and 1970, most were from the estuary, but birds were also noted as far afield as Gloucester, Redmarley and the river Coln. There is no obvious seasonal pattern, and there have been no records during the past decade.

RAZORBILL, *Alca torda*

A very scarce visitor to the Severn Vale.

Mellersh mentions several from last century, but with little detail.[40]

The only dated records are of an immature found alive in Stroud, October 1959; one, Prestbury, Cheltenham, September 1962; one in flight over the Severn at Awre, May 1970; a bird off the New Grounds, April 1972, and one found dead at Aylburton Warth, in May of the same year.

LITTLE AUK, *Alle alle*

Occasionally found along the river Severn and inland following gales (see page 62).

Several were noted in the Severn Vale after a violent storm in October 1841[68][82], and Mellersh[40] lists about ten between 1850 and 1900, including one or two on the Cotswolds.

Records for the present century also number about ten, including one at Cirencester, February 1912 (*Brit. Birds*, V, p.286); one at Claypits, Frampton-on-Severn, in January 1943;[77] and three from different localities during the "wreck" of February 1950. One was seen at Frampton Pools in December 1957 and another, also near Frampton, in December 1960. A bird was found, recently dead, at Bourton-on-the-Water gravel-pits in

January 1975, and another was swimming in a pit near Cerney Wick, Cotswold Water Park, in November of the same year.

PUFFIN, *Fratercula arctica*

An occasional storm-driven visitor.

Mellersh *et al.*[40] [80] report several records from the Cotswolds and the Vale between 1870 and 1900. Single birds were found at Bourton-on-the-Water in January 1920; Sherborne in December 1934; Calmsden in October 1935 and at Uley, October 1957. The only recent reports are of one found exhausted at Guiting Power, September 1974, and one flying over Frampton Pools in August 1977.

PALLAS'S SANDGROUSE, *Syrrhaptes paradoxus*

Formerly a sporadic visitor, but no records for more than 90 years (see also page 60).

Small parties occurred in Vale and Cotswold localities during both the 1863 and 1888 irruptions, some specimens being obtained, others seen. These reports include one of fifteen birds "on the hill over Coombe" (near Wotton-under-Edge), in June 1863; eight or ten flying overhead "down the Gloucester Canal" on 3 June 1888, and one bird shot at Naunton in October 1888, having "associated for two months with Partridges". Five were also seen at Ullenwood, near Cheltenham, in June 1888, and six or seven "between Cirencester and Northleach" a few days later (*Zool.* 1864 and 1888;[40] [41] [77] [80]).

STOCK DOVE, *Columba oenas*

A common resident, and probably a winter visitor from more northerly parts of Britain.

Already widely known by the close of the nineteenth century and well distributed at least on the Cotswolds, where winter flocks of fifty birds were often seen[41].

The Stock Dove is probably now considerably more plentiful than formerly, breeding in all parts of the county, and forming large feeding flocks, sometimes in excess of 200 birds, in winter and even into May. These may consist partly of birds which have moved in from the north and east, and this no doubt explains the huge flock of 1,200 to 1,500 birds seen at Didbrook in the severe weather of February 1979.

The decrease noted in parts of southern and eastern Britain in the late 1950s seems not to have extended to Gloucestershire.

WOODPIGEON, *Columba palumbus*

An abundant resident, nesting in all parts of the county, and a pest of some importance to agriculture.

Numbers are increased in autumn and winter by influxes of birds from eastern and northern Britain and sometimes, perhaps, from abroad, especially in severe weather. Flocks of 3,000 or more may be noted, especially during weather-movements or when feeding in favourable sites on the Cotswolds or in the Vale. Considerable numbers may also invade the Forest of Dean to feed on beech-mast or acorns.

COLLARED DOVE, *Streptopelia decaocto*

A common resident, breeding throughout the county in suitable areas.

Following its arrival in Britain (Norfolk, 1955), the bird reached this county in 1961, when about six birds were present at Gloucester Docks (see *Glos. Bird Report*, 1963). Breeding was first proved in 1963 at Gloucester, in the Wildfowl Trust enclosures, and at Sherborne and Coln St. Aldwyns on the Cotswolds. Numbers at Gloucester Docks exceeded 50 by late 1963.

Increase in numbers, and spread throughout the county, were very rapid thereafter. By the end of 1966, the Wildfowl Trust population had reached 200, and birds had been reported from many places as far apart as Stroud, Tetbury, Lechlade, Chipping Campden, Lydney (where breeding may have occurred in 1964), and Cannop in the Forest of Dean. Birds reached the mouth of the Wye by 1968, but remained scarce in, or absent from much of the Forest itself.

The largest concentrations are now to be found at the Wildfowl Trust (900 birds in February 1974), Gloucester Docks and throughout the City, and at such places as Bourton-on-the-Water, where grain is put out for captive birds of other species. (See also page 86).

TURTLE DOVE, *Streptopelia turtur*

A summer visitor, not uncommon, but rather sparsely distributed. There appears to have been no major change since the end of the last century[10,40,41,80].

The bird now breeds quite commonly in the Forest of Dean in scrub and along woodland margins; rather sparingly, although locally numerous, in the Severn Vale; and in suitable localities all over the Cotswolds and in the Thames Area. Flocks of twenty to forty birds were reported not infrequently during the 1960s but not recently, there being some evidence of a decline during the past decade.

CUCKOO, *Cuculus canorus*

A widespread summer visitor, whose numbers vary from year to year.

Breeding reports are from all parts of the county and from a wide variety of habitats. There appears to have been a gradual decline in numbers since about 1955.

Recorded host species in Gloucestershire: Skylark, Tree Pipit, Meadow Pipit, Grey Wagtail, Pied Wagtail, Wren, Dunnock, Robin, Nightingale, Sedge Warbler, Marsh Warbler, Reed Warbler, Whitethroat, Blackcap, Spotted Flycatcher, Nuthatch,[77] Starling,[77,12] Chaffinch, Greenfinch, Linnet, Yellowhammer and Reed Bunting. A fledged juvenile in Nagshead

Cuckoos

Reserve, Forest of Dean, was seen being fed by a Wren and by a female Pied Flycatcher on the same day in 1978.

BARN OWL, *Tyto alba*

Resident, widely but locally distributed.

There is some evidence that the bird was more plentiful at the end of the last century than now[10 40 52 75], but the pattern of distribution has changed little.

The Barn Owl is still very scarce in the Forest of Dean, although up to three pairs have been suspected of nesting near Mitcheldean. It seems to have declined recently in the Severn Vale, where it is least numerous in the north. On the Cotswolds, which have always been its stronghold, it is still widespread and not rare; a few pairs are believed to nest in the Thames Area also. (See also pages 88, 89, 92, 98).

A bird showing some characters of the dark-breasted north-eastern race, *T. a. guttata*, was seen in the Forest of Dean in May 1977, and another near Eastleach in March and April 1979.

LITTLE OWL, *Athene noctua*

A widespread resident, breeding over most of the county.

Following the rapid spread from centres of introduction (notably in

Northants and Kent) in the late nineteenth century, Little Owls may have reached Gloucestershire before 1900[40][41], but the earliest reliable record is apparently that of a bird at Fairford, 20 February 1908 (*Brit. Birds*, I, p.388; *Zool.*, 1908, p.113). The earliest record of breeding seems to be that at Newent in 1916[77].

The bird was probably not uncommon over much of the county by the 1920s[77] and continued to spread and increase until at least 1940. The *Report of the Little Owl Food Inquiry* (1936–37)[34] mentions nineteen gizzards supplied from a single estate at Ampney St. Peter. There are sharp declines during severe winters, and following that of early 1963 numbers seem not to have reached their earlier levels.

The Little Owl is now uncommon in the well-wooded parts of the Forest of Dean, and breeding is not often confirmed in the Forest area generally. The bird is widespread and quite numerous over the Cotswolds; less so in the Severn Vale and the Thames Area. (See also pages 88, 92, 93).

TAWNY OWL, *Strix aluco*

A widespread resident, breeding in suitable areas all over the county.

It is most plentiful in the Forest of Dean, the Wye valley, and along the wooded parts of the main Cotswold valleys, and least so on the open hills and perhaps in the Thames Area. Breeding has been noted also in the urban areas of Gloucester, Cheltenham and elsewhere.

There has probably been a considerable increase during the present century due to a decline in persecution by man.

LONG-EARED OWL, *Asio otus*

A former resident. After a long interval there have been some recent records, but only one of confirmed breeding.

Towards the close of last century, and during the first twenty years of so of this, the bird was known as a scarce but widespread resident on the Cotswolds, at least from Cirencester northwards[40][41][77][80]. A.G. Tayler[1] stated that Long-eared Owls nested quite commonly in the Bourton-on-the-Water area until about 1930, then suddenly decreased and disappeared.

Thereafter there were no satisfactory records until 1975, when, following a large autumn influx to Britain, several birds were found roosting in hawthorn scrub near Eastleach, on the Cotswolds. A peak number of seventeen was reached in February 1976, and a few birds have been noted there in the following years. 1976 also produced records of one or two individuals from several other localities. There are no certain reports from the Forest of Dean and Wye valley. (See *Glos. Bird Report*, 1976, pp.27–29).

An adult was seen feeding two young in June 1979, in a locality in the Severn Vale where a pair had been seen for three years. This is the only breeding record since about 1930. At least one bird was present near Great Rissington, January 1980.

SHORT-EARED OWL, *Asio flammeus*

A winter visitor and passage migrant in small but variable numbers.

Mellersh[41], in 1902, described it as a winter visitor, almost entirely to the Cotswolds, but the Severn Vale is now the chief source of records. Well over 100 birds have been reported since 1960, all but about ten from October to April inclusive, with December the peak month.

Most records, accounting for the majority of individuals, have come from Vale localities, especially from the New Grounds, where up to eight are sometimes seen. Cotswold records are fewer but widespread, usually of single birds, but up to five together have been noted.

There are very few reports from the Cotswold Water Park; one from Tutshill near the river Wye, and apparently none from the Forest of Dean. The bird is said to have nested on Painswick Hill in 1904 (Mellersh[40]), but there is no confirmed breeding record.

NIGHTJAR, *Caprimulgus europaeus*

A regular but very local summer resident, more widespread and much more plentiful at the close of last century than now.

The Forest of Dean region has long been the main stronghold, providing a sequence of habitats, some always suitable for Nightjars. Nicholls[47], in 1858, wrote "The fern owls are very numerous", and Mellersh[41] stated in

Nightjar: in 1902, W.L. Mellersh described this bird as "a frequent summer visitor to most Cotswold woods". Now seldom found on these hills, and the bird is decreasing even in the Forest of Dean.

Swifts breed in many towns and villages throughout the county, and there are old reports of nests in rock-sites on Cleeve Hill and in the Wye valley.

1902 that they are found "in great profusion" in the Forest. During this period the bird was widespread on the Cotswolds and bred also at Highnam and Michael Wood in the Severn Vale[40 41 75 80].

The decline this century appears to have been gradual, with an acceleration from the 1940s. Ten pairs, at least, were still nesting in the Forest in 1973, and a survey in 1979 also recorded ten pairs. On the Cotswolds, however, there have been rather few reports of breeding, or probable breeding, during the past 30 years, and none since 1970.

There are no reports from the Thames Area, although Bowly[10] in 1856 stated that he had seen them in "two or three summers" near Siddington.

SWIFT, *Apus apus*

A common and generally distributed summer visitor.

Breeding pairs or colonies occur in towns and villages all over the county, considerable numbers nesting in the larger towns such as Gloucester, Cheltenham, Stroud and Cirencester. Nests were formerly not unusual under loose-fitting stone roofing-tiles in Cotswold villages, but these colonies diminished in number as the old roofing materials were replaced by new. Several pairs bred for some years in natural rock-crevices in quarries on Cleeve Hill (G.L. Charteris[1]), and Mellersh[40] (under House Martin) mentions Swifts breeding in rocks at Lancaut on the river Wye.

Large flocks of birds on passage may be seen in both spring and late summer, particularly in the Severn Vale (see page 55), but also over the gravel-pits of the Cotswold Water Park. Such places also attract large numbers of birds all through the summer for feeding purposes.

Late migrants are not infrequently noted in September, much less often in October, and there are one or two November records. A bird was reported over Cheltenham on 1 and 2 December 1951.[18 31] An unusually heavy late passage in 1977 included 166 birds counted on 2nd September, flying south to south-west over Hatherley, Cheltenham (*Journal*, Glos. Nat. Soc., Nov.[31]). In 1980 a pair were still feeding young in Stroud on 22 September.

ALPINE SWIFT, *Apus melba*

Two old reports, not fully documented, and two in recent years.

Mellersh[40 41] mentions a bird killed near Cirencester in 1863, and another at Seven Springs, near Colesborne, about 1869.

One was seen over Cainscross, Stroud, on 16 April 1970, and another was observed flying above South Cerney sewage-farm on 1 June 1977.

KINGFISHER, *Alcedo atthis*

A resident of local distribution, but more widespread after the breeding season.

The Severn Vale and the gravel-pits of the Cotswold Water Park are the most favoured areas. It is seen also on most Cotswold streams but breeding reports from these are fewer than might be expected, on account of the scarcity of suitable nesting banks. For the same reason nesting in the Severn Vale tends to be along side streams flowing towards the main river.

The development of the Water Park in the Thames Area was attended by an increase of the local Kingfisher population and, in 1976, birds were reported from 24 different gravel-pits. At least eight or nine pairs bred there in 1978.

Kingfishers are sometimes reported from the Wye valley and from Cannop, Parkend and Westbury Brook in the Forest of Dean, from where there are two or three records of suspected breeding.

Records seem to suggest on autumn influx from outside the county, but this is not supported by ringing evidence in the Severn Vale. Late summer and autumn numbers in the Water Park, however, sometimes appear to be higher than can be accounted for by a purely local post-breeding dispersal, and it may be that some birds are arriving from elsewhere, the population declining again before the next breeding season.[35][65] Exceptionally hard winters may cause high mortality, but recovery is usually fairly rapid. (See also pages 50, 51, 88, 89).

BEE-EATER, *Merops apiaster*

A rare vagrant.

Mellersh[40][41] records a Bee-eater having been killed at Shurdington, near Cheltenham, about 1871, and one in the Cheltenham Museum bears a card giving "Gloucestershire" as the locality, but no other data.

The only fully satisfactory record is of a bird seen at South Cerney, following a thunder-storm, 31 May 1979.

HOOPOE, *Upupa epops*

Formerly a somewhat irregular visitor from March to November. Now reported almost annually.

Mellersh[41] recorded that ten were killed between 1870 and 1902, "generally in the autumn" but the latter comment is at variance with his manuscript entries[40] which include several spring reports. Records for the first half of this century were relatively few[77], but become more frequent and regular from the late 1940s.

Of forty or more birds reported since 1955, three-quarters were noted in April and May, from one to six being seen in most years, nearly always singly. Approximately equal numbers were noted from the Cotswolds and the Severn Vale, while a few were observed in the Forest of Dean and Thames Areas.

The only breeding record is of a pair which reared young in an old pollard willow at Hope's Brook, Longhope, in 1925 (C.G. Grosvenor[1]). A bird was seen entering and leaving a hole in a birch-tree near Cannop, Forest of Dean, in early May 1966 but not subsequently; a pair were present near St. Briavels in late June and early July 1974; two birds were seen together in a Forest locality in early summer 1978, and in 1980 two were present for a fortnight near Gloucester, late May and early June, but in none of these cases was breeding indicated.

WRYNECK, *Jynx torquilla*

Formerly known as a regular summer resident, breeding in moderate numbers. Now a very scarce visitor, chiefly in autumn.

Bowly[10], in 1856, described it as a constant summer visitor to Siddington, near Cirencester, and Wheeler[75], in 1862, regarded it as generally distributed in the Cheltenham area. It was still widely known some 30 years later and Mellersh[40][41] in 1902 held that it was "not common" on the Cotswolds but widely distributed in the Forest of Dean region, while having its chief haunts in the Severn Vale. Decline must thereafter have been very rapid, but is poorly documented. Breeding probably ceased quite early in the present century[52], and few occurrences of any kind were recorded in the 1940s and 1950s (see page 85).

Since 1960 only twenty birds have been reported, and seven of these were seen in 1976. Nearly all were in Severn Vale localities, but singles were noted at Slad and Painswick on the Cotswolds and at Meysey Hampton in the Thames Area.

GREEN WOODPECKER, *Picus viridis*

A widespread and fairly common resident.

This bird may have been somewhat less plentiful at the end of last century than now, Mellersh[41] regarding it as scarce in many districts on the Cotswolds but abundant in and around the Forest of Dean. It is still common in the Forest region, though not in dense woodland, and occurs throughout the Severn Vale and in most suitable Cotswold localities. It appears to be least numerous in the Cotswold Water Park.

Numbers are seriously reduced by severe winters, and recovery from that of 1963 has been slow, at least on the Cotswolds where the bird is at present less plentiful than the Great Spotted Woodpecker.

GREAT SPOTTED WOODPECKER, *Dendrocopos major*

A fairly numerous and widespread breeding resident which has increased during the twentieth century.

Mellersh, in 1902, described it as most numerous in the Forest of Dean and on the Cotswolds, but scarce in the Severn Vale, where it seems to have been less common than the Lesser Spotted Woodpecker: it "scarcely if ever enters Cheltenham"[41].

There has been a general increase this century, especially since about 1930, with extension into urban habitats, where bird-tables are often visited. The bird is now the commonest woodpecker over much of the county in woodland and other well-timbered habitats, most plentiful in the

Woodpeckers

Forest of Dean and perhaps least so in the Thames Area and, of course, on the open Cotswolds.

LESSER SPOTTED WOODPECKER, *Dendrocopos minor*

A widespread but thinly distributed resident, with no evidence of any marked change since last century.

The bird breeds locally in small numbers in mature broad-leaved woodland in the Forest of Dean and Wye valley region. It occurs sparingly throughout the Severn Vale and locally on the Cotswolds, but has seldom been seen in the Thames Area of the county. The near absence of reports from the north-east, around Great Barrington, Stow-on-the-Wold and Moreton-in-Marsh, may reflect the distribution of observers rather than of this somewhat elusive bird[62].

WOODLARK, *Lullula arborea*

Formerly an uncommon local resident, but there have been no reports of nesting, and very few other records, since the late 1960s.

There are few references from last century[10] [60] [75], but Saunders[60] mentions Gloucestershire as one of the counties in which it was "most frequent", and Mellersh[40] [41] reports it from the Cotswolds and the Forest of Dean.

The Woodlark used to breed in several parts of Gloucestershire especially along the Cotswold escarpment, but there are no recent records.

Breeding in the present century occurred on the Cotswolds in scattered localities from Chipping Camden in the north at least as far south as Dursley and Wotton-under-Edge, the majority of haunts lying north of the Stroud valley. Most territories were on or close to the escarpment edge, but a few lay at some distance down the dipslope. There is some evidence of an increase between 1920 and the 1940s (A.G. Tayler and G.L. Charteris;[1] *Brit. Birds*, XVIII, p.218 and XLI, p.331). A drastic decline set in about 1956, however, and the latest reported Cotswold nest was at Stanway in 1961 (see pages 35, 86).

The Woodlark's early history in the Forest of Dean is obscure, but some pairs continued to nest on spoil-heaps and in young plantations in the Forest until about 1968[49][62] (and see page 19). A few pairs were also occasionally found up to the 1950s in the vicinity of Redmarley.

In autumn and winter small parties or single birds were to be met in lowland districts as well as on higher ground, but the only relatively recent reports of any kind are of a bird in song near Berkeley, April 1968, and one seen near Ebworth, November 1978.

SKYLARK, *Alauda arvensis*

Present at all seasons in large numbers, but population far from static on account of considerable movements from autumn to spring, often related to weather conditions.

Breeds plentifully on pasture and arable alike in most parts of the county, including oolitic downland on the Cotswolds, riverside pastures in the Severn Vale and in open areas of the Forest of Dean. Migrating parties or winter flocks of up to 200 birds, and sometimes many more, are by no means uncommon

SHORE LARK, *Eremophila alpestris*

A very scarce visitor.

Several are noted by Mellersh[40][41] as having been killed or seen between about 1870 and 1900, but evidence of identification is given only for a bird seen on Robin's Wood Hill, Gloucester, 20 October 1911. The description is brief but adequate: ". . .yellow forehead and another patch of yellow on its throat. . . a black band across the uppermost part of the breast, making a border to the yellow patch on the throat. It also had a black crest"[40]

The only recent reports are of one in adult plumage near Frampton-on-Severn breakwater, 1 November 1958, and another at the New Grounds, 8 November 1969.

SAND MARTIN, *Riparia riparia*

A summer visitor and passage migrant.

Many nesting colonies are small and more or less temporary, and may be found sparingly along the banks of the Severn from Tewkesbury to south of Gloucester, beside the river Wye, at sand-pits and other sites in the Severn

Vale and, much more plentifully, at Thames Area gravel-pits.

These Water Park colonies vary much in size and location from year to year. In 1977, for example, at least 1,100 nest-holes were counted in seventeen colonies, varying in size between ten and 288 holes, while in 1978 there were about 470 nest-holes at thirteen sites, in colonies of eight to 120 holes per colony. Numbers in the Water Park are now much greater than they were in the 1950s.

The bird is very scarce in the Forest of Dean and few are seen over most of the Cotswolds, even on migration, except perhaps in the Windrush valley. Two hundred were found using the big Swallow roost at Frampton-on-Severn in August–September 1980.

SWALLOW, *Hirundo rustica*

A summer visitor, breeding in farm buildings and at other suitable sites throughout the county. There may have been some general decrease this century, but the evidence is not clear.

The bird is least plentiful in heavily wooded areas such as parts of the Forest of Dean, and on high agricultural land of the Cotswolds where farms are large and breeding sites correspondingly sparse. Mellersh[40,41] mentions large roosts at Lechlade and Apperley, and others have been noted from time to time, usually in willows or reeds, but in 1980, at Frampton-on-Severn, in reedmace, where 1,248 birds were ringed. (See *Journal*, Glos. Nat. Soc., November–December 1980 and March 1981).

A series of several recoveries of birds ringed in the Severn Vale as *pulli* illustrates pre-migratory dispersal as far afield as Staffordshire, Yorkshire, Lincolnshire, Suffolk and Surrey[61].

HOUSE MARTIN, *Delichon urbica*

Summer visitor, breeding in some numbers on houses and other buildings in most areas.

Mellersh[40,41] regarded the bird as decreasing, but the evidence for this is not convincing. The location of colonies frequently change for various reasons. At present the bird is perhaps more abundant on the Cotswolds than in lowland regions.

A few pairs used to nest on cliff sites near Chepstow and at Woodcroft[40], both on the river Wye, and nests have also been recorded on bridges across the Wye[49].

RICHARD'S PIPIT, *Anthus novaeseelandiae*

Mellersh refers to "one near Cheltenham about 1888, caught with Larks", but details of identification are not given[40,41].

The only satisfactory record is of a bird caught by a dog at Moreton Valence, 14 December 1931 (*Brit. Birds*, XXV, p.301.)

TREE PIPIT, *Anthus trivialis*

A widespread but somewhat local summer visitor.

It is probably most plentiful in the Forest of Dean area, where considerable numbers nest on clear-felled ground, rough, bushy hillsides and in open woodland: in 1979 at least fifteen pairs bred in the Nagshead Reserve, Parkend, and nineteen in 1980.

The bird tends to be scarce on the low-lying land of the Severn Vale, but is quite numerous on the Cotswold hills, where bushy downland and young plantations are favoured. A decline, however, has been noted on the Cotswolds since the 1950s, and also in the Thames Area where the bird was never common. In the Cotswold Water Park few if any pairs now breed.

MEADOW PIPIT, *Anthus pratensis*

A local summer resident, but better known as a winter visitor and passage migrant.

Breeds sparingly on open ground in and around the Forest of Dean, in scattered places along the river Severn, and locally on the Cotswolds, notably the Cleeve Hill region, but apparently now scarcer on the hills than indicated by Mellersh in 1902.[41] There appear to be no breeding records from the Thames Area, including the Cotswold Water Park.

Much more widespread on passage and in winter, when the bird is common in the Severn Vale, but less so in the Forest, Cotswold and Thames areas of the county. Movement in autumn and winter is much influenced by hard weather.

RED-THROATED PIPIT, *Anthus cervinus*

The only record of this northern Palaearctic species is of one in summer plumage in the Hundred Acre Field at Frampton-on-Severn, New Grounds, 18 April to 7 May 1980. (See *Journal,* Glos. Nat. Soc,. June–July 1980).

ROCK PIPIT, WATER PIPIT, *Anthus spinoletta*

The Rock Pipit, *A.s. petrosus,* is a regular autumn to spring visitor along both sides of the Severn estuary as far up-stream as Frampton-on-Severn, presumably moving into Gloucestershire from the Bristol Channel. Most birds have been seen in the period October to February; frequently also in September and March, but birds are absent from April to August. Rock Pipits are also reported occasionally away from the river at Witcombe reservoirs and Frampton Pools, and there are two or three records from the Cotswold Water Park. There are no confirmed breeding records from the county, but Mellersh[40][41] refers to the bird as resident in the lower Wye valley and at Beachley, where nesting may have been overlooked.

The Water Pipit, *A.s. spinoletta,* has been reported from the Severn Vale on three or four occasions since 1950, and in the Cotswold Water Park several times since 1972, involving in all about nine different birds in March and April. There is a single record (New Grounds, February 1967) of a bird showing several plumage characters fitting *A.s. littoralis* from north-west Europe. (Mellersh's references[40][41][60] to a nest of this race (= *A. rupestris*) in the Wye valley in 1854 most probably represents a mis-identification).

YELLOW WAGTAIL, BLUE-HEADED WAGTAIL, *Motacilla flava*

The Yellow Wagtail, *M.f. flavissima*, is a regular summer visitor and passage migrant, occurring in variable numbers in the lowland country of the Severn Vale and the Thames Area, but scarce or absent on the higher ground of the Cotswolds and in the Forest of Dean.

Its main nesting areas are in the Vale where, although pairs may be found away from the Severn (Frampton Pools, Witcombe reservoirs, Alderton, Brockhampton, etc.), breeding is largely restricted to riverside fields and marshes.

Breeding also occurs sparingly near many of the gravel-pits of the Cotswold Water Park in the Thames Area, from Poole Keynes to Lechlade with some pairs found also up the Windrush valley to Bourton-on-the-Water. The Water Park population has built up since the early 1950s.

In some years, passage migrants pass through the Severn Vale and the Water Park in considerable numbers, but few birds are noted on the Cotswolds apart from those in the Windrush valley. There are two winter records: singles at South Cerney sewage-farm in December 1970, and at Aylburton in February 1977.

Birds showing characters of the Blue-headed Wagtail, *M.f. flava*, have been reported occasionally. Singles were seen in the New Grounds — Frampton area in April 1952[11], August 1966, April 1977 and May 1978. The female of a pair at Twyning, Tewkesbury, in June 1979 appeared to be of this race, and three birds were seen at Berkeley in May 1980. The Cotswold Water Park produced records of single birds showing these characters in May 1971, May and July 1975 and April 1976. In 1972 and 1973 a male *flava* bred with a typical *flavissima* female at Dudgrove pit near Fairford.

An adult male showing characters of the grey-headed race, *M.f. thunbergi*, of northern Europe was seen at the New Grounds, Slimbridge, in May 1969.

GREY WAGTAIL, *Motacilla cinerea*

Resident, with local movement outside the breeding season.

At the end of last century Mellersh[41] considered the bird to breed in Gloucestershire almost exclusively to the west of the Severn estuary. He mentions one or two nests found at Cheltenham on the east side of the river, but "only exceptionally" did birds breed on the Cotswolds.

Following an increase and spread during the first half of the present century, the Grey Wagtail now breeds on suitable streams and rivers in most parts of the county, notably in the Wye valley — Forest of Dean region and along Cotswold rivers. It is less numerous in the Severn Vale, and relatively uncommon in the Thames Area and in the district round Newent and Redmarley in the north-west of the county.

Although some birds do not desert their summer haunts after breeding, the species is noticeably more widespread in autumn and winter, and numbers appear in the Severn Vale during hard weather.

PIED WAGTAIL, WHITE WAGTAIL, *Motacilla alba*

The Pied Wagtail, *M.a. yarrellii*, is present and widespread at all seasons, breeding in small or moderate numbers over most of the county, except in the heavily wooded parts of the Forest of Dean and on the higher Cotswolds, although upland quarries may attract nesting pairs.

Numbers on the Cotswolds are diminished in severe winter weather, while an increase may be noted in the Severn Vale due to immigration as well as to movement of local birds off the hills.

Large roosts have been found in the Vale in recent years, building up from August or September to hold peak numbers from November to January, and usually dispersing in early spring. Urban sites have been used in such centres as Cheltenham and Gloucester, the birds resting in trees and on buildings. A rural roost in reedmace at Frampton-on-Severn pond held 1,000 to 1,500 birds in November 1978, and over 1,000 have been ringed there between 1976 and 1980. Smaller roosts have been reported in young spruce plantations and in quarry rubble in the region of the Forest of Dean. (See pages 24, 62, and *Glos. Bird Report*, 1979, p. 42).

Ringing recoveries support the view that most, but not all, Gloucestershire breeding birds move south during autumn and winter, some travelling as far as France and Spain, and are replaced by birds of Scottish and other northern localities. Peak movements are in October and early March. There is also ringing and retrapping evidence to show that some adults and young remain in the county and use the same roosts throughout the year[61].

The White Wagtail, *M.a. alba*, is a passage migrant, almost all birds being noted in April and from localities in the Severn Vale. Occasional records come also from the Cotswold Water Park, where from one to six birds, occasionally more, may be noted in spring, and there are two or three reports from the Cotswold hills. There are very few satisfactory autumn records, birds then being less readily identified.

WAXWING, *Bombycilla garrulus*

A scarce winter visitor from late October to early April, reported through the years from many localities and now observed almost annually, usually in very small numbers (see page 60).

The earliest notice, and one of the first for Britain, is contained in

Journeys of Thomas Baskerville[5], and records two birds, one being killed, four miles from Gloucester in January 1683 (see transcript, p. 65; and *Zool.* 1894, pp. 62-3).

Among records for the nineteenth century, Wheeler[75] reports seven obtained at "Cleeve" and others at Birdlip in 1858, while Mellersh[41] makes particular mention of the winter of 1866-67, when numbers were killed chiefly on the Cotswolds.

There appear to have been very few reports during the first forty years of the present century, but early in 1947 there were several records, including one of twenty birds or more at Longney (K.D. Pickford;[1] and see *Brit. Birds*, XLI, pp. 2 and 34).

Since 1960 the Waxwing has been noted almost every year, the majority of birds having been seen in and close to the Severn Vale. Most records refer to one or a very few individuals, flocks of more than six being unusual. The winter of 1965-6 produced more reports than usual, including flocks of nine and thirteen near Cheltenham.

Most Cotswold records come from close to the escarpment edge, but birds have been seen also near Cirencester, and up to six appeared at Elkstone in late October 1972. There are no reports from the Cotswold Water Park and only two from the Forest of Dean area, but one of these was of 30 birds seen at Drybrook quarry in mid-December 1970.

DIPPER, *Cinclus cinclus*

A local resident, breeding on the more rapid streams in various parts of the county.

An early reference is contained in a letter from John Aubrey to John Ray, dated 15 December 1692, where we read: "Sir, — There are Water Blackbirds about Rentcomb in Cotswald, which I never heard of before. . ."[58]. During last century the bird was well known on the Cotswolds and in the Forest of Dean[40 41 47 75], and these are still its main strongholds. A few nests may also be found where streams run out into the Severn Vale and the Wye valley. Breeding sites on the Cotswolds are almost always associated with weirs or other man-made features which produce broken water (see page 42; and jacket).

Birds tend to move off the Cotswolds during severe winter weather and may then be seen on streams and other waters where they are not normally known. They soon return to the hills.

A black-bellied bird, considered to be of the nominate race *C.c. cinclus*, was seen at a South Cerney gravel-pit on 17 December 1972.

WREN, *Troglodytes troglodytes*

Found abundantly throughout the county in a very wide variety of habitats.

Severe reduction of numbers occurs during prolonged hard weather in some winters, but recovery is usually rapid. An exceptionally large roost was found in the Forest of Dean near Lydney, early in 1979, where 96 birds were counted entering a small hole in the loft of a house on 15 February (*Brit. Birds*, 73, p.104). A census in the Nagshead Reserve, Forest of Dean, in 1980, recorded 90 pairs.

Most recoveries of Gloucestershire-ringed birds have been within three miles of the ringing site, but a juvenile ringed at Frampton in June 1980 was controlled at Portland Bill in September of the same year[61].

DUNNOCK, *Prunella modularis*

A common and widespread resident, breeding throughout the county.

It is most abundant in hedgerows, gardens and coppiced woodland; least so on high open ground of the Cotswolds and in continuous mature woodland such as in the Forest of Dean. The bird is basically sedentary with little sign of any but very local movement, even in hard weather. Mortality may then be very high, but recovery is generally rapid.

ALPINE ACCENTOR, *Prunella collaris*

The only record is of one shot on Leckhampton Hill, Cheltenham, sometime previous to 1860 (*Zool.*, 1860, p.6889). Mellersh[41] gives the record as ". . .1860 shot by J.T. White" (a local taxidermist). (*Handbook*[81]: "Gloucester(1)".)

ROBIN, *Erithacus rubecula*

A common species throughout the year, and in a wide variety of habitats in all parts of the county.

Common in all types of woodland, especially where coppiced; abundant also in hedgerows, and a favourite bird of gardens and parkland. Ringing returns show that many are breeding residents, but some depart in autumn and other doubtless reach the county from elsewhere and remain through the winter. There is no ringing evidence of continental birds in the county.[61]

NIGHTINGALE, *Luscinia megarhynchos*

A summer visitor found locally in several parts of the county.

There appear to have been fluctuations in both numbers and distribution in the county during the past 100 years or so. Nicholls[47], in 1858, stated that Nightingales "abound" in the neighbourhood of the Forest of Dean (but not in the Forest itself); Mellersh[40][41] shows them to have been more widespread and perhaps more numerous at the turn of the century than now, and Bowly[10] (1856) stated that they were "formerly abundant at Furzenlease. . ." near Siddington. M.P. Price[56] (1950, 1961), reporting a local study near Gloucester from 1927 to 1960, noted an increase followed in the late 1950s by a decline to a low level (see also *Brit. Birds*, V, pp.2–9).

Nightingales often favour woodland managed as coppice-with-standards, having a rich and varied ground flora. Preferred sites appear to be those with coppice between five and eight years old (Stuttard, P. and Williamson, K: *Bird Study*[8], 18, No. 1.). The practice of rotation-coppicing of this type has declined in Gloucestershire as elsewhere during the past 30 to 50 years, with consequent loss of suitable Nightingale habitats. However, the bird has increased recently, adopting new sites, notably those associated with gravel workings as at Frampton Pools and at various Cotswold Water Park localities. A survey in 1976 (Hudson, R: *Bird Study*[8], 26, No.4) reported 30 singing males from fourteen localities in this county. The corresponding numbers from the 1980 survey by the British Trust for Ornithology are 62 birds from 29 localities, an increase in line with the national trend. (Hale, J.W., and Sanders, J.D.: *Glos. Bird Report*, 1980, pp. 53–6).

Thus the Nightingale now breeds rather sparingly in Gloucestershire in suitable localities in the Severn Vale north to the Worcestershire border near Tewkesbury; a few pairs may still be found along the south-eastern fringes of the Forest of Dean region, but birds have not been reported recently from the Lower Wye, where they used to occur thinly, and are seldom noted in the Forest proper. Some birds are still found along the foot of the Cotswold scarp, but reports from dipslope localities are now less frequent than during the 1960s. Even then sites were seldom occupied for more than two or three years consecutively. Some reports were of solitary singing males and breeding has seldom been proved. Recorded localities on the hills are widely spread and include such places as Birdlip, Sapperton, Miserden, Chedworth and Stow-on-the-Wold; also near Chipping Campden in the extreme north of the county, and from the low-lying country round Moreton-in-Marsh and Daylesford. Several pairs may be present annually along the Thames and the lower reaches of its tributaries from Lechlade westwards, as well as in the newly-colonised Water Park gravel-pits previously mentioned. (See also Sharrock, J.T.R.,[62] pp. 352–3 and 462).

BLUETHROAT, *Luscinia svecica*

An adult male of the white-spotted race, *L. s. cyanecula*, preserved in Cheltenham College collection (recently transferred to Liverpool Museum), bears on what appears to be the original label the inscription "Blue-throated Robin; Stonehouse, Glos. 1872." This seems to be a hitherto unrecorded specimen[81]. Mellersh[40][41] mentions a bird (race not specified) at Cheltenham in autumn about 1875, but details are lacking.

The only subsequent reports are of a male of the red-spotted *L. s. svecica* at the New Grounds, April 1951[11][78], and another red-spotted male at Brockworth, Gloucester, May 1975, later caught and ringed. A bird is reported to have been seen at a bird-bath near Newent in May 1976 (*Brit. Birds*, 69, p. 375) but further details were not received; and a female or immature visited the New Grounds, Slimbridge, in October of the same year. The latest report is of one, perhaps two, near Frampton-on-Severn, April 1978.

BLACK REDSTART, *Phoenicurus ochruros*

A passage migrant and winter visitor in small numbers, and occasionally seen in summer also.

The bird was noted irregularly but fairly frequently in former years[40][41][75][77], and much more often since the 1950s. In all, over 50 birds have been recorded since 1957. Most have been seen in Severn Vale localities, but several on the Cotswolds and rather fewer in the Thames Area. The only Forest of Dean report is of a male at Cinderford in October 1978.

Most records fall in the periods March to May and October to December, with the highest number in October. A male in first summer plumage was to be heard singing in Cheltenham from May to July 1958, but there was no evidence of breeding. Single adult males have also been reported in late May and June from Coombe Canal, Up Hatherley and Colesbourne, in 1959, 1965 and 1972 respectively, but again with no indication of nesting.

REDSTART, *Phoenicurus phoenicurus*

A summer visitor, breeding throughout the county.

The bird's distribution at the end of last century appears to have been much as now[40][41][75], and the decline which occurred over a large part of southern and eastern England, noted prior to 1940[52], was not conspicuous in Gloucestershire until much later.

The Redstart is now commonest in the Forest of Dean region, probably always its main stronghold. Nest-boxes in Forest study areas have sometimes been used by this species[13]. It is found, but more sparsely, throughout the Severn Vale and over most of the Cotswolds, especially in the main river valleys of the latter, and along the escarpment edge. The bird is uncommon in the Thames Area, and there appears to have been a considerable decrease there in recent years, and possibly also on the Cotswolds.

WHINCHAT, *Saxicola rubetra*

A summer visitor which declined strikingly during the first half of the present century.

A widespread nesting species during the nineteenth century[40][41][42], found commonly in the Forest of Dean, on May Hill, in riverside meadows of the Severn Vale, and on rough ground and lane-side verges over much of the Cotswold hills.

A decrease set in early in this century, and by 1950 the Cotswolds were virtually deserted, although a few pairs lingered on in the Windrush valley. The Severn Vale population was also decreasing fast and very few breeding records have come from that region since about 1970 (see page 91). Even in the Forest of Dean numbers have fallen, but a sparse breeding population is still present each summer, mainly in young plantations: twenty pairs were noted in 1980.

Spring and autumn passage is reported annually, chiefly from the Severn Vale, but birds also appear in small numbers on the Cotswolds and at the Thames Area gravel-pits.

STONECHAT, *Saxicola torquata*

Formerly a widespread and not uncommon resident[10,40,41,75]. Now very much scarcer.

A marked decline set in during the 1920s and the population, already small, was virtually exterminated by the severe winters of 1940 and 1947. A recovery was heralded by a steady increase in reports of non-breeding birds from many parts of the county, commencing about 1957.

A pair bred on Leckhampton Hill, Cheltenham, in 1959. In the Forest of Dean, where a few pairs may have survived undetected, nests were found in 1958, 1961 and 1962 and then from 1973 onwards, while breeding was resumed at Cleeve Hill on the Cotswolds from 1974. The total number of nesting pairs in the county at present probably does not exceed ten.

Reports of non-breeding birds, from summer to late winter, have come increasingly in recent years from all parts of the county, including the Thames Area gravel-pits. (See pages 36, 88, 91).

WHEATEAR, *Oenanthe oenanthe*

Occurs chiefly as a passage migrant, but a few pairs stay to breed.

Mellersh[41], writing in 1902, described the species as "fairly common everywhere on the hills" (Cotswolds), but even if passage birds are included this is no longer true.

The decrease probably began in the 1920s and, although ten pairs nested on Cleeve Common in 1951, numbers are now very low. A few pairs still nest on Cleeve and perhaps at other open localities on the higher Cotswolds, preferred sites being old quarries and stone walls, but even in these places the birds are now of irregular occurrence.

Nicholls, in 1858[47], and Machen[39] referred to Wheatears as nesting in old stone walls in the more open parts of the Forest of Dean during the first half of the nineteenth century, and a few pairs still bred on ancient spoil-heaps in the Forest until the 1950s, but apparently not subsequently. Breeding has also been suspected on occasion along the banks of the Severn below Frampton-on-Severn, but the bird is best known in the Vale as a passage migrant. (See page 91). The main spring and autumn passage is noted in the Severn Vale, with a sparse movement also over the Cotswold dipslope and through the Water Park in the Thames Area.

Birds of the larger Greenland race, *O. o. leucorhoa*, especially bright-plumaged males, are usually not difficult to recognise in spring, and have been reported frequently from both Vale and Cotswolds. Autumn reports of this race are relatively few.

WHITE'S THRUSH, *Zoothera dauma*

The only adequate record of this Asiatic species from within the present county boundaries is of a bird at Lechlade, 30 October 1966.

Mellersh's manuscripts[40] include the following entry: "One seen by Earl of Gainsborough at Campden 20 Sept. 1903 (Campden, in litt. 27-8-1903". There appears to have been no evidence of identification.

(There is also an 1859 report of one at Welford-on-Avon, now in Warwickshire[41,60,81].)

RING OUZEL, *Turdus torquatus*

Former status uncertain, but now a passage migrant in small numbers, occurring chiefly in March-April and in October.

According to Wheeler[75] and Mellersh[40,41], this bird seems to have been more frequently noted towards the close of the last century than now, and it is reputed to have bred. Yarrell[82] states that the Ring Ouzel, "according to Mr. More, breeds regularly every year" in Gloucestershire[44], and Mellersh refers to several nests (some in improbable localities), although he appears not to have seen any of these himself. In no case is a nest clearly shown to have been that of a Ring Ouzel, but Wheeler states "I have both bird and eggs obtained from Cleeve Hill".[75]

Almost all reports during the past 30 years have been from the high ground along the Cotswold escarpment edge, with a large majority of birds seen on Cleeve Hill. Flocks of up to seventeen have been reported from this locality and from Leckhampton Hill and Cam Long Down in both spring and autumn. In recent years there have been isolated records also from the Severn Vale and once from near Tidenham in the Forest and Wye region.

BLACKBIRD, *Turdus merula*

No doubt Gloucestershire experienced the widespread extension by the Blackbird during the nineteenth century from its original semi-woodland habitats to hedgerows, parks and gardens, including those of large towns, but documentation is lacking. The bird is now abundant in all parts of the county.

The spring and summer population is increased by immigration from October to March. Ringing studies at Minsterworth[61] indicate an influx in mid-October of birds presumed to be of continental origin. Considerable winter gatherings are sometimes reported, notably one of 300 birds feeding on fallen apples at Minsterworth in January 1979: large numbers of these were caught and ringed, and many had wing-lengths greater than those of resident birds.

Blackbirds are better able to withstand the effects of severe winters than are Song Thrushes and this may have contributed to the development of the present high population.

FIELDFARE, *Turdus pilaris*

A widespread winter visitor and passage migrant from the first half of October to April or May.

In general a common bird, but numbers vary considerably, with flocks of up to 1,500 birds or more sometimes reported. Hard weather causes a general departure from the high Cotswold ground where, even in mild winters, autumn numbers are seldom maintained after mid-December.

The bird is widespread in pasture land, and in severe weather considerable numbers may congregate in orchards and large gardens. 750 birds were feeding on fallen apples at Minsterworth in January 1979, and 300 were caught and ringed. Of these only four were subsequently retrapped, suggesting that the birds were moving further west or south-west.[61]

A bird was caught near Rendcomb on 9 June 1961.

SONG THRUSH, *Turdus philomelos*

A common and widespread breeding species found in a variety of habitats and in most parts of the county, being least plentiful on the more open parts of the Cotswolds. This species suffers considerable losses during hard winters, such as those of 1940, 1947 and 1963. Recovery has been fairly rapid, but the overall trend at present seems to be towards decrease.

Nearly 40 recoveries of locally-ringed birds suggest that some Gloucestershire individuals are sedentary. Of several more distant returns, one was from Ireland, the rest from other parts of England. Many birds are winter visitors or passage migrants to this county, probably from elsewhere in Britain, and some at least in transit to southern England.[61]

REDWING, *Turdus iliacus*

A common and widespread winter visitor and passage migrant from October to early April.

Mellersh[41], in 1902, regarded the Redwing as much less numerous on the Cotswolds than the Fieldfare. This is not now noticeably the case but, like the Fieldfare, this bird tends to desert the higher ground at the onset of hard winter weather. Flocks numbering 1,000 to 2,000 birds are sometimes noted in Vale and Cotswold localities, and 5,000 were reported in the New Grounds area, December 1980.

MISTLE THRUSH, *Turdus viscivorus*

A common and widespread breeding species.

The great increase during the first half of last century[52] was not documented in Gloucestershire, but the bird was already plentiful by 1900[40,41]. There has been, if anything, a further increase up to the present, and the Mistle Thrush is now to be found quite commonly in all parts of the county. Post-breeding season flocks in excess of 60 birds are sometimes reported from August onwards.

GRASSHOPPER WARBLER, Locustella naevia

A summer visitor, widely but locally distributed over much of the county, but of somewhat erratic occurrence in any particular locality.

The grasshopper Warbler is widespread in Gloucestershire, but more often heard than seen. Its reeling song is sometimes mistaken for that of the Nightjar.

It breeds in moderate numbers in very young plantations and rough common-land in the Forest of Dean area. In the Severn Vale, favoured places are rank, marshy areas near the river, while on the Cotswolds most territories are on bushy slopes with coarse grassland vegetation, and again in young forestry plantations. The bird appears to be uncommon in the Thames Area.

AQUATIC WARBLER, Acrocephalus paludicola

An immature bird was caught in a reed-bed at Frampton-on-Severn on the evening of 12 August 1979, when a considerable movement of Sedge Warblers was in progress. (See *Journal*, Glos. Nat. Soc., September 1979.)

SEDGE WARBLER, Acrocephalus schoenobaenus

A summer visitor occuring in some numbers in suitable localities.

The bird is uncommon in the Wye valley and Forest area, but singing males have been noted in several places. In the Severn Vale, it breeds along streams and ditches, at pools and along the Severn margins, but has declined in recent years. Over most of the Cotswolds, Sedge Warblers are merely very scarce visitors, and there appears to be no more than an insignificant movement along the dipslope river valleys in both spring and autumn. Breeding occurs along these rivers only in the lower, south-eastern reaches as they flow out to join the Thames, and especially in the lower Windrush system.

Birds have probably always nested along the upper Thames as far as the Kemble district, and with the development of the gravel workings between Lechlade and Poole Keynes the population has expanded greatly, so that the bird is now common in the Cotswold Water Park, which seems to be its chief stronghold at present.

Passage movements of variable magnitude occur annually in the Severn Vale and probably also in the Cotswold Water Park. Peak passage times in the Vale are in early May and mid-August, and most birds have left by the end of August[61].

MARSH WARBLER, *Acrocephalus palustris*

Formerly a summer resident breeding annually in small numbers, mainly in the Severn Vale. Now reduced almost to extinction in this county.

The Marsh Warbler was not recognised as a distinct species until 1798, and the earliest Gloucestershire record appears to be that of a nest and eggs found near the Thames-Severn Canal at Siddington, near Cirencester, in June 1886 (*Zool.*, 1887, pp.264–5. The locality is there given as "Liddington", but the context makes it clear that Siddington is meant, Liddington being near Swindon, Wilts., and several miles from the old Thames-Severn Canal).

By the close of last century birds had been identified in a number of localities in the Severn Vale, where up to ten pairs or more were to be found nesting in each of several favoured sites. Birds continued to breed in eight or ten localities from Purton to Tewkesbury up to the 1930s or later. (Mellersh[40]; Wild[77]; G.L. Charteris[1]; W.C. Taunton[1]; *Brit. Birds*, III, p.158; W.H. Hudson[36].)

Data are somewhat scanty between 1920 and 1950, by which year a decline was already obvious. Throughout the 1960s annual totals from the Severn Vale localities fluctuated between about twelve pairs and a single pair. An extensive search in 1974 revealed only five singing males, of which two were presumed to have bred. Repeat investigations in the next two seasons produced no records, but a pair bred in 1977 and song was heard at two other sites. Singing birds were also present in two localities in 1978 and 1979, and at one in 1980.

At gravel-pits in the Thames Area (now in the Cotswold Water Park), two or three pairs bred in 1955 and one to three singing birds were reported there in 1961, 1966 and 1977. (See also pages 25–26, 85–86, 90).

REED WARBLER, *Acrocephalus scirpaceus*

A summer visitor, breeding locally in small or moderate numbers.

There are no breeding records, and very few other reports, from the Forest of Dean area. In the Severn Vale there are breeding sites on both sides of the river up to the county boundary near Tewkesbury. Nests are by no means restricted to pure reed-beds and in earlier years, when Marsh Warblers were more numerous, there was considerable overlap of habitats between the two species.

Birds used to breed in Northwick Park, near Blockley, but over the Cotswolds as a whole Reed Warblers are exceptional, even in the river valleys during spring and autumn passage. In the Thames Area, however, small colonies have been known at gravel-pits from Lechlade to Poole Keynes since the early 1950s, and their number tends to increase with the development of the Water Park system of pits. As in the Severn Vale, breeding is not restricted to reed-beds, but frequently occurs in the mixed marsh vegetation, with or without reeds, beneath willows.

Ringing data disclose much interchange of birds between various colonies along the Severn Vale and as far south-west as Chew Valley Lake (Avon). Peak periods of passage in the Vale are in early May and late August, most birds having left by early September[61].

GREAT REED WARBLER, *Acrocephalus arundinaceus*

A male was present near Fairford, in the eastern part of the Cotswold Water Park, from 23 to 26 June 1979. It was discovered while singing in a small reed-bed at a gravel-pit. (See page 87, and *Journal*, Glos. Nat. Soc., August 1979).

BARRED WARBLER, *Sylvia nisoria*

One record of this central Palaearctic species.

An immature bird was trapped near Minsterworth in the Severn Vale on 26 August 1979 (not the 28th as stated in *Glos. Bird Report*, 1979. See also page 57, and *Journal*, Glos. Nat. Soc., October 1979[31]).

LESSER WHITETHROAT, *Sylvia curruca*

A summer visitor to most parts of the county.

Breeds sparingly in the Forest of Dean, but chiefly in marginal land and other more open areas. Not uncommon in the Severn Vale and towards Newent and Redmarley, but much more local on the Cotswolds, where it is most numerous along the larger valleys, while scarce or absent on the higher, open ground. It breeds also in the Thames Area, but in small numbers.

The main passage in the Vale is in early May and in late August and early September. The south-easterly migration of this species is illustrated by four recoveries of Frampton-ringed birds in Italy, Albania and Egypt[61].

WHITETHROAT, *Sylvia communis*

A widespread and usually common summer visitor, breeding in all parts of the county.

An exceptional and sudden decline in numbers was noted in Britain as a whole in 1969, when few birds were seen in Gloucestershire. A slow recovery was made during the next ten years, but in 1979 the Severn Vale Ringing Group[61] reported that numbers in the Vale were still only one third of those estimated in 1968.

Peak passage times in the Severn Vale are in early May and early August[61], (and see *Bird Study*: 21, No. 1). A bird was reported to have been seen at Woodmancote, near Cheltenham on 17 December 1967.

GARDEN WARBLER, *Sylvia borin*

A widespread and fairly common summer visitor, breeding over much of the county.

In the Forest of Dean it is a bird of marginal land and young plantations, but occurs also in high forest with a good shrub layer. It is well distributed in the Severn Vale, but avoids the higher, open Cotswolds, being most numerous in the main river valleys there, and occurring also throughout the low-lying Thames Area. (See also Price, 1950, 1961[56]).

Spring passage in the Severn Vale is thin, but the autumn movement in late August and early September is more noticeable[61].

BLACKCAP, *Sylvia atricapilla*

A well known summer visitor, breeding throughout the county. An increasing number of birds are wintering in Gloucestershire.

The bird is nowhere more plentiful as a nesting species than in the Forest of Dean, and in wooded localities generally it tends to be more numerous than the Garden Warbler, although the two species may often be found together, most frequently, perhaps in the valleys of the Cotswolds.

Mellersh[41] (1902) refers to only four reports of wintering birds, and few other winter records were made prior to 1959–60. Thereafter up to twelve or more individuals were noted in each of several winters, during the months November to February. Many of these records have come from the Cheltenham, Gloucester and Stroud districts; fewer from the Cotswolds and hardly any from the Forest of Dean and the Thames Areas. A survey by the British Trust for Ornithology produced a surprising total of more than 150 birds in the county during the period January to March 1979. (*Bird Study*, Vol. 28, No. 1).[8]

The recovery in January 1968 of a Norwegian-ringed bird at Amberley fits the view that some at least of British-wintering Blackcaps are of continental origin. Peak passage times in the Severn Vale are in mid-April and from late August to early September[61]. (See also Price, 1950, 1951[56]; *Journal*, Glos. Nat. Soc., February–March 1979; *Bird Study*, Vol. 26, No. 4.)

YELLOW-BROWED WARBLER, *Phylloscopus inornatus*

The only record is of one shot on the river Chelt at Sandford Mill, Charlton Kings, Cheltenham, on 11 October 1867 (*Ibis*, 1869, p.128;[40][41][81]). This appears to have been the third British record of this Siberian drift migrant. (See also page 57).

WOOD WARBLER, *Phylloscopus sibilatrix*

A summer visitor, breeding in several parts of the county and occurring more widely on passage.

The bird nests in considerable numbers in the Forest of Dean, and in outlying woods of the region such as those near Symond's Yat, Newent and Highnam, but it is scarce or absent from the denser woods of the Wye valley. Few, if any, pairs breed in the low-lying land of the Severn Vale. (See Price, 1950, 1961[56]).

On the Cotswolds small numbers are to be found in scattered places in the beechwoods of the escarpment edge, notably from Stanway south to the Dursley area, although there appears to have been a decline here in recent years.

From remarks made by Mellersh in 1902[40][41], it seems that the bird has decreased also on the Cotswold dipslope, where it now appears only in very small numbers and is not noted every year. Reports in this region have come from localities as far apart as Westonbirt, Sapperton, Colesbourne, Corndean, Guiting, Chipping Campden and Moreton-in-Marsh.

There have been no breeding records from the Thames Area, and very few of passing birds. (See also pages 15, 17, 19, 34, 40).

CHIFFCHAFF, *Phylloscopus collybita*

A common summer visitor in all suitable areas.

Most plentiful in the Forest of Dean and in the woodland parts of the main Cotswold river valleys. It is relatively less common as a breeding bird in the more open parts of the Severn Vale, Cotswold dipslope and Thames Area. (See also Price[56]).

Birds of the nominate race, *P.c. collybita* have been reported during winter months from time to time in the past, and almost annually since 1960. Most such records, from December to February, are from localities in or near the Severn Vale, but there are several from the Water Park and the Cotswolds.

A bird seen at Frampton-on-Severn in the winter of 1968–9, and then thought to be of the north Siberian race, *P.c. tristis*, was almost certainly of the race *abietinus* (Scandinavia and western Russia) (J.D. Sanders[1]). A bird of the race *tristis* was seen at Cheltenham on various dates between 23 January and 8 April 1980, and another was trapped and ringed at Frampton Pools, 6 April 1980 (see *Glos. Bird Report*, 1980, pp. 57–8).

Main periods of passage in the Severn Vale are from early to mid-April and early to mid-September. There are four recoveries south to Iberia of birds ringed in Gloucestershire, and one control in this county of a bird ringed south of the Sahara, in Senegal[61].

In spite of comments by Mellersh[41] in 1902, most reports of spring arrivals in March now refer to Vale localities and not to the Cotswold river valleys, although birds often arrive at the Cotswold Water Park simultaneously with those in the Vale (see page 53).

WILLOW WARBLER, *Phylloscopus trochilus*

An abundant and widespread summer visitor, breeding throughout the county.

Price[56], during his studies of oak woods near Gloucester from 1927 to 1960, noted a marked decline in numbers, but there is little indication that this was of more than local extent.

The bird occurs in large numbers in and around the Forest of Dean and throughout the Severn Vale. Some nest even on the higher Cotswold hills, and commonly elsewhere on the dipslope and throughout the Thames Area.

Peak passage times in the Vale are mid-to late April and mid-to late August[61].

GOLDCREST, *Regulus regulus*

A widespread breeding species, present at all seasons.

Although sometimes occurring in purely deciduous woodland, conifers are preferred, so that the heaviest populations are found in plantations of these trees in many parts of the Forest of Dean and on the Cotswolds. Birds are also present in parks and large gardens in all parts of the county, and even a single large yew or spruce tree may be sufficient to attract a breeding pair.

Outside the nesting period, Goldcrests are much more widely dispersed, and less inclined to remain in conifers. The species suffers severe declines in hard winters, such as those of 1940, 1947, 1963 and 1979, but recovery is rapid. Ringing returns show a marked peak passage in October with no more than a slight return movement detected in spring[61].

FIRECREST, *Regulus ignicapillus*

Formerly no more than a scarce visitor, but records have recently become more frequent.

Wheeler[75] refers to one having been shot in "the Park", Cheltenham, some time prior to 1860, and preserved in Gloucester Museum, while Mellersh and others[40,41,80] mention a number of reports from last century, but in no case is evidence of identification given.

A bird was found dead at Shurdington in March 1938[77]. Between November 1968 and March 1970 there were several reports of one or two birds at Frampton Pools. One was seen also at the Wildfowl Trust's Decoy Wood in late March, 1970; another at Charlton Kings, Cheltenham, in the same month, and in May of that year a bird was trapped at Quedgeley near

Gloucester. One was noted at the New Grounds in December 1971, and 1975 brought reports of four birds, all in the Severn Vale, in January, March and October. Records in 1976 came from Cranham, Cheltenham and the Forest of Dean in February, March and the late autumn respectively, and one bird, perhaps accompanied by a second, was seen at Rendcomb Lake, March 1978.

In 1979 birds were seen at Birdlip and in the Forest of Dean where breeding was suspected at two sites. In 1980 a singing male was present at one site in the Forest, and another male, plus a nest-building pair, in another locality in June. (See also pages 87, 94).

SPOTTED FLYCATCHER, *Muscicapa striata*

A common summer visitor, breeding throughout the county.

This species subsists mainly upon insects caught in flight during sallies from perches, and is thus most numerous in areas of high forest, woodland rides and margins, timbered parks and gardens. It is common in the Forest of Dean, in the Severn Vale and along the Cotswold edge and main dipslope river valleys; less so on the open wolds and over much of the Thames Area. Many nests are on or close to human dwellings and other buildings.

There are few ringing data for spring, but the main arrival is probably in the second week of May. Peak autumn passage in the Vale is in early September, and there are three recoveries in Portugal and Spain of birds ringed as *pulli* in Gloucestershire[61].

Spotted Flycatchers are typical village birds, but often nest also in open woods and in parkland.

RED-BREASTED FLYCATCHER, *Ficedula parva*

A male, said to have been accompanied by a female, was reported at Kempsford Manor, Fairford, on 21 August 1935 ([81]; C.E. Bryant[1]). A single bird was seen near Churchdown, Gloucester, on 25 September 1977, and a female was present at the Wildfowl Trust enclosures on 19 September 1980. (See page 57). (Attempts to trace the origin of a report in *The Birds of Gwent* (1977) of a bird at the Wildfowl Trust, July 1973, have not so far been successful).

PIED FLYCATCHER, *Ficedula hypoleuca*

A summer visitor breeding in the Forest of Dean and, on rare occasions, to the east of the Severn. Very few are seen on passage in either spring or autumn.

Early writers refer to the bird as scarce on spring passage, and there are few references to breeding[40, 41, 75, 80, 82]. Mellersh[41], however, states that "at least four nests have been recorded since 1880, but always in the Western half of the county"; also that it "occasionally nests near Gloucester and in other parts of the county". H. Hook[1] notes that he remembers birds if not nests in the Forest in the years about 1910, but records of any kind for this species between 1900 and 1940 are very few. It seems probable that Pied Flycatchers have always bred in the Forest of Dean in small numbers.

Some nest-boxes were erected at Sallowvallets in the Dean about 1928, but records were not preserved. In February 1942 the Forestry Commission set up 84 boxes near Parkend, and fifteen were occupied the same year by Pied Flycatchers. This scheme has continued up to the present. The number of boxes was increased and, in 1951, a hundred breeding females were recorded (some males are polygamous). Numbers then declined and fluctuated somewhat during the next twenty years. A more drastic 40% reduction in the population then occurred in 1972–73, coinciding with Forestry Commission management operations. Less than 40 boxes a year have been occupied during the late 1970s (B. Campbell[13]; P.E. Newberry[1]; *Bird Study*[8]; *Brit. Birds*, XXXVI, pp.179, 201; see also under Redstart, Blue Tit and Great Tit; and see pages 17, 70–71).

Other nest-boxes were put up at Betty Daw's Wood near Newent in 1963, Blakeney Hill in 1964 and at Cannop in 1966. A few pairs of Pied Flycatchers have bred in each of these localities. Nesting has also been noted in natural sites in the Forest, and has been suspected on rare occasions on the Cotswolds in the past. Young were seen in an east Cotswold locality in 1979, and a pair bred near North Nibley in 1980.

As a passage migrant, the Pied Flycatcher is noted in most years, but only in very small numbers. The majority of records are in April, May and August, and most are from the Severn Vale and Cotswold edge localities (and see page 55).

A remarkable series of recoveries of birds ringed in the Forest of Dean shows a clear migratory movement down the western edge of Europe, with most recoveries from Portugal and Spain and three from north-west Africa. A male was recovered in Italy on return (spring) passage[61].

BEARDED TIT, *Panurus biarmicus*

A visitor of irregular occurrence, but reported fairly frequently during the past twenty years.

Several nineteenth century authors refer to birds having been seen near Gloucester and others up the Thames valley to Gloucestershire[42,55,60,82]. A pair, formerly in the Cheltenham College Museum, labelled "Stonehouse, Glos. (?)", may have been two of the three reported by Mellersh as having been obtained between 1865 and 1870. He also mentions that eggs are said to have been found, but evidence is lacking[40,41].

The first records for the present century were of at least two birds at Frampton Pools in the winter of 1959–60. Two were again noted in the corresponding period in 1965–6, and at least three were present there in the autumn of 1966, one, a male, having been ringed in Holland in September of that year. A bird was also seen near Splatt Bridge about that time. A party of five frequented the Pools during the winter of 1968–9, the last being seen on 23 March

In 1972, one or two birds were again present in autumn at Frampton Pools and the New Grounds, and a party of twelve moving northwards, was seen at Awre on 16 October. A single was observed at the New Grounds, November 1973, and no less than eleven at Walham Pools, October 1978 (J. Rowe[1]).

A male and female or immature at a gravel-pit near Poole Keynes, November 1980, provide the first Water Park record.

LONG-TAILED TIT, *Aegithalos caudatus*

A common breeding resident found in all parts of the county.

Perhaps especially plentiful in and around the Forest of Dean, along the scarp-face of the Cotswolds and down the chief dipslope river valleys. Numbers are severely reduced by hard winters but recovery is then rapid. Ringing shows the birds to be basically sedentary, although they wander about in autumn and winter in mixed flocks with other tits.

MARSH TIT, *Parus palustris*

Resident and moderately common.

Most numerous in well-wooded areas such as the Wye valley, Forest of Dean and the Cotswold valleys and escarpment edge. Least plentiful on the higher open parts of the Cotswolds and not very common in the Thames Area. More widespread in winter, when birds often join in flocks of other species of tit. At this season, also, they are frequent visitors to gardens and bird-tables.

Long-tailed Tit

WILLOW TIT, *Parus montanus*

An uncommon but fairly widespread breeding species.

The Willow Tit was not discovered in Britain until 1900, and for many years after this most black-capped tits were probably regarded uncritically as Marsh tits. This must have applied to Gloucestershire, for Witherby and Nicholson, in their 1937 summary of the known distribution of Willow Tits in Britain, could include only three localities for this county (a fourth is now in Avon): near Tewkesbury, near Rendcomb, and in "one regular locality north of the Cotswolds" (*Brit. Birds*, XXX, p.361; G.L. Charteris[1]).

Mellersh, in 1902, did not include the Willow Tit in his book[41], and the only reference in his manuscript notes[40] is to a bird of the northern race, *P. m. borealis*, shot near Tetbury in March 1907. (Mellersh calls it the Northern Marsh Tit and puts the year as 1908.) This was the first British record of the Scandinavian form, and the specimen is preserved in the British Museum (Nat. Hist.) (*Brit. Birds*, II, p.277).

A steady increase in records began in the 1950s, and birds have been noted annually since 1962. Reports have come from widely scattered places in all the major regions of the county and in every month. Nevertheless the bird appears to be very thinly distributed.

Breeding has been reported since 1966 in all four main regions, but only infrequently. In view of the considerable number of birds seen in April and May, it may be that actual breeding is still often overlooked, and could be more widespaced than the B.T.O. *Atlas* map indicates[62].

CRESTED TIT, *Parus cristatus*

Apart from two old and unsatisfactory reports mentioned by Mellersh[40,41], the only record is of a bird seen "in the arboretum at Weston Birt, Sir George Holford's place on the Wiltshire-Gloucestershire boundary" in December 1930. (*Brit. Birds*, XXV, p.84. The entry is headed "Probable Crested Tit in Wiltshire", and appears in the *Handbook*[81] as a "sight" record under *P. c. cristatus*. The new county boundary (1974) places the whole of the arboretum, Silk Wood and Westonbirt School in Gloucestershire, which necessitates the inclusion of the record here).

COAL TIT, *Parus ater*

Not uncommon as a breeding species and found throughout the county, with a strong but not exclusive preference for areas with coniferous trees. It is therefore more numerous in the Forest of Dean and on the Cotswolds than in the Vale and Thames areas.

A juvenile ringed at Stroud, November 1969, was caught in Germany in December 1971, the first control of a British-ringed Coal Tit from that country[61].

BLUE TIT, *Parus caeruleus*

An abundant breeding species, occurring throughout the county.

The bird is very common in all four major regions of Gloucestershire, and one of the best known of garden birds. In the Forest of Dean nest-box area at Nagshead, Parkend, Blue Tits completed first clutches in from 30 to 97 boxes annually in the study-period 1948–1967[13], and in 1979 the Nagshead area held a breeding population of about 150 pairs (see also Pied Flycatcher).

Most ringing recoveries are local, but there is a suggestion of a southerly movement for the winter[61]. (See Great Tit).

GREAT TIT, *Parus major*

A common breeding species, occurring in all parts of the county, and in a wide variety of habitats.

Great Tits occupied from fifteen to 70 nest-boxes annually (completed first clutches) during the period 1948 to 1967 in the Forest of Dean study area at Parkend[13] (and see Pied Flycatcher). Usually less abundant than Blue Tits, but both species show considerable population fluctuations.

NUTHATCH, *Sitta europaea*

A widely distributed resident found in suitable habitats throughout the county.

Most plentiful in the Forest of Dean and in the more wooded parts of the Cotswolds, but frequent also in parks, large gardens and wherever there are mature broad-leaved trees in some numbers. In autumn and winter, birds frequently join with mixed feeding flocks of tits.

There is somewhat inconclusive evidence of an increase since the earlier years of the present century.

TREECREEPER, *Certhia familiaris*

Resident and widespread, breeding in all but the most open parts of the county.

Very numerous in the Forest of Dean and all other well-wooded areas, breeding mostly in deciduous and mixed woods; less plentifully in pure coniferous plantations, where the trees are seldom allowed to reach the age which provides suitable nest sites. Much less common over the more open Cotswolds and in the Thames Area.

Widely distributed in winter, when birds are often seen with mixed feeding parties of tits, and sometimes in country not inhabited during the breeding season.

GOLDEN ORIOLE, *Oriolus oriolus*

A scarce visitor.

There are several reports from the nineteenth century, but without conclusive detail[40][41][80]. Mellersh also refers to one at the Cheltenham sewage-farm in November 1908[40].

Accepted records since then are of one near Gloucester, May 1920 (*Brit. Birds*, XIV, p.45); two males at Cheltenham, July 1949 (*Brit. Birds*, XLIII, p.151); a first-summer male at Elmore near Gloucester, June 1962; an adult male at Cheltenham, June 1970, and a male at Quedgeley in April and May 1977. A first-summer male was heard in song near Leonard Stanley in May, and an adult male was singing at Brockworth in July 1979. (Written reports of females and young all too often fail to eliminate the possibility of confusion with Green Woodpecker, when flying birds are seen briefly.)

RED-BACKED SHRIKE, *Lanius collurio*

Formerly a widespread summer visitor, and probably not uncommon in some areas. Now a very scarce bird chiefly seen in May and June, but with no recent reports of breeding.

In 1902, Mellersh stated that Gloucestershire is "visited. . . regularly by large numbers of the Red-backed Shrike in the summer"[41]. A decline set in early this century, but the primary stages are poorly documented. The species continued to be fairly well known on the Cotswolds and in the Severn Vale until about 1930, after which the decrease became rapid and there were few if any records on the Cotswold dipslope after 1940. A very few pairs continued to breed irregularly in the Vale until 1964, notably near Cheltenham.

The former position in the Forest of Dean is unclear but here also the bird had become very scarce by the late 1940s. A few pairs continued to nest, chiefly in the Yorkley and Speech House districts, until 1966.

Data from the Thames Area are very meagre. Bowly[10], in 1856, stated that there were usually two or three pairs in Siddington parish, but there seem to be no recorded occurrences of breeding this century and scarcely any other records, the latest being of two birds near Fairford in July 1967.

The only reports from anywhere in the county since 1970 are of single birds at Frocester Hill, May 1971; near Daglingworth, May 1973 (*Glos. Bird Report*, 1975); and at Ozleworth, June 1976. (See also pages 85, 90).

GREAT GREY SHRIKE, *Lanius excubitor*

An occasional winter visitor from November to March or early April. Mellersh's statement, in 1902[41], that one or two were recorded in most winters, was perhaps an exaggeration, for there are scarcely any published reports for last century[28,80,83], and Mellersh himself, in manuscript notes[40], mentions only about a dozen instances since 1875, while Wheeler, in 1862[75], had described it as "of rare occurrence".

The only reports for the first 60 years of the present century are of one shot at Tibberton near Gloucester in November 1914[77], and two (or one seen twice) in the Windrush valley, Bourton-on-the-Water, November and December, 1928 (*Brit. Birds*, XXII, p.211).

Since 1960, fourteen birds have been noted, mostly from Cotswold and Severn Vale localities, but including one near Tidenham, and another "all winter" near Parkend in the Forest of Dean.

Apart from Bowly's comment[10] in 1856, "sometimes seen" at Siddington, the only Thames Area report is of one near Cerney Wick, December 1979.

WOODCHAT SHRIKE, *Lanius senator*

A very scarce visitor.

Mellersh refers to three as having been obtained near Cheltenham since 1852 — probably those mentioned in his manuscript notes as killed at Dowdeswell Wood before 1875, and at Shurdington and Badgeworth in 1893[40,41]. (See page 69).

The first conclusive record is of a bird which remained for several days in May 1905 in the vicinity of Westcot Heath (Glos.) and Fifield Warren Farm (Oxon.). Wild states that this bird usually inhabited a hedge on the county boundary[77]. Witherby[81] does not record the species for Gloucestershire, and it is clear that the above occurrence has previously been reported in print for Oxfordshire only[2].

Notices for recent years are of an adult seen on the Cotswolds near Dursley, 27 May 1958[11], and another at Coombe Canal, 6 June 1961.

JAY, *Garrulus glandarius*

A common resident in wooded areas and found increasingly also in large gardens and parks, including occasionally those of the larger towns.

The Jay has always been most plentiful in the Forest of Dean and other large woodlands. Mellersh records that 300 were killed in 1900 by one keeper over about 1,000 acres of the Forest[41]. The bird is still a common breeding species there.

Although locally distributed throughout the Severn Vale and quite common in parts of the Cotswolds, Jays are much less numerous in the more open regions of these hills and in the Thames Area, where relatively few are found.

MAGPIE, *Pica pica*

A common resident breeding in all regions.

There has been a marked increase in numbers in all parts since the 1940s, and birds are now found regularly even in town parks and far up on to the higher Cotswolds. In the Forest of Dean it is chiefly a bird of marginal ground rather than of dense woodland, and much less numerous than the Jay.

Outside the breeding season, flocks of 30 or more are sometimes reported, and as long ago as 1878 seventy birds were seen together[80].

Magpie

NUTCRACKER, *Nucifraga caryocatactes*

Mellersh records that one was seen by T. White at Shurdington, near Cheltenham, in 1866, but gives no other details[41].

The only fully acceptable report is of one seen at Humblebee Wood, Belas Knap, near Winchcombe, on 28 September 1963. The unprecedented influx to Britain in 1968 produced no satisfactory record for Gloucestershire.

JACKDAW, *Corvus monedula*

An abundant and widespread resident, which has increased considerably during this century, at least since the 1940s if not earlier.

Birds breed freely in holes in trees all over the county; also in quarries and cliffs on the Cotswolds and in the Wye valley, while many are found in village and urban sites. Considerable numbers consort with Rooks to visit the Forest of Dean woods during heavy infestations by defoliating caterpillars (see Rook), and to feed on agricultural land throughout the county.

ROOK, *Corvus frugilegus*

An abundant resident.

Mellersh[40][41], in 1902, made several references to roosts of 20,000 to 25,000 birds in various parts of the county, but it is not possible to decide whether the Rook was then more or less plentiful than now. There appears to have been an increase in Gloucestershire during the period 1930 to 1950, when numbers in Britain as a whole rose by some 30%, only to decline again during the past twenty years or so.

Local surveys (see references, below) in north Gloucestershire, and astride what is now the new county boundary with Avon, provide interesting information on distribution and tree-preferences for nesting (especially in relation to Dutch elm disease), but little assistance in assessing population changes in the county as a whole, beyond indicating a recent general decline. The 1975 National Census of Rookeries discovered 849 rookeries in the county, with a total of 13,563 nests, but these figures are not strictly comparable with those of a previous survey (Fisher) in 1944–46, which used the pre-1974 county boundary. Results of the survey of 1975 and 1980 in Gloucestershire are compared by Pierce (*Journal*, Glos. Nat. Soc., October 1980).

During the Dutch elm disease outbreaks in the 1960s and 1970s, there were marked decreases in Rooks in the Severn Vale where elms were the predominant trees, but birds also moved to other tree species in the district, and Pierce listed 27 such species in 1976.

Destruction of elms on the Cotswolds had less effect on the Rook population than in the Vale, for beech and ash are the principal trees on the hills and widely used for nesting purposes. The Cotswolds, in fact, have one of the highest average nest-densities in Britain, with over ten nests per square kilometre.

In the Forest of Dean, rookeries tend to be widely scattered, and most are small. Nicholls[47], in 1858, referred to Rooks invading the Forest from elsewhere, "when the oaks are much blighted, to feed on grubs, and in such quantities that the trees are quite black with them. They come from a distance... and never breed in the Forest". This practice of feeding in large numbers on defoliating caterpillars still continues (see Jackdaw).

(Selected references: Yapp, W.B: *Journ. Animal Ecol.*, 3, pp.77–80, and 20, pp.169–172. Fisher, J: *Agriculture*, 55, pp.20–23; and unpublished summary for the 1944–46 investigation, Edward Grey Institute, Report R4. Bristol Nat. Soc., Ornith. Sect., *Fieldwork Review*, 1957; and *Bristol Bird Report*, 1962, 1964. Brit. Trust for Ornithology: records for survey of 1975; and *Bird Study*, 25, pp.64–81 (Sage B.L. and Vernon J.D.R.). Pierce, L.C.: Glos. Nat. Soc. *Journal*, 1969, 1973, 1974, 1976, 1980. Ogilvie, M.A.: ditto, 1972).

CARRION CROW, HOODED CROW, *Corvus corone*

The Carrion Crow, *C. c. corone*, is a common resident in all parts of the county and it seems probable that there has been a considerable increase during this century.

Although usually seen singly or in pairs, considerable numbers often gather at refuse-tips and sometimes on the Severn-side salt-marshes, while winter roosts of up to 40 birds or more have been reported in various places. (See also page 93).

The Hooded crow, *C. c. cornix*, is now an irregular and uncommon winter visitor. Bowly[10], in 1856, wrote: "some years since the Royston Crow was always to be seen at Aldsworth as you travelled from Cirencester to Burford", and Mellersh recorded at the turn of the century that it used to appear annually on the Cotswolds, and sometimes in flocks of up to ten[40,41].

There seems to have been a lack of reports from then until the 1940s, but since 1946 the bird has been noted irregularly up to the present, with a total of nearly 30 birds, mostly seen singly. The majority in recent years were at the New Grounds or on the Cotswolds; two reports come from the Forest of Dean, but none from the Thames Area.

RAVEN, *Corvus corax*

The history of this species is one of decrease followed by partial recovery. It now breeds in very small numbers.

The bird was still fairly numerous in the Wye valley and Forest of Dean until the mid-nineteenth century, when a decline, already in progress, became noticeable, and it is doubtful if any were still breeding there in 1880[40,41,47].

Ravens also bred during the last century in scattered localities on the Cotswolds, but in decreasing numbers, and no nests were reported on these hills from about 1875 until very recently. Former Cotswold localities included Witcombe Woods, Whittington, Hilcot, Barnsley and Barrington.

Breeding was again reported from the Forest of Dean and the Wye cliffs from about 1952, and up to four pairs at least have nested there almost annually to the present, using both tree and rock sites.

Since 1950, isolated birds, pairs and small groups have been reported from many Severn Vale and Cotswold edge localities; a few reports have come from well down the Cotswold dipslope, and one or two even from the Thames Area. The only evidence of resumed breeding anywhere on the east side of the Severn, however, is that of a pair which built a nest near North

Nibley in 1972, but no young were seen. (*per* Miss S.M. Butlin[1]). A pair with two juveniles was noted at the New Grounds, Slimbridge, in June 1965, but these may have come from the Forest or the Wye valley.

STARLING, *Sturnus vulgaris*

An abundant species found throughout the county in all months.

It seems probable that Gloucestershire experienced a decline in Starling numbers, as did other parts of western Britain, during the first part of the nineteenth century. This was followed by a progressive increase to the present state of abundance.

The bird is now a common breeding species in all parts of the county except on the higher, relatively treeless parts of the Cotswolds. The main sedentary breeding population is much increased by immigration from October to December, most visitors leaving again between February and April. Many ringing recoveries show the origins of the winter flocks in Gloucestershire to include Belgium, Holland, Denmark, Germany, Poland, Finland and western Russia.[61]

Mellersh[41] (1902) described a roost near Gloucester containing perhaps a million birds, and other large roosts have been noted in various localities in the county. Their locations tend to change every few years or at shorter intervals. (See page 62).

ROSE-COLOURED STARLING, *Sturnus roseus*

Mellersh[41] (1902) reports "6 killed since 1855", but lists only five in his manuscripts[40]: Bibury, 1855; Seven Springs, 1857; Tewkesbury Road, Cheltenham, 1861; Colesbourne, about 1875; and Shurdington Road, near Cheltenham, 1890. No details of identification are given, but the Colesbourne bird was preserved, until recently, in Cheltenham College Museum.

The only subsequent records are of single adult birds on Cleeve Hill, 30 March 1952, and at Tewkesbury, 17 July 1961 (the latter was regarded by the *British Birds* Rarities Committee as possibly an escaped bird).

HOUSE SPARROW, *Passer domesticus*

A very common resident, breeding throughout the county, by far the greater number in close association with houses and other buildings.

Large numbers depend on farms both for breeding sites and for feeding grounds, considerable flocks being found in the fields in late summer and autumn. Mellersh[41], in 1902, recorded that in "one large field of grain, no fewer than two thousand birds were killed". The species still does much damage to agriculture.

A colony of exposed nests on electricity cable brackets outside houses in South Cerney, reported in 1966, is said to have been there for the previous 25 years (*Brit. Birds*, 59, p.114).

TREE SPARROW, *Passer montanus*

A local resident, but more plentiful than is often realised, and distributed at least thinly in all parts of the county.

Mellersh mentioned that the Severn Vale was its main breeding area, and that few nested on the Cotswolds where it was chiefly known in the winter[41]. Bowly, however, in 1856, had noted it as not uncommon in winter round Siddington, near Cirencester[10].

Whatever its distribution at the end of last century, it is now widespread in all major regions of the county. On the Cotswolds it is found mainly along the sides of the river valleys, but small colonies also occur up to 650 feet or more above sea-level. It is more widespread in winter, and flocks of up to 300 birds have been reported in both Vale and Cotswold localities, the resident population perhaps being augmented by winter visitors. It is found also in the Forest of Dean, avoiding coniferous and other dense woodland.

CHAFFINCH, *Fringilla coelebs*

An abundant resident, breeding throughout the county, and a winter visitor from September to April in all areas.

Most abundant as a breeding bird in deciduous woodland; less so in conifers. Very common also in parkland, gardens and throughout the agricultural areas of the county wherever there is a good sprinkling of trees and tall hedgerows.

Numbers are greatly increased by autumn influxes from late September into November: winter feeding flocks of 400 to 500 birds are not rare, especially on agricultural land. The return movement is chiefly in March and April. Ringing and wing-length measurements indicate that many of these winter immigrants to the county are of the nominate race *F. c. coelebs* coming mainly from Belgium and Holland, but also from as far to the north-east as Finland. Our breeding birds (*F. c. gengleri*) appear to be mainly sedentary[61]. (See Greenfinch.)

BRAMBLING, *Fringilla montifringilla*

A winter visitor in very variable numbers from October to March and early April.

It occurs annually in and around the Forest of Dean, mostly in small numbers, but up to 400 or more were seen at Serridge, near Cinderford, early in 1957. In the Severn Vale numbers are often lower than on the Cotswolds, but over 1,000 birds were noted in a flax-field near the Worcestershire border, January 1955, with other species.

Large numbers are not infrequent in Cotswold edge and dipslope localities in some years. Mellersh[40] states that "about 1850 Lord Ducie used to see flocks of 200–1,000 or more after Beech mast in Woodchester Park". In early 1953, 500 birds were seen at Stanway, but most Cotswold flocks do not exceed 100 to 200, and are usually much smaller.

Bowly[10], in 1856, recorded Bramblings as not uncommon round

Siddington near Cirencester in severe winters, but in the Thames Area generally the species is not numerous, although flocks of up to 50 birds have been noted near Lechlade.

SERIN, *Serinus serinus*

There are only three records of this species, which has recently been extending its European range northwards (page 87).

A male was observed feeding on thistles in the Wildfowl Trust enclosures, Slimbridge, on 13 and 16 July 1961[11], and a bird was seen and heard calling in flight at the New Grounds, Slimbridge, on 6 April 1968. A male was seen near Sandhurst, Gloucester, 7 September 1979 (*Glos. Bird Report*, 1980).

GREENFINCH, *Carduelis chloris*

A common and widespread resident, least numerous on the higher, more open parts of the Cotswolds and in continuous woodland of the Forest of Dean.

Many birds move to agricultural land in autumn and winter where, in hard weather, their numbers may be augmented from elsewhere. Mellersh[41] states that during the nineteenth century the Greenfinch used to be the commonest species of seed-eating bird on the Cotswolds, but that by 1900 it was "far outnumbered by the Chaffinch". Winter flocks of up to 450 birds have been reported on a number of occasions in recent years, and one containing some 2,500 was seen in January 1955 in a flax-field in the north of the Vale. About 1,000 birds roosted at Lilley Book, Cheltenham, in January 1961.

Ringing data suggest that many of the birds wintering in Gloucestershire have come from the north and east of England.[61]

GOLDFINCH, *Carduelis carduelis*

Resident and widespread, breeding in moderate numbers in suitable localities throughout the county.

The bird has increased since the end of last century, partly at least as a result of legislation against bird-catching. (cf. Mellersh[40,41], and see passage on page 90). Autumn and winter flocks of up to 50 birds are now quite usual, and much larger numbers are occasionally reported, such as a gathering of 400 at Lechlade in January 1958, and of 200 near Milkwall on the western fringe of the Forest of Dean, in October 1965[49]. Ringing results show that many birds move south to Spain in autumn and winter[61].

SISKIN, *Carduelis spinus*

A winter visitor, usually in small numbers, but plentiful in some years, and has bred occasionally.

Autumn and winter flocks of up to 50 birds are not uncommon wherever alders and birches are numerous. Birds may therefore be found in many parts of the Forest of Dean region, where over 1,000 were present near Cinderford, January 1971. Numbers up to 250 or more are sometimes observed at Frampton Pools and elsewhere in the Severn Vale, while on the Cotswolds most records come from the river valleys, exceptionally large flocks approaching 200 strong having been noted. There are few observations from the Thames Area.

From early 1970 onwards, Siskins have been seen visiting bird-tables, and this habit has now been recorded from several towns and villages in the Vale and on the Cotswolds.

A nest was reported to have been found in the county in 1865 (*Ibis*, 1865, p.129), and Mellersh refers inconclusively to other early instances of breeding[40]. Apart from these, for which escaped cage-birds could have been responsible, the only breeding record is of two pairs which nested in the Forest of Dean in 1977, although there were earlier reports of probable breeding.

LINNET, *Carduelis cannabina*

A common and widespread breeding bird in suitable places throughout the county.

Flocks of up to 250 birds or more are not unusual from August to October, and one of 1,300 was reported at Birdlip in February 1978. The winter population, however, is often much lower than that in summer and autumn, presumably as a result of southward movement of many birds to France and Spain. The breeding population builds up again in March and April.

TWITE, *Carduelis flavirostris*

A scarce and irregular visitor, although perhaps overlooked.

Mellersh[41], in 1902, considered the Twite to be an uncommon visitor, chiefly to the higher Cotswolds, and in decreasing numbers, but a manuscript entry[40] suggests that flocks might be seen in the 1880s on Cleeve Hill.

Single birds, probably of this species, were seen near Bourton-on-the-Water in January and February, 1932 (A.G. Tayler[1]). All other reports except one, are from the New Grounds and Frampton area in the Severn Vale: one, December 1966; one in February and two in October 1967; one on the early date of 19 August in 1971, and one or two over the New Grounds in November 1980.

A party of 25 birds near South Cerney in the Cotswold Water Park was seen on 23 November 1980, and is the only flock reported this century.

REDPOLL, *Carduelis flammea*

The "Lesser Redpoll" (*C. f. cabaret*) was formerly regarded as a scarce but more or less regular breeding species at least around Cheltenham; also as a winter visitor in small numbers[40,41,75,80].

There appear to have been no confirmed breeding reports since the early years of the present century until 1976, when a family party was seen near Parkend in the Forest of Dean. At least one pair bred, also in the Forest, in 1977; nesting was suspected at Parkend in the two following years, and a family was seen in 1980. Occasional summer records come from other parts of the county and possible breeding has been reported several times.

The bird is now best known as an autumn and winter visitor in variable numbers, with a considerable increase noted since the 1950s. Most winter reports come from the Forest, Severn Vale and Cotswolds, where groups of up to 30 birds are now frequent. Occasional parties of much larger size are noted, such as one of 130 birds in the Forest in April 1977. Redpolls are uncommon in the Thames Area, although flock of up to 30 have been seen there, chiefly near Lechlade.

Birds showing characters of the race *C. f. flammea* (the Mealy Redpoll) have been reported from time to time. Records include a bird at Wick Rissington, April 1934, and three, same place, November 1937[77]; a party of four at the New Grounds, Slimbridge, October 1976, and six birds at Gloucester in January 1979. Older records lack details of identification[40 41 80].

CROSSBILL, *Loxia curvirostra*

A visitor in most years but in very variable numbers. Occasionally a few birds remain to breed.

In some years few if any birds are reported, but following "irruptions" from the continent of Europe considerable numbers may appear in the county (see page 60). Mellersh[41] refers to "the great invasion of 1868", while a notable influx early this century was in 1909–10. After a major arrival in 1929, "thousands of Crossbills remained throughout the winter on the Cotswolds" (Chelt. and Dist. Nat. Soc., 1952–3[31]).

Immigrants may appear almost anywhere from July to March, either singly or in parties of up to 30 or more, in the Forest of Dean, the Vale and on the Cotswolds, but the only report so far from the Thames Area is of six birds seen near Fairford, July 1962.

The earliest notice of breeding appears to be that for 1839 (Yarrell[82]); and Mellersh, in 1902, refers to Crossbills as "resident" and nesting both in the Forest of Dean and on the Cotswolds[41]. In manuscript[40] he lists several instances of breeding, but with little detail. Nests were found, however, at Cheltenham and Stroud in 1910;[40] (*Brit. Birds,* IV, pp. 81, 329–30; *Field,* March 1910), and at Stonehouse in 1930. Attempted breeding was reported from the Forest of Dean in 1957 and 1958[49]; at Cheltenham in 1959 and perhaps also in 1962; several pairs again nested in the Forest in 1971, and two pairs in 1977. A pair with at least one juvenile was seen in the Forest in April 1980.

PARROT CROSSBILL, *Loxia pytyopsittacus*

Of three crossbills killed near Cheltenham in late November 1861, two were identified as *L. pytyopsittacus*, preserved and checked by H.F. Witherby in 1935 (*Zool.,* 1862, p.7844; *Handbook*[81]; B.O.U. List, 1971[65].)

BULLFINCH, *Pyrrhula pyrrhula*

Resident and widespread.

According to Mellersh there were no actual breeding records from the Severn Vale at the turn of the century, although birds were present in early spring and autumn[41]. Bullfinches appear to have been present in other parts of the county, but evidently much less plentifully than now.

The increase became apparent in the 1950s, and Bullfinches now breed commonly over most of the county, although scarce or absent on the higher, open Cotswolds.

A female of the northern race, *P. p. pyrrhula*, is said to have been taken near Gloucester in 1889, but the record has never been fully accepted (*Brit. Birds*, II, p.411; Wild mss.[77]).

HAWFINCH, *Coccothraustes coccothraustes*

An uncommon and elusive resident.

The bird was probably quite rare in the early years of the nineteenth century[42,52], but increased steadily thereafter and, according to Mellersh, was "not uncommon anywhere" in the county at the beginning of the twentieth century[41].

Wild gives numerous records for the first half of this century[77], and during the past 30 years the bird has been reported widely, but only in very small numbers, from the Cotswolds and Severn Vale (including several breeding records), and especially from the Forest of Dean area. Breeding in the Forest has often been noted, and in 1978 five pairs were thought to have had nests in one small district. Two birds were seen in the Cotswold Water Park in 1976. (See also pages 89, 92).

SLATE-COLOURED JUNCO, *Junco hyemalis*

A male of this North American relative of the buntings was present at Haresfield, near Stroud, from 1 to 12 April 1975, and constitutes the first record for Gloucestershire and the sixth for Britain (*Brit. Birds*, 69, p.358). The species is kept in captivity in Britain, but spring records are perhaps more likely to be of wild vagrants than of escaped birds. The possibility of assisted passage by ship is another factor to be considered.

LAPLAND BUNTING, *Calcarius lapponicus*

A scarce and irregular visitor.

The first report was of a first-winter female, taken at Wotton-under-Edge, in October 1956, when found alive in a shed housing canaries and other caged birds. Its appearance and behaviour were those of a wild bird[11].

There have been five subsequent records. Single birds were seen or heard, all at the New Grounds, Slimbridge, in November 1967, September 1968 and 1972, and in October 1977. Two immatures were noted, also at the New Grounds, in December 1977.

SNOW BUNTING, *Plectrophenax nivalis*

An irregular winter visitor, occurring singly or in small parties of less than ten birds.

In former years, according to Mellersh[40] [41], most birds were seen on the Cotswolds and especially in severe weather, but in the past 30 years, at least, reports have come chiefly from Severn localities between Purton and Fretherne and, on the west side of the river, from Aylburton Warth. Other reports are from Vale localities away from the river, including several close to Cheltenham. The only records from the Cotswolds during this period are of a male on Haresfield Beacon, April 1951[18], and a surprising report of another seen among the buildings of a school near Dursley on the late date of 6 May 1958[11].

Most birds appear in the period October to March, with the majority during the three mid-winter months, notably in January.

(The possibility of confusion with partial albinos of other species should be borne in mind.)

YELLOWHAMMER, *Emberiza citrinella*

A widespread breeding species, and present at all seasons.

Mellersh, in 1902, claimed a decrease in the Severn Vale as a result of replacement of cereals by grazing, and that the bird no longer bred there[41]. Even if that were the case 80 years ago, the bird is now found quite commonly in all the main regions of the county, and is probably most numerous on the agricultural land of the Cotswold dipslope. In the Forest

Yellowhammers

of Dean, Yellowhammers tend to be birds of marginal ground and very young plantations. Winter flocks containing from 100 to 200 birds are sometimes noted in the Vale and in Cotswold and Thames Area localities, and these birds are probably mostly of fairly local origin.

CIRL BUNTING, *Emberiza cirlus*

A former resident, well distributed in the Severn Vale but seldom seen on the Cotswolds. No recent records.

Montagu[42], who discovered this bird in the West Country at the beginning of the nineteenth century, made no mention of it farther east than Glastonbury. Some 80 years later Yarrell's 4th edition ([82], 1871–85) stated that it breeds in Gloucestershire but seems to be "confined to very few spots", and Saunders ([60], 1889) noted it along the Thames and its tributaries as far as Gloucestershire. Witchell and Strugnell ([80], 1892) described it as "generally distributed, but nowhere abundant"; and around Stroud there was perhaps one pair per square mile (*Zool.*, 1892, p.121). Mellersh, ten years later, recorded that in some parts of the Severn Vale one was more likely to meet Cirl Buntings than Yellowhammers[41].

Wild reported it as still breeding sparsely in the 1930s between Gloucester and Berkeley, on Churchdown Hill and near Cheltenham[77]. Apart from this, the decline in numbers was poorly documented until the early 1950s, when reports of breeding, or breeding-season records, were still fairly frequent from the neighbourhoods of Tewkesbury, Apperley, Cheltenham, Highnam, Minsterworth and other Vale localities, and also from places in the Stroud district. The number of birds, however, was already small, and the decrease thereafter rapid.

A few reports have come also from Cotswold edge localities such as Pitchcombe, Amberley and Wotton-under-Edge, but notices from places down the dipslope are very few indeed. Mellersh saw several birds at 800 feet above sea-level near Chedworth in 1919[40] and, more recently, two were noted at Beverston near Tetbury, June 1951[11].

The only Thames Area record this century appears to be of three birds at a gravel-pit near Fairford in March 1959, and there are no reports from the Wye valley and Forest of Dean region. The latest records from anywhere in the county were in 1967, when there was an unsuccessful nesting at Taynton, and single males were heard in song at Hartpury and Hasfield. (See also page 85).

REED BUNTING, *Emberiza schoeniclus*

Present at all seasons and not uncommon in suitable habitats.

Breeding pairs are found locally in small numbers in the Forest of Dean area, and more commonly throughout the Severn Vale, especially in the larger marshy regions. A few pairs may be found in scattered localities on the Cotswolds but in general the bird is scarce on these hills.

In the Thames Area the Reed Bunting used to be rather uncommon, but numbers grew with increase in the number of gravel-pits, and birds are now found quite plentifully throughout the Cotswold Water Park.

This species becomes more widespread in autumn and winter, and flocks of up to 30 or 40 birds, occasionally more, have been noted along the Severn marshes, at Walmore Common and in the Water Park, especially in March and during the autumn when passage is in progress.

An immature female, ringed at Frampton-on-Severn in late March 1966 and retrapped there a week later, was then found dead in May of the same year in Jamtland, Sweden — the first British-ringed recovery from that area[61].

CORN BUNTING, *Miliaria calandra*

Resident and perhaps a local migrant. Widespread and not uncommon on the Cotswolds; scarcer in the Severn Vale and Thames Area. There are no reports from the Forest of Dean and Wye Valley.

Bowly[10] (1856) notes it as common round Siddington near Cirencester, and Wheeler (1862) describes it as "generally distributed" in the Cheltenham district[75]. According to Mellersh, however, in 1902[41], "this species is more local in the Cotswold than in the Vale grain districts".

Since about 1950, when more detailed recording began, the Corn Bunting has been noted in small numbers in the breeding season around Tewkesbury, eastwards to the foot of the Cotswolds, southwards towards Gloucester and, increasingly of late years, also between Arlingham and the New Grounds, to the south of the City. The bird is now found locally over most of the Cotswolds throughout the length of Gloucestershire, and from the escarpment edge in the west to the borders of Oxfordshire and Wiltshire. In the Thames Area it is much scarcer, but there are irregular breeding-season reports from a few localities scattered between Lechlade and Somerford Keynes.

There is an apparent reduction in population in autumn and winter, when small numbers (occasionally up to 50 birds) are reported among flocks of other species. At present it is not clear whether winter flocking accounts for all our local breeding birds, or whether some of these move away from the county. (See also pages 85, 89).

APPENDIX ONE

List of Birds Reputed to have Occurred in Gloucestershire but not Accepted for Present Purposes

Some species which have been reported in the county are omitted from the Systematic Section of this book because the evidence on which acceptance must rest appears to be less than satisfactory. Some records are rejected on account of inadequate evidence of identification (eg: Lesser Kestrel, Marsh Sandpiper); others, especially some old reports involving birds killed, because doubt exists about the Gloucestershire origins of the specimens (eg: Dartford Warbler; and see page 68), or their status as wild birds (eg: Ruddy Shelduck). For discussion see Chapter Six.

On the other hand, species which are establishing self-maintaining (feral) breeding populations originating from escaped birds are included in the main Systematic Section (eg: Red-crested Pochard, Mandarin).

Species claimed as new to the county, but for which all records have been rejected by the County Advisory Committee (since 1963), or by the *British Birds* Rarities Committee (since 1958), are not included in the following list of reputed Gloucestershire birds, but the details are retained by the organisations concerned.

The sources of records referring to rejected species in the list are indicated briefly. Indices refer to the Bibliography (page 217). English names are from *The "British Birds" List of Birds of the Western Palearctic* (1978).

Ruddy Shelduck	Witchell and Strugnell[80]; Cotteswold Nat. Field Club.[18] Glos. Nat. Soc.[31] (No satisfactory evidence of a wild bird.)
King Eider	Mellersh[40].
Surf Scoter	Mellersh[40,41].
Velvet Scoter	Witchell and Strugnell[80]; Mellersh[41].
Buffelhead	Mellersh[40,41].
Hooded Merganser	Mellersh[40]; *Handbook*[81], and letter, Oct. 1912, from F.C.R. Jourdain to W.L. Mellersh.
Black-shouldered Kite	Mellersh[40]; *Nat. Journ.*[46].

Swallow-tailed Kite (*Elanoides forficatus*)	Mellersh[40]; *Nat. Journ.*[46].
White-tailed Eagle	Mellersh[40]; I.C.T. Nisbet, pers. comm.
Spotted Eagle	Mellersh[40]; *Nat. Journ.*[46].
Golden Eagle	Mellersh[40,41]; *Nat. Journ.*[46]. A 1954 report[31] was later shown to refer to an escaped bird (J.R. Lowe, pers. comm.).
Lesser Kestrel	Mellersh[40].
Red Grouse	Mellersh[40,41].
Capercaillie	Mellersh[40,41].
Black-winged Stilt	Mellersh[40,41].
Upland Sandpiper	Witchell and Strugnell[80]; Mellersh[40,41]; Morris.[45]
Marsh Sandpiper	Mellersh[40].
Black Guillemot	Mellersh[40].
Rock Dove	Witchell and Strugnell[80]; Mellersh[40,41].
Great Spotted Cuckoo	Mellersh[40].
Black-billed Cuckoo	Mellersh[40], and letter, Aug. 18th, 1912, from H.F. Witherby to W.L. Mellersh.
Scops Owl	Mellersh[41]; *Nat. Journ.*[46] Two, Hook collection, may have been obtained in the Forest of Dean.
Tengmalm's Owl	Mellersh[40,41]; *Nat. Journ.*[46].
Roller	Mellersh[41].
Black Woodpecker	*Brit. Birds,* L, p. 84
Eastern Meadow Lark (*Sturnella magna*)	Witchell and Strugnell[80]; *Brit. Birds,* XLVIII[12]; *Zool.,*[83] 1871.
Dartford Warbler	Witchell and Strugnell[80]; Mellersh[40,41].
Ruby-crowned Kinglet (*Regulus calendula*)	Mellersh[40]; *Brit. Birds,* XLVIII[12].
Two-barred Crossbill.	Mellersh[40,41]; and a 1980 record currently under review by the *British Birds* Rarities Committee.
Pine Grosbeak	Mellersh[41].
Ortolan Bunting	Wheeler[75]; Witchell and Strugnell[80]; Mellersh[40,41].

A record of a Semi-palmated Sandpiper (New Grounds, 13 October 1968) was withdrawn by the observer "when the full complexities of stint identification became apparent" (*Brit. Birds,* 72, p.265; *Glos. Bird Report,* 1968.).

APPENDIX TWO
Scientific Names of Plants Mentioned in the Text

Scientific names of Angiosperms, Gymnosperms and Pteridophyta are taken from *Flora of the British Isles* (Clapham, Tutin and Warburg, Ed. 2, 1962).

Alder, *Alnus glutinosa*.
Amphibious Bistort, *Polygonum amphibium*.
Ash, *Fraxinus excelsior*.
Beech, *Fagus sylvatica*.
Birch, *Betula pendula, B. pubescens*.
Bracken, *Pteridium aquilinum*.
Bulrush (and see Reedmace), *Schoenoplectus lacustris*.
Coltsfoot, *Tussilago farfara*.
Crack Willow, *Salix fragilis*.
Elm, *Ulmus glabra, U. procera*.
Fir, *Abies* spp., *Pseudotsuga menziesii* (Douglas fir).
Gorse, *Ulex europaeus*.
Hawthorn, *Crataegus monogyna*.
Heather, Ling, *Calluna vulgaris*.
Heather, Bell-, *Erica cinerea, E. tetralix*.
Larch, *Larix decidua, L. leptolepis*.
Oak, *Quercus petraea, Q. robur*.
Osier, *Salix viminalis*.
Pine, *Pinus sylvestris* and other species.
Pondweed, *Potamogeton* spp.; *Elodea canadensis; Lagarosiphon majus*.
Reedmace ("Bulrush"), *Typha latifolia*.
Rush, *Juncus* spp.
Sedge, *Carex* and other genera.
Sow-thistle, *Sonchus* spp.
Spruce, *Picea abies, P. sitchensis*.
Sweet Chestnut, *Castanea sativa*.
Water-Crowfoot, *Ranunculus* spp. (white-flowered aquatics).
Water-milfoil, *Myriophyllum* spp.

Willow, *Salix* spp. (see Crack Willow, Osier).
Willow-herb, *Epilobium hirsutum* and other species, and *Chamaenerion angustifolium*.
Yew, *Taxus baccata*.

APPENDIX THREE
Bibliography

For the method of using the bibliography please see the note in the introduction to the Systematic Section on page 102.

1. Personal communication.
2. Alexander, W.B. : *A Revised List of the Birds of Oxfordshire* (1947).
3.   : *The Woodcock in the British Isles* (1934–5). (Ibis, 87, pp. 512–550).
4. Alexander, W.B. and Lack, D. : *Changes in Status among British Breeding Birds*. (*British Birds*, XXXVIII).
   Atlas of Breeding Birds in Britain and Ireland (1976): see Sharrock, J.T.R.
   Atlas of European Birds: see Voous, K.H.
5. Baskerville, Thomas: *Journeys of Thomas Baskerville* (Portland mss). (Welbeck Abbey), Hist. Mss. Commission, 13th Report, 1893; Zoologist, 1894, pp. 62–63
6. Berkeley, Hon. Grantley: *Reminiscences of a Huntsman* (1854).
7. Bewick, Thomas: *History of British Birds* (1797–1804).
   Bird Notes: Journal of the Royal Society for the Protection of Birds.
8. *Bird Study*: (Organ of the British Trust for Ornithology). Selected references (volume and number given): See also Campbell, B.; Moore, N.W.; and the Systematic Section under Pied Flycatcher and Rook.
   Hickling, R.A.O.: *The Wintering of Gulls in Britain*: Vol.1, No.4.
   Brown, R.G.B.: *The Migration of the Coot in Relation to Britain*: Vol.2, No.3.
   Great Crested Grebe studies: *Enquiry*, 1931: *British Birds*, Vol. XXVI. *Sample Census*, 1946–55: *Bird Study*, Vol.6, No.1 (Glos. not included in the sample).
   Census, 1965: Vol.13, No.2. Census, 1975: Vol.26, No.4.
   Hickling, R.A.O.: *The Coastal Roosting of Gulls in England and Wales, 1955–56*: Vol.7, No.1.

Barnes, J.A.G.: *The Winter Status of the Lesser Black-backed Gull, 1959–60*: Vol.8, No.3.
Breeding Season Census of Common Birds ("Common Bird Census"): trial run, 1960, 1961: Vol.9, No.1. Census still continuing.
Peakall, D.B.: *The Past and Present Status of the Red-backed Shrike in Great Britain*: Vol.9, No.4.
Moore, N.W.: *Pesticides in Birds: a Review of the Situation in Great Britain in 1965*: Vol.12, No.3.
Hickling, R.A.O.: *The Inland Wintering of Gulls in England, 1963*: Vol.14, No.2.
Ogilvie, M.A.: *The Numbers and Distribution of the European White-fronted Goose in Britain*: Vol.15, No.1.
Hope Jones, P.: *The Migration of the Pied Flycatcher from and through Britain*: Vol.24, No.1.

9. Blathwayt, Rev. F.L.: *Gloucestershire Wild Geese*: (in *Gloucestershire Countryside*, Vol.1, No.2; 1932).

10. Bowly, E.: *List of Birds seen in Siddington, Glos.* (1856). (Proc. Cotteswold Nat. Club, Vol.2, 1860.)

11. Bristol Naturalists' Society: *Proceedings*, and annual *Bristol Bird Report*; also *Fieldwork Reviews*.

12. *British Birds* (periodical, 1907 to present). Detailed references in the text.
British Ornithologists' Union: see *Ibis*; and *Status of Birds in Britain and Ireland*.
British Trust for Ornithology: see *Bird Study*; and Sharrock, J.T.R.

13. Campbell, B.: *Acta XI Congressus Internationalis Ornithologici*, 1954, pp.428–434. *Bird Notes*, XXIII, p.224. *Bird Study*, I, p.82; 2, pp.26 and 179; 12, pp. 305–318. *British Birds*, XLIII, p.13.
British Breeding Distribution of the Pied Flycatcher, 1953–62: a Report to the British Trust for Ornithology. Reports (duplicated) to the Nature Conservancy. *Forestry*, 41, pp.27–46 (1968). (All refer to Pied Flycatchers in the Forest of Dean; and see also *Bird Study*, Vol.24, No.1.)

14. Carson, R.: *Silent Spring* (1963): see also the Review by D.A. Ratcliffe, *British Birds*, LVI, pp.222–4.
Cheltenham and District Naturalists' Society: see Gloucestershire Naturalists' Society.

15. Cheltenham Examiner (journal).
Cheltenham Working Naturalists' Association: *Minutes* (1861–3): see Wheeler.

16. Cotswold Water Park Joint Committee: *Draft Report* (1969; Gloucestershire and Wiltshire County Councils.)

17. *Cotswold Water Park, Aquatic Nature Reserve: Draft Recommend-*

ations (1974) and *Report* (1975) of the Technical Working Party (duplicated).

Cotswold Water Park, Birdwatching in the: see Holland, S.C. and Mardle, D.V.

18. Cotteswold Naturalists' Field Club: *Proceedings* for the appropriate years. See also Bowly, E.
19. *Country-Side* (periodical). Some references given in the text.
20. Cramp, S: *Toxic Chemicals and Birds of Prey (British Birds*, LVI, pp.124–139).
21. Davis, H.H. *A Revised List of the Birds of the Bristol District. (Proc. Bristol Nat. Soc.*, XXVII, Part IV, 1947).
22. Dreghorn, W.: *Geology Explained in the Forest of Dean and Wye Valley* (1968).
23. ————— : *Geology Explained in the Severn Vale and Cotswolds* (1967).
24. Dursley Birdwatching and Preservation Society: *Bulletin*.
25. Edlin, H.E. (ed.): *Dean Forest and Wye Valley* (Nat. Forest Park Guides, H.M.S.O., 1956).
26. Evans, E.E.: *The Birds of Gloucestershire*, in *Trans. Stroud Nat. Hist. and Field Soc.* (1878–81).
27. Evans, M.E.: *The Effect of Weather on the Wintering of Bewick's Swans. . . at Slimbridge, England (Ornis Scandinavica*, 10, pp. 124–132).
28. *Field* (periodical, from 1853). Some references given in the text.
29. Gibbs, J.A.: *A Cotswold Village* (1898).

Gloucestershire Bird Report: annual publication. See Gloucestershire Naturalists' Society.

30. *Gloucestershire Countryside*: (periodical). References in the text.
31. Gloucestershire Naturalists' Society: see also Cheltenham and District Naturalists' Society and North Gloucestershire Naturalists' Society, these being former names of the same organisation (see p. 72). Publications under each of these three names are indicated here, including the *Gloucestershire Bird Report* (p. 72). Also the Society's *Journal*: March 1950 to Jan. 1954: ed. W.E. Handover; Feb. 1954 to Sept. 1962: ed. R.J.M. Skarratt; Oct. 1962 to May 1965: ed. R.J.M. Skarratt and Mrs. S.C. Holland; from June 1965: ed. Mrs. S.C. Holland.

Handbook of British Birds, The: see Witherby; H.F. *et al.*

32. Harting, J.E.: *A Handbook of British Birds* (1872; revised 1901).
33. "Hastings Rarities, The": see *British Birds*, LV, pp.281–384; LVI, pp.33–38; 62, pp.364–381; 63, pp.89–90.
34. Hibbert-Ware, A.: *Report of the Little Owl Food Inquiry* (1936–37; Brit. Trust for Ornithology: *British Birds*, XXXI).

35. Holland, S.C. and Mardle, D.V.: *Birdwatching in the Cotswold Water Park* (Glos. County Council, 1977).
36. Hudson, W.H.: *Adventures among Birds* (1913; revised 1924).
37. *Ibis* (the organ of the British Ornithologists' Union). References in the text.
    Journal of the Gloucestershire Naturalists' Society: see Gloucestershire Naturalists' Society.
38. Knapp, J.L.: *Journal of a Naturalist* (ed. 2, 1829).
39. Machen E: Papers. Deposited in Gloucestershire Record Office.
40. Mellersh, W.L.: Manuscript notes (in Cheltenham Library and Museum).
41. ———: *A Treatise on the Birds of Gloucestershire* (1902). Migration studies: see list of references on pp.63–4,Chapter Five.
42. Montagu, G.: *A Dictionary of Birds* (1802, and *Supplement*, 1813; ed. 3, E. Newman, 1866).
43. Moore, N.W.: *Toxic Chemicals and Birds*. (*British Birds*, LV, pp. 428–434; and *Bird Study*, 12, no.3).
44. More, A.G.: *Ibis* (new series) I, pp.1–27; 119–142; 425–458.
45. Morris, F.O.: *A History of British Birds* (1870).
    Mullens, W.H., Swann, H.K. and Jourdain, F.C.R.: *A Geographical Bibliography of British Ornithology* (1919).
46. *Naturalists' Journal*: ed. H.K. Swann *et al.* (periodical, 1892–1900).
47. Nicholls, H.G.: *The Forest of Dean* (1858; ed. C. Hart, 1966).
48. Nicholson, E.M.: *Birds in England* (1926).
49. Niles, J.R.A. and Cooper, S.: *Birds of the Dean Forest Park* (1969).
    North Gloucestershire Naturalists' Society: see Gloucestershire Naturalists' Society.
50. Ogilvie, M.A.: *Ducks of Britain and Europe* (1975).
51. ———: *Wild Geese* (1978).
52. Parslow, J.L.F.: *Changes in Status among Breeding Birds in Britain and Ireland* (*British Birds*, 60 and 61).
53. Payne, G.E.: *Gloucestershire: a Survey* (J. Bellows Ltd., n.d.).
54. Payne-Gallwey, R.: *Letters to Young Shooters* (1896).
55. Pennant, T.: *British Zoology* (1766 *et seq.*).
56. Price, M.P.: (1935) *Notes on population problems and terrestrial habits of Chiffchaffs and Willow-Warblers* (*British Birds*, XXIX, pp.158–166).
    ———: (1950) *Influences causing fluctuation of warbler population in cultivated lands and oak woods in the Severn Valley* (*British Birds*, XLIII, pp.345–351).
    ———: (1961) *Warbler fluctuations in oak woodland in the Severn Valley* (*British Birds*, LIV, pp.100–106).

57. Ratcliffe, D.A.: *Organo-chlorine Residues in some Raptor and Corvid eggs from Northern Britain (British Birds*, LVIII, pp.65–81).
58. Ray, J.: *The Correspondence of John Ray* (ed. E. Lankester, 1848).
59. Roberts, M.: *Annals of my Village* (1831).
60. Saunders, H.: *An Illustrated Manual of British Birds* (1888–9; ed. 3, W.E. Clarke, 1927).
61. Severn Vale Ringing Group: *Annual Report* and *News Letter*, also R.K. Bircher and J.D. Sanders (pers. comm.); and see *Journals* of the Gloucestershire Naturalists' Society.
62. Sharrock, J.T.R. and the British Trust for Ornithology: *The Atlas of Breeding Birds in Britain and Ireland* (1976).
63. Simms, E.: *Bird Migrants* (1952); Chapter 8: *The Cotswold Corridor.*
64. ——— : *Autumn Bird-migration across the South Midlands of England (British Birds*, 43, pp.241–250).
65. *Status of Birds in Britain and Ireland, The*: (Records Committee of the British Ornithologists' Union, 1971).
66. Swaine, C.M.: *Birds and Bird Watching in Gloucestershire* (1969; North Gloucestershire Naturalists' Society).
67. Tetley, H. (former Curator of Bristol Museum): Manuscript list of specimens in Bristol Museum, sent to O.H. Wild in 1935.
68. *Tewkesbury Yearly Register and Magazine*: Vol. I, 1830–1839; Vol. II: 1840–1849. (Pub. James Bennett, Tewkesbury).
69. Trueman, A.E.: *Geology and Scenery in England and Wales* (Penguin Books, 1972).
70. *Victoria History of the County of Gloucester* (1907).
71. *Victoria History of the County of Warwick* (1901).
72. Voous, K.H.: *Atlas of European Birds* (1960).
73. Wallace, D.I.M.: *A Tentative Management Plan for the Severn and New Grounds* (duplicated; 1967).
74. Webster, B. and Wood, G.: *Guide to Birds in Gloucestershire with part of Avon* (duplicated; 1976).
75. Wheeler, –: *Minutes* of the Cheltenham Working Naturalists' Association, 1861–63: *The Birds of the District.* (Read in 1862).
76. White, G.J.: *Rarae Aves that have passed through the hands of T. White and Son (Naturalists' Journal.* Vol.2, Nos. 16 and 17; 1893).
77. Wild, O.H.: Manuscript notes.
78. Wildfowl Trust: *Annual Report* (from 1948). See also list of selected publications, page 83.
79. Willis, L.J.: *The Palaeogeography of the Midlands* (Univ. Press of Liverpool, 1950).

80. Witchell, C.A. and Strugnell, W.B.: *Fauna and Flora of Gloucestershire* (Stroud, 1892).
81. Witherby, H.F. *et al.*: *The Handbook of British Birds* (1938–41).
82. Yarrell, W.: *History of British Birds* (1843; ed. 4, A. Newton and H. Saunders, 1871–85).
83. *Zoologist* (periodical, 1843–1916; incorporated in *British Birds Magazine* in 1917). Detailed references (at least the year) given or implied in the text.

APPENDIX FOUR

Gazetteer

Place-names mentioned in the text and others of general use. Ordnance Survey sheets, 1:50,000, which cover Gloucestershire are: 149, 150, 151, 162, 163, 172 and 173 (the two last include only very small areas of the county.

For each place listed, a four-figure national grid reference is given. See also separate list of Nature Reserves page 80.

A

Ablington	1007
Adlestrop	2427
Alderley	7690
Alderton	0033
Alderton Hill	0034
Aldsworth	1510
Alvington	6000
Amberley	8501
Ampney Crucis	0601
Ampney St. Mary	0802
Ampney St. Peter	0801
Andoversford	0219
Apperley	8628
Arlingham	7111
Ashchurch	9233
Ashleworth	8125
Ashleworth Ham N.R.	8326
Aston Blank	1219
Aston Magna	2035
Aston Subedge	1341
Avening	8897
Avon (river): see Warwickshire Avon and Little Avon	
Awre	7008
Aylburton	6101
Aylburton Warth	6200

B

Badgeworth	9019
Bagendon	0106
Barnsley	0705
Barnwood	8518
Barrington Bushes	2116
Batsford Park	1833
Baunton	0204
Beachley Point	5490
Belas Knap	0125
Berkeley	6899
Berkeley Pill	6600
Berry Hill	5712
Betty Daw's Wood	6928
Beverston	8693
Bibury	1106
Bigs Weir	5304
Birdlip	9214
Bishop's Cleeve	9627
Bisley	9006
Blackpool Bridge	6508

Blaisdon	7016	Chestnuts Hill	6714
Blaize Bailey	6711	Chipping Campden	1539
Blakeney	6707	Churchdown Hill	8819
Blakeney Walk	6409	Churn (river)	0206 & 0497
Blockley	1635	Cinderford	6513
Boddington	8925	Cirencester	0201
Bourton Downs	1331	Cirencester Park	9902
Bourton-on-the-Hill	1732	Clanna	5902
Bourton-on-the-Water	1620	Claypits	7606
Bourton Woods	1633	Clearwell	5708
Bowmoor Lake: see		Cleeve Hill	9826
Dudgrove Pit		Coaley	7701
Boxwell	8192	Coaley Peak	7901
Bream	6005	Coates	9800
Brimpsfield	9312	Coberley	9615
Brockeridge Common	8838	Cockshoot Wood	6407
Brockhampton,		Coldwell Rocks	5715
Cheltenham	9426	Coleford	5710
Brockhampton Park	0322	Colesbourne	9913
Brockweir	5401	Colesbourne Lake	0013
Brockworth	8916	Collinpark Wood	7528
Bromsberrow Heath	7333	Coln (river)	1205 & 1898
Brookthorpe	8312	Coln Rogers	0809
Buckholt Wood	8913	Coln St. Aldwyns	1405
Buckland	0836	Coln St. Dennis	0811
Buckle Wood	9113	Compton Abdale	0616
Bull Cross	8708	Condicote	1528
		Coombe, Wotton-u-Edge	7694
C		Coombe Canal	8626
Cainscross	8405	Coombe Hill, Cheltenham	8827
Calmsden	0408	Coombe Hill, Wotton-u-	
Cam Long Down	7799	Edge	7694
Cambridge	7403	Cooper's Hill	8914
Cannop Ponds	6010	Corndean	0126
Cassey Compton	0515	Corse	7826
Cerney Wick	0796	Cotswold Water Park: see p. 101	
Chaceley	8530	Cotswolds: see map, p. 100	
Chalford	8903	Cowley	9614
Charlton Kings	9620	Cranham	8912
Chace End Hill	7635	Crickley Hill	9216
Chatcombe Wood	9717	Cutsdean	0830
Chedworth	0511		
Chedworth Woods	0513	D	
Cheltenham	9522	Daglingworth	9905
Chepstow bridges	5394	Daneway	9403
Cherington	9098	Daylesford	2425

Appendices 225

Deerhurst	8729
Didmarton	8287
Dikler (river)	1723
Donnington	1928
Dowdeswell reservoir	9919
Down Ampney	1097
Down Hatherley	8622
Drybrook, East Dean	6417
Dudgrove Pit	1899
Dumbles: see New Grounds, Slimbridge	
Dumbleton	0136
Duntisbourne Abbots	9708
Dursley	7598
Dymock	6931
Dymock Wood	6828

E

East Dean	6520
Eastcombe	8904
Eastington, Stonehouse	7705
Eastington, Northleach	1313
Eastleach	2005
Ebley	8205
Ebrington	1840
Ebworth	9011
Edge	8409
Edgeworth	9406
Elkstone	9612
Elmore	7915
Elmore Back	7616
Elmstone Hardwicke	9226
English Bicknor	5815
Epney	7611
Estcourt Park, Tetbury	8991
Evenlode (river)	2227
Ewen	0097
Eyford Park	1424

F

Fairford	1501
Farmington	1315
Fiddington, Tewkesbury	9231
Flaxley Abbey	6915
Ford	0829
Forest of Dean: see map. p.	100

Forthampton	8532
Foss Cross	0609
Fossebridge	0811
Foxes Bridge	6312
Framilode	7510
Frampton Mansell	9202
Frampton Marsh	7407
Frampton-on-Severn	7407
Frampton Pools	7507
Fretherne	7309
Frocester	7803
Frocester Hill	7901
Frome (river)	9303

G

Gatcombe Wood	8799
Gloucester	8318
Gloucester-Berkeley Canal	7304
Gloucester Docks	8218
Gotherington	9629
Great Barrington	2013
Great Rissington	1917
Great Witcombe	9114
Greet	0230
Guiting Power	0924
Guiting Wood	0726
Guscar Rocks	6098

H

Hailes Wood	0530
Hailey Wood	9500
Hardwicke	7912
Haresfield	8110
Haresfield Beacon	8108
Hartpury	7925
Hasfield	8227
Hasfield Ham	8326
Hatherop	1505
Haw Bridge	8427
Hawling	0623
Hazleton	0818
Hempsted	8117
Hewelsfield	5602
Hewlett's reservoirs	9722
Highnam	7819
Highnam Woods	7719

226 BIRDS OF GLOUCESTERSHIRE

Hilcot, Withington	9916	Lower Swell	1725
Hilcot Wood	9816	Lydbrook	6015
Hills Flats (part)	6397	Lydney	6303
Horcott, Fairford	1400		
Hornsleazow	1232	**M**	
Horsley	8398		
Hucclecote	8717	Mailscot Wood	5614
Huntley	7219	Maisemore	8121
K		Maisemore Ham	8220
		Marsden	0111
Kemble	9997	May Hill	6921
Kempsford	1696	Meysey Hampton	1100
Keynes Park, Shorncote	0295	Michael Wood	7095
Kineton	0926	Mickleton	1643
King's Stanley	8103	Milkwall	5809
Kingswood	7492	Minchinhampton Common	8501
Knockall's Inclosure	5411	Minsterworth	7717
L		Miserden	9308
		Mitcheldean	6618
Lancaut	5396	Moreton-in-Marsh	2032
Lasborough Park	8193	Moreton Valence	7809
Lassington	7921	Mythe, Tewkesbury	8934
Lea Bailey	6320		
Leach (river)	2102	**N**	
Leadon (river)	7627		
Lechlade	2199	Nagshead Plantation	5909
Leckhampton	9419	Nailsworth	8499
Leckhampton Hill	9418	Naunton	1123
Ledgemore Bottom	8696	Netherswell	1824
Leigh	8726	New Grounds, Lydney	6300
Leighterton	8291	New Grounds, Slimbridge	7205
Leonard Stanley	7903	Newent	7226
Lidcombe Wood	0732	Newent Woods	7022
Lilley Brook, Cheltenham	9619	Newland	5509
Little Avon (river)	6897	Newnham	6911
Little Barrington	2012	Noose, Slimbridge	7207
Little Dean	6713	North Cerney	0207
Little Rissington	1919	North Nibley	7495
Longborough	1729	Northleach	1114
Longford	8320	Northleach Downs	1216
Longhope	6919	Northwick Park	1736
Longlevens	8520	Norton	8524
Longney	7612	Notgrove	1020
Lower Lode, Tewkesbury	8731	Nottingham Hill	9828
Lower Parting, Gloucester	8118	Noxon Pond	5806
Lower Slaughter	1622	Nympsfield	8000

Appendices 227

O

Oakenhill Wood, Yorkly	6207
Oakley Wood, Cirencester	9703
Oddington	2225
Old Bargains Wood, Lydney	6003
Old Park Wood, Lydney	6103
Over Bridge, Gloucester	8119
Overley Wood, Cirencester	9705
Owlpen	8098
Oxenhall Wood	6828
Oxenton	9531
Oxenton Hill	9731
Ozleworth Bottom	7892

P

Painswick	8609
Painswick Beacon	8612
Pamington	9433
Paradise, Painswick	8711
Parkend	6108
Parkend Walk	6007
Paxford	1838
Pen Moel, Woodcroft	5495
Perrott's Brook	0106
Pitchcombe	8508
Poole Keynes	0095
Postlip Valley	9926
Poulton	1001
Prestbury	9723
Preston	0400
Prinknash Park	8713
Puckham Woods	0022
Puesdown	0717
Purton, Lydney	6704
Purton, Sharpness	6904

Q

Quedgeley	8114
Queen's Wood, Newent	6727
Queen's Wood, Southam	9825
Quenington	1404

R

Redbrook	5309
Redmarley d'Abitot	7531
Rendcomb(e)	0109
Robins Wood Hill	8415
Rodborough Common	8503
Rodmarton	9498
Roel Gate	0524
Ruardean	6117
Russell's Inclosure	6110

S

St. Briavels	5504
Sallowvallets Inclosure	6013
Sandhurst Pools	8123
Sapperton	9403
Saul Worth	7408
Sedbury Cliffs	5593
Sedbury Park	5593
Selsley Common	8202
Serridge Inclosure	6113
Seven Springs, Coberley	9617
Seven Springs, Upper Slaughter	1322
Sevenhampton	0321
Severn (river)	8834 & 7112
Severn estuary	7005
Severn Ham, Tewkesbury	8832
Severn House Farm	6498
Severn Vale: see map, p. 100	
Sezincote	1731
Sharpness	6702
Sheepscombe	8910
Sherborne	1714
Shipton Moyne	8989
Shipton Oliffe	0318
Shorncote Pits: see Keynes Park	
Shurdington	9218
Shuthonger, Twyning	8935
Siddington	0399
Silk Wood, Westonbirt	8489
Slad, Stroud	8707
Slimbridge	7303
Snowshill	0933
Somerford Keynes	0195
Soudley Ponds	6610 & 6611

South Cerney	0497	Todenham	2436
South Cerney sewage-farm	0396	Tredington	9029
Southam	9725	Tuffley	8315
Southrop	2003	Turkdean	1017
Speech House	6212	Tutshill, Tidenham	5394
Splatt Bridge, Frampton	7406	Twigworth	8522
Standish	8008	Twyning	8936
Stanton	0634	Twyning Green	9036
Stanway	0632	Tyley Bottom, Wotton	7794
Staunton, Coleford	5412		
Staunton, Tewkesbury	7829	U	
Staverton	8923	Uckington	9124
Stinchcombe	7398	Uley	7998
Stinchcombe Hill	7498	Ullenwood	9416
Stoke Orchard	9228	Up Hatherley	9120
Stone Bench	7914	Upleadon	7527
Stonehouse	8005	Upper Slaughter	1523
Stow-on-the-Wold	1925	Upper Swell	1726
Stowell Park, Yanworth	0813	Upton St. Leonards	8614
Stroud	8505		
Stroudwater Canal: see		W	
Thames Severn Canal		Wainlode Hill	8425
Sudleley Castle	0327	Walham Pools	8220
Swindon, Cheltenham	9325	Walmore Common	7415
Syde	9410	Warwickshire Avon (river)	9237
Symonds Yat	5615		& 8933
Syreford	0220	Waterley Bottom, Nibley	7696
		Westbury-on-Severn	7114
T		Weston Subedge	1240
Taynton	7321	Westonbirt Arboretum	8589
Teddington	9633	Westonbirt Park	8689
Temple Guiting	0928	Westridge Wood, Wotton	7595
Tetbury	8993	Wheatenhurst	7609
Tewkesbury	8932	Whelford Pools	1799
Thames (river)	0294 & 1896	Whitcliff Park, Berkeley	6697
Thames Area: see map, p. 100		Whitecroft	6206
Thames Head	9899	Whitminster	7708
Thames-Severn Canal	7707	Whittington	0120
	& 0498	Wick	7196
Thornhill Waters, Fairford	1700	Wick Rissington	1921
Tibberton	7622	Wigpool Common	6519
Tidenham	5595	Wildfowl Trust, Slimbridge	7205
Tidenham Chase	5598	Willersey	1039
Tirley	8328	Williamstrip Park	1505
Toadsmoor Valley	8804	Winchcombe	0228
Toddington	0333	Windrush	1913

Windrush (river)	1816	Woodmancote, North	
Winson	0908	Cerney	0009
Winstone	9509	Woolaston	5899
Wintour's Leap, Wye	5496	Wormington	0436
Witcombe reservoirs	9014	Wotton-under-Edge	7593
Witcombe Wood	9113	Wye (river)	5514
Withington	0315		& 5491
Withington Woods	0314	Wye Valley and Forest	
Wolford Wood and Heath (part)	2232	Region: see map, p. 100	
Woodchester Park	8101	Y	
Woodcroft, Wye	5495		
Woodmancote, Bishop's Cleeve	9727	Yanworth	0713
		Yorkley	6306

Index

Figures in **bold type** indicate the principal entries in the systematic section. Scientific names of birds are not included in the Index (see page 101). Place-names are indexed only for particular purposes (see Gazetteer, page 223).

Accentor, Alpine **182**
Agricultural chemicals (toxic) 91–92
Agriculture, effects of: see Changes in the use of Land
Alder *(Alnus)* 19, 44
Amphibious Bistort *(Polygonum)* 47
Ash *(Fraxinus)* 16, 34
Ashleworth Ham Nature Reserve 28
Atlas of Breeding Birds in Britain and Ireland (B.T.O.) 76, 95–97
Auk, Little 62, **164**
Avocet 29, 68, **141**

Baskerville, Thomas 65
Beech *(Fagus)* 16, 34, 40
Bee-eater 51, **172**
Berkeley, G. 66
Bewick, T. 66
Bibliography 102, 217–222
Birch *(Betula)* 19
Bird-catching 88, 90
Bittern 26, 69, **109**
    Little 30, **110**
Blackbird 95, **186**
Blackcap 24, 40, 53, 56, 96, **191**
Bluethroat 57, **183**
"Bottoms" (dry valleys) 38, 43
Bourton gravel-pits 42
Bouly, E. 66
Bracken *(Pteridium)* 20
Brambling 56, **205**
Bristol Bird Report 7
Bristol Channel 23, 62

Bristol Naturalists' Society 7, 71, 72
British Birds (periodical) 66, 71
    Rarities Committee 30, 51, 213
British Birds Magazine: see *British Birds*
British Trust for Ornithology 73, 74, 76, 95
Bufflehead 213
Bullfinch 96, **209**
Bulrush *(Schoenoplectus)* 47
Bunting, Cirl 24, 85, 96, **211**
    Corn 24, 38, 85, 89, 96, **212**
    Lapland **209**
    Ortolan 68, 214
    Reed 48, 56, 96, **212**
    Snow 28, **210**
Bustard, Great **141**
    Little **141**
Buzzard 15, 17, 36, 40, 89, 92, 96, **133**
    Honey 40, 92, **131**
    Rough-legged **133**

Campbell, B. 70, 71
Cannop Ponds 20
Capercaillie 214
Carboniferous limestone 13–15
Carboniferous Period 12–15, 16
"Carr" (willow) 48
Cattle, grazing by 38
Chaffinch 31, 57, 61, 96, **205**
Changes in use of land 16–17, 23, 34, 81, 84, 91–93
Changes in status of birds: see Status, change in
Chara (alga) 47

Index

Charteris, G. L. 71, 72
Chedworth Woods 40
Cheltenham and District Naturalists' Society (see also Gloucestershire Naturalists' Society) 71, 72–73
Chepstow 15
Chestnut, Sweet *(Castanea)* 16
Chiffchaff 40, 53, 96, **192**
Cirencester Park 40, 42
Clay, Lias 22, 23, 25
   Oxford 43, 44, 46
Cleeve Hill 34, 35, 36–37
Cliffs 10, 13–15, 34, 35–36
Climate, changes in (and see Storms; Weather; Winter) 84, 85–88
Coltsfoot *(Tussilago)* 47
Coombe Canal 27, 28
Cooper, S. 73
Coot 21, 26, 42, 47, 49, 50, 95, **140**
Cormorant 15, 50, **109**
Corncrake 28, 38, 91, 96, **139**
Cotswold Water Park 11, 42, 44, 53, 66, 76, 79, 94, 101
Cotswolds 11, 31–42, 53
   Geological history 22–23, 33–34
Cotteswold Naturalists' Field Club 71, 72–73
County Advisory Committee (bird records) 72–3, 213
Crake, Baillon's 30, **139**
   Little 30, 31, **139**
   Spotted **138**
Crane 30, **140**
   White-naped **140**
Crossbill 19, 60, 92, 96, **208**
   Parrot **208**
   Two-barred 214
Crow, Carrion 39, 93, 96, **203**
   Hooded **203**
Cuckoo **166**
   Black-billed 214
   Great Spotted 214
Curlew 26, 28, 55, 56, 57, 62, 68, 89, **151**

Davis, H. H. 71
Dean: see Forest of Dean
Deer, grazing effects 19
Devonian Period 12, 13–15, 23
Dipper 15, 20, 39, 42, 61, 96, **181**
Dipslope (Cotswolds) 11, 37–38, 101
Diver, Black-throated **104**
   Great Northern **105**
   Red-throated **104**
Divers 26, 50
Dotterel 36, **143**
Dove, Collared 31, 86, 96, 97, **166**
   Rock 214
   Stock 20, 95, 165
   Turtle 19, 53, **166**
Duck, Ferruginous **126**
   Long-tailed 26, **128**
   Ring-necked 30, 31, 51, **126**
   Ruddy 31, 94, 95, **130**
   Tufted 26, 47, 48, 49, 50, 60, 62, 96, 97, **126**
Dunlin 29, 55, **147**
Dunnock 95, **182**
Dursley Birdwatching and Preservation Society 72, 75, 78–79
Dutch elm disease 23, 202
Dymott, P. H. 76, 95

Eagle, Golden 68, **214**
   Spotted 68, 214
   White-tailed 214
Egg-collecting 88, 90
Egret, Cattle 30, **110**
   Little 30, 31, **111**
Eider **127**
   King 213
Elm *(Ulmus)* 23, 202
Elmore 28
Evans, E. 66

Falcon, Red-footed 30, 51, **134**
Feral bird-populations 31, 87, 94
Field (periodical) 66
Fieldfoere 56, 57, 61, 66, **187**
Fir *(Abies, Pseudotsuga)* 19
Firecrest 87, 94, **193**
Flocking of birds (and see Roosts) 39, 62
Flycatcher, Pied 17, 55, 70–71, 92, 96, **195**
   Red-breasted 57, **195**
   Spotted 40, 96, **194**
Forest of Dean 10, 11, 15–21, 31–32, 35, 66, 92, 101
   geological history 15–16
Forestry Commission 16
Forestry, effects of 15, 16–17, 34, 92
Frampton Marsh 28
Frampton Pools 25–26, 77
Fulmar **107**

Gadwall 26, 31, 49, 87, 95, **121**
Game rearing and gamekeepers 40, 84, 88–90
Gannet 30, 62, **108**
Garganey 28, 49, 50, **123**
Gazetteer 223–229
Geological map (Gloucestershire) 9
Geological Periods, Table of 12
Gibbs, J. A. 66
Gloucester — Berkeley Canal 28
Gloucestershire Bird Report (annual) 7, 10,

50, 72-73, 76, 101
Gloucestershire, boundaries old and new 7, 8 (map), 71
 climate 10
 geographical position 10
 geological map 9
 ornithological regions 11, 100 (map)
 topographical map 8
Gloucestershire Naturalists' Society 72-73, 75-77, 219
 Table of annual publications 72-73
Gloucestershire Trust for Nature Conservation 20, 73, 75, 76, 79-80
 List of selected nature reserves 80
Godwit, Bar-tailed 29, 55, **150**
 Black-tailed 29, 55, **150**
Goldcrest 19, 88, 92, **193**
Goldenege 26, 50, 60, **128**
Goldfinch 90, 96, **206**
Goosander 26, 50, **130**
Goose, Barnacle 60, 94, **118**
 Bean 60, **115**
 Brent 60, **119**
 Canada 94, 97, **118**
 Egyptian 94
 Greylag 60, 94, 97, **117**
 Lesser White-fronted 28, 30, 60, **117**
 Pink-footed 28, 60, **116**
 Red-breasted 28, 30, 60, **119**
 Snow 28, **117**
 White-fronted 28, 56, 59, 60, 81, **116**
Gorse *(Ulex)* 20, 91
Goshawk 40, 94, **132**
Gravel extraction 25, 42, 44-47, 92-93
Gravel, oolitic limestone 25, 42, 43
Gravel-pits 10, 25, 42, 44-51, 61, 101
 deep water 45, 48-49
 diagram of section 46
 shallow, drained 45, 47-48
Grazing effects: see Cattle; Deer; Rabbits; Sheep
Grebe, Black-necked 43, **107**
 Great Crested 26, 42, 49, 50, 97, 103, **105**
 Little 21, 26, 42, 47, 49, **105**
 Red-necked **106**
 Slavonian 43, **106**
Grebes 26, 50
Greenfinch 31, 61, 96, **206**
Greenshank 47, 55, **153**
Grosbeak, Pine 214
Grouse, Black **136**
 Red 214
Guillemot **164**
 Black 214
Gull, Black-headed 30, 38, 50, 55, 94, **156**
 Common 30, 38, 50, 55, 66, **157**

Glaucous **160**
Great Black-backed 93, **160**
Herring 14, 15, 24, 30, 50, 93, 95, **159**
Iceland **159**
Ivory 30, **161**
Lesser Black-backed 24, 30, 50, 55, 93, 95, **158**
Little 26, 87, **156**
Mediterranean **156**
Gull-roosts: see Roosts
Guscar Rocks 29
Gyrfalcon 30, **135**

"Hams", Severn flood-plain 26-28
Harrier, Hen **132**
 Marsh 26, **131**
 Montagu's **132**
Harriers 28
Hasfield Ham 28
Hastings Rarities, The 67-68
Hawfinch 15, 17, 40, 89, 92, 96, **209**
Hawthorn *(Crataegus)* 35
Hayward, L. W. 72
Heather *(Calluna, Erica)* 20
Heathland 19-20
Heron, Grey 15, 40, 88, 92, **111**
 Night 30, 31, **110**
 Purple 30, **111**, **112**
 Squacco 30, **110**
Highnam Woods 21
Hobby 24, 39, 49, 50, 90, 95, 96, **135**
Holland, S. C. 50, 73, 101
Hoopoe 172

Ibis (periodical) 66
Ibis, Glossy **112**
Ice-ages: see Pleistocene glaciation
Industries, rural 92-93
Insecticides: see Agricultural chemicals
"Irruptions": see Migration, irregular

Jackdaw 19, 20, 35, 62, 96, **202**
Jay **200**
Jourdain, F. C. R. 68
Junco, Slate-coloured **209**
Jurassic Period 10, 12, 22, 43

Kestrel 20, 39, 89, **134**
 Lesser 213, 214
Kingfisher 15, 42, 49, 50, 51, 88, 89, 96, **171**
Kinglet, Ruby-crowned 214
Kite, Black-shouldered (= Black-winged) 68, 213
 Red 89, 92, **131**
 Swallow-tailed 68, 214
Kittiwake 30, 56, **160**

Knot 29, 89, **145**

Lakes: see Bourton pits, Cannop Ponds, Cirencester Park, Frampton Pools, Gravelpits, Marl lakes, Noxon Pond, Rendcomb Lake, Reservoir, Sandhurst Pools, Soudley Ponds, Walham Pools, Wildfowl Trust, Woodchester Park
Lancant (Wye) 15
Lapwing 26, 38, 47, 61, 62, 95, **144**
Larch *(Larix)* 16, 19
Lark, Eastern Meadow 214
  Shore **176**
Leckhampton Hill 35, 36
Limestone, Carboniferous 13–15, 33
  Oolitic 22, 25, 33–34, 35, 43
Linnet 96, **207**

Machen, E. 66
Magpie 39, 96, **201**
Maisemore Ham 28
Mallard 20, 40, 42, 49, 50, 60, 88, 95, **122**
Malvern Hills 16
Man: effects of human activity (and see Changes in use of land; Forestry) 42, 88–94
Mandarin 31, 94, **120**, 213
Maps: geology 9
  migration 54, 58
  ordnance survey 223
  ornithological regions 100
  topography 8
Mardle, D. V. 50, 73, 101
Marl lakes 49–50
Martin, House 40, 55, 95, **177**
  Sand 50, 55, 96, **176**
May Hill 16
Mellersh, W. L. 7, 67–69, 89
Merganser, Hooded 213
  Red-breasted 26, **129**
Merlin 28, 68, **134**
Michael Wood 23–24
Migration 52–64, 74
  autumn 57–60
  Cotswolds 53, 55–56, 59–60
  drift- 55, 56, 57
  irregular 60
  maps 54, 58
  moult- 29, 56–57
  peak passage times (table) 53
  references 63–64
  Severn — east coast route 55, 56, 57–59
  Severn Vale 53, 55–60
  spring 53–57
  Water park 47, 55, 56, 59
Minsterworth Ham 28

Montagu, G. 66
Moorhen 21, 31, 40, 47, 49, 88, 95, **139**
Moreton-in-Marsh 34
Myxomatosis virus 35, 86, 91, 133

National Wildfowl Count Scheme 50
Naturalists' Journal (periodical) 68
Nature reserves, list of 80
Nest boxes 17, 70–71, 76
New Grounds, Lydney 101
New Grounds, Slimbridge 26, 28, 29, 59, 71, 101
Newent 21
Nicholls, H. G. 66
Nightingale 15, 24, 40, 44, 48, 53, 90, 96, **182**
Nightjar 19, 20, 24, 35, **169**
Niles, J. R. 73
Nomenclature used in this book (birds) 101
North Gloucestershire Naturalists' Society (see also Gloucestershire Naturalists' Society) 72–73
Noxon Pond 20, 21
Nutcracker **201**
Nuthatch 19, 40, **198**

Oak *(Quercus)* 16
Oriole, Golden **199**
Ornithological regions of Gloucestershire 11, 100 (map), 101
Ornithology in Gloucestershire: history 65–74
Osier *(Salix viminalis)* 25, 48
Osprey 26, 50, **134**
Ouzel, Ring 36, 68, **186**
Owl, Barn 20, 39, 88, 89, 92, 98, **167**
  Little 39, 44, 88, 92, 93, 94, **167**
  Long-eared 38, 94, **168**
  Scops 68, 214
  Short-eared 28, 36, **169**
  Tawny 20, 40, 89, 95, **168**
  Tengmalm's 68, 214
Oystercatcher 29, **141**

Partridge, Grey 38, **137**
  Red-legged 38, 93, 96, **136**
Payne-Gallwey, R. 66
Peregrine 14, 15, 28, 90, **135**
Persecution of birds by man 88–90
Pesticides: see Agricultural chemicals
Petrel, Leach's 30, 62, **108**
  Storm 30, **108**
Phalarope, Grey **155**
  Red-necked **155**
  Wilson's 30, **154**
Pheasant 93, 95, **137**

Pigeon, Passenger 66
Pine *(Pinus)* 19
Pintail 49, 60, **122**
Pipit, Meadow 26, 36, 56, 57, 61, 62, **178**
  Red-throated 30, **178**
  Richard's **177**
  Rock 28, **178**
  "Scandinavian" Rock 68
  Tree 19, 20, 35, 91, **178**
  Water **178**
Plant names (scientific) 215–216
Plant succession 19, 35, 47, 48
Pleistocene glaciation 12, 13, 16, 23, 25, 34, 43, 84
Plover, Golden 28, 39, 89, **144**
  Grey 29, **144**
  Kentish 29, 47, **143**
  Lesser Golden 30, **144**
  Little Ringed 47, 86, 93, 94, 96, **142**
  Ringed 29, 39, 50, 55, 94, **143**
Pochard 50, 60, 94, 95, **125**
  Red-crested 31, 87, 94, 95, 97, **125**, 213
Pondweed *(Potamogeton)* 47
Pratincole, Collared 51, **142**
Pre-Cambrian Era 12, 15–16
Price, M. P. 21
Puffin 39, **165**

Quail 38, 95, 96, **137**
Quarries, disused 20

Rabbit, grazing effects 19, 35, 38, 86, 91, 133
Rail, Water 26, **138**
Raven 15, 20, 35, 89, 92, 96, **203**
Razorbill **164**
Records Committee: see County Advisory Committee
Records, evaluation of: see *British Birds* Rarities Committee; Chapter Six; County Advisory Committee; 30, 51, 72–73, 102, 213
Redbrook (Wye) 15
Redmarley 21
Redpoll 40, **207**
  Mealy **208**
Redshank 26, 47, **152**
  Spotted 29, 55, 102, **152**
Redstart 15, 17, 40, 44, 53, 95, **184**
  Black 24, **184**
Redwing 56, 57, 61, 66, 78, **187**
Reed *(Phragmites)* 25, 28, 47, 48
Reedmace *(Typha)* 47
Refuse tips, birds at 24, 30, 93
Rendcomb Lake 41
Reservoir, Dowdeswell 25
  Hewletts 25

Witcombe 25
Ringing of birds: see Severn Vale Ringing Group: Wildfowl Trust.
River Avon (Warwickshire) 23
  Churn 40, 41, 42
  Coln 40, 42
  Dikler 42
  Evenlode 40
  Frome 25, 39
  Leach 40
  Leadon 21, 23
  Severn 10–11, 15, 21, 26, 29–30
  Thames 11, 22, 23, 39
  Windrush 40, 42, 55
  Wye 10–11, 13–15, 16, 23
Roberts, M. 66
Robin 90, 95, **182**
Roller 214
Rook 19, 23, 39, 62, 96, **202**
Roosts, gull 30, 38, 50, 62
  Pied Wagtail 24, 62, 180
  Starling 62
  Swallow 177
  Wren 181–182
Royal Society for the Protection of Birds 76, 80, 90
Ruff **148**
Rushes *(Juncus)* 47

Sanderling 39, **145**
Sanders, J. D. 73
Sandgrouse, Pallas's 30, 60, **165**
Sandhurst Pools 25
Sandpiper, Bairds 30, **146**
  Broad-billed 30, **148**
  Buff-breasted 30, 51, **148**
  Common 15, 55, 68, **154**
  Curlew 29, 55, **147**
  Green 47, 55, **153**
  Marsh 213, 214
  Pectoral 47, **146**
  Purple 29, **147**
  Semi-palmated 214
  Upland 214
  White-rumped 30, **146**
  Wood 47, 55, **153**
Saunders, H. 66
Scarp-face, scarp-slope (Cotswolds) 11, 31, 34–36, 101
Scaup 26, **127**
Scientific names: birds 101; and see Systematic Section.
  plants 215–216
Scoter, Common **128**
  Surf 213
  Velvet 213

Scott, P. 80, 114
Sedges (*Carex*, etc.) 47
Serin 30, 87, **206**
Severn Bore 26
Severn estuary: see River Severn
Severn, geological history 23–24
Severn Ham, Tewkesbury 28
Severn Vale 11, 21, 22–32, 101
Severn Vale Ringing Group 52, 53, 62, 73, 75, 77–78, 101
Severn Wildfowl Trust: see Wildfowl Trust
Sewage-farm, South Cerney 50–51
Shag 30, **109**
Shearwater, Manx 30, 39, 62, **107**
Sheep, grazing effects 19, 35, 38
Shelduck 15, 29, 56, **119**
    Ruddy 213
Shooting 88–90
Shoveler 49, 50, 60, 94, 95, **124**
Shrike, Great Grey 66, 102, **200**
    Red-backed 19, 35, 85, 90, 96, **199**
    Woodchat 69, **200**
Silurian Period 12, 23
Siskin 19, 40, 92, **206**
Skua, Arctic 30, 55, **155**
    Great 30, **156**
    Long-tailed 30, **156**
    Pomarine 30, **155**
Skylark 38, 56, 57, 61, 95, **176**
Slaughter, Lower 39
Smew 26, **129**
Snipe 47, **149**
    Great 30, **149**
    Jack 47, **148**
Soudley Ponds 20
Sow-thistle (*Sonchus*) 47
Sparrow, House 90, 93, 96, **204**
    Tree 44, 96, **205**
Sparrowhawk 19, 40, 89, 92, **133**
Spoonbill **112**
Spruce (*Picea*) 16, 19
Starling 19, 28, 62, 93, 96, **204**
    Rose-coloured **204**
Status of birds, changes in 84–94, 102
Stilt, Black-winged 214
Stint, Little 29, 55, **146**
    Temminck's 26, 47, **146**
Stonechat 20, 36, 88, 91, 95, 97, **185**
Stone-curlew 38, 69, 90, 91, **142**
Stork, White 51, **112**
Storms, effects of 30, 39
Strugnell, W. B. 67
Swaine, C. M. 72–73
Swallow 40, 52, 55, 95, **177**
Swan, Bewick's 26, 31, 56, 59, 82, **114**
    Mute **113**
    Whooper 21, **115**
Swift 40, 55, 57, 93, 95, **170**, **171**
    Alpine 51, **171**
Symond's Yat (Wye) 15
Systematic Section 99–212
    Classification employed in 101
    Introductory notes to 102

Taxidermists and taxidermy 67, 68, 69, 89
Teal 49, 50, 60, 62, 88, **121**
    Blue-winged 30, 31, **124**
Tern, Arctic 30, 55, 57, **162**
    Black 26, 50, 55–56, **163**
    Caspian 30, **161**
    Common 30, 50, 55, 57, **161**
    Gull-billed 30, **161**
    Little 30, 102, **162**
    Roseate **161**
    Sandwich 30, 57, **161**
    White-winged Black 30, 51, **164**
Thames Area 11, 25, 34, 38, 43–51, 101
    geological history 43
Thames, river: see River Thames
Thames — Severn Canal 25
Thrush, Mistle 88, 95, **187**
    Song 61, 88, 90, 95, **187**
    White's 51, **186**
Tidenham Chase 20
Tit, Bearded 26, **196**
    Blue 96, **198**
    Coal 19, 92, 96, **198**
    Crested 67, **198**
    Great 96, **198**
    Long-tailed 88, 96, **196**, 197
    Marsh 96, **196**
    Willow 40, 102, **197**
Tits 17, 19, 62, 90
Topography (Gloucestershire) 8 (map), 10–11
Treecreeper 19, 40, 96, **199**
Triassic Period 12, 21, 22, 23
Turnstone 29, **154**
Twite **207**

Urban areas 93

Wagtail, Blue-headed **179**
    Grey 15, 20, 39, 42, 61, **179**
    Grey-headed **179**
    Pied 24, 95, **180**
    White **180**
    Yellow 26, 48, 53, 57, 96, **179**
Walham Pools 25
Walmore Common 28, 77
Warbler, Aquatic 30, **188**
    Barred 57, **190**

Cetti's 87
Dartford 68, 213, 214
Garden 19, 35, 40, 53, 96, **191**
Grasshopper 19, 35, **188**
Great Reed 51, 87, **190**
Marsh 25-26, 28, 48, 85-86, 90, **189**
Reed 21, 25, 26, 44, 48, 53, 96, **190**
Savi's 87
Sedge 21, 25, 40, 44, 48, 53, **188**
Willow 19, 20, 35, 53, 56, 95, **193**
Wood 15, 17, 19, 34, 40, **192**
Yellow-browed 57, **192**
Water-Crowfoot *(Ranunculus)* 47
Water meadows 44
Water-milfoil *(Myriophyllum)* 47
Water Park: see Cotswold Water Park
Waxwing 60, 65, **180**
Weather-movements (see also Winter; "Wrecks") 30, 39, 61-62
Webster, B. 73
Wheatear 19, 28, 36, 53, 91, **185**
  Greenland **185**
Wheeler — 66
Whimbrel 28, 55, 57, **150**
Whinchat 19, 20, 53, 57, 91, 97, **184**
White, J. T. 68, 69
White, T. 68
Whitethroat 19, 35, 53, 95, **191**
  Lesser 19, 53, **190**
Wigeon 28, 49, 50, 60, 62, 68, 88, **120**
  American 30, **121**
Wild, O. H. 71
Wildfowl Trust 28, 31, 50, 52, 59, 61, 71, 72,
73, 75, 80-83
references to research 83
Willow *(Salix)* 44, 48
Willow-herb *(Chamaenerion, Epilobium)* 47
Winter: effects of severe weather (see also Weather movements) 88
Wintour's Leap (Wye) 15
Witchell, C. A. 67
Withington Woods 40
Wood, G. 73
Woodchester Park 42
Woodcock 17, 19, 40, **149**
Woodland (and see Forest; Forestry)
  coniferous 16-17, 19, 40
  deciduous 10, 15-19, 23, 34, 35, 40
Woodlark 19-20, 21, 35, 85, 86, 95, 96, **175**
Woodpecker, Black 214
  Great Spotted 40, 95, **173**
  Green 44, 88, **173**
  Lesser Spotted 40, **175**
Woodpeckers 17, 174
Woodpigeon 61, 62, 88, 95, **165**
"Wrecks" of sea-birds 62
Wren 88, 90, 95, **181**
Wryneck 85, **173**
Wye Valley 13-15, 101
  geological history 13-15

Yarrell, W. 66
Yellowhammer 38, 57, 96, **210**
Yellowlegs, Lesser 30, **153**

Zoologist (periodical) 66